An Introduction to Literary Chinese

Harvard East Asian Monographs 176

An Introduction to Literary Chinese

Revised Edition

Michael A. Fuller

Published by the Harvard University Asia Center
and distributed by Harvard University Press
Cambridge, Massachusetts, and London
2004

The Harvard University Asia Center publishes a monograph series and, in coordination with the Fairbank Center for East Asian Research, the Korea Institute, the Reischauer Institute of Japanese Studies, and other faculties and institutes, administers research projects designed to further scholarly understanding of China, Japan, Vietnam, Korea, and other Asian countries. The Center also sponsors projects addressing multidisciplinary and regional issues in Asia.

Library of Congress Cataloging-in-Publication Data

Fuller, Michael Anthony.
  An introduction to literary Chinese / Michael A. Fuller.-- Rev. ed.
    p. cm. -- (Harvard East Asian monographs ; 176)
  Includes bibliographical references and index.
  ISBN 0-674-01726-9 (pbk. : alk. paper)
  1. Chinese language--Textbooks for foreign speakers. 2. Chinese language--Grammar--Textbooks for foreign speakers. I. Title. II. Series.
  PL1128.F85 2004
  495.1'82421--dc22

                    2004016243

Index by the author

⊛   Printed on acid-free paper

Last figure below indicates year of this printing
                    09

1st edition, 1999; revised edition, 2004

Note: Portions of Lessons 4, 11-14, and 18 have been revised.

Contents

Part II: Intermediate Texts

Part III: Advanced Texts

Part IV: 唐宋文選

Selected Táng and Sòng Dynasty Writings

Appendixes

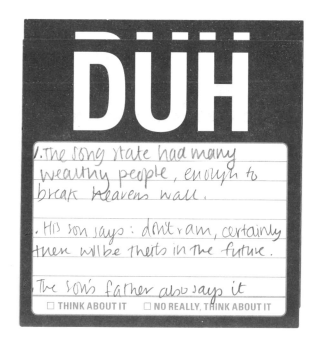

Preface

Like most teachers of literary Chinese, I have slowly assembled an array of materials and techniques to bring to the classroom. I have taken the further step of organizing those materials into this textbook because—quite simply—I have found that the approach works. Those who adopt and apply the analytic approach to syntax stressed in this textbook will, by the end of the book, be well on their way to becoming good readers of the classical language.

Precisely because this book grew by accretion and refinement, it is important to acknowledge its sources. When I began teaching at the University of California, Irvine, I brought with me the first-year reader used at Harvard, which has a good selection of short passages. These in turn seem to have derived from *Fifty Chinese Stories*, which I consulted next. To these texts I added my own revised version of the overview of classical grammar in Hugh Stimson's *Fifty-five T'ang Poems*.[1] Reorganized, rethought, and expanded, these materials evolved into the present textbook.

1. Y. C. Liu and Walter Simon, *Fifty Chinese Stories, Selected from Classical Texts, romanized and translated into Modern Chinese* (London: Lund Humphries, 1960). Hugh M. Stimson, *Fifty-five T'ang Poems* (New Haven: Far Eastern Publications, 1976), pp. 7–21.

The textbook's approach to literary Chinese largely follows what Prof. Stimson taught me twenty-five years ago.[2] Where I have ventured to innovate, I have had the good fortune of being able to discuss these matters with the linguists at University of California, Irvine. In particular, James C. T. Huang, Lisa Cheng, and Shi Dingxu, who now teaches at Hong Kong Polytechnic, were very helpful as I began to clarify the formal issues. I was also extremely lucky to be able to attend the UCI graduate seminar on Chinese historical syntax organized by Wei P'ei-ch'üan, Cao Guangshun, and James C. T. Huang in spring 1996. I am grateful for their patience with my layman's questions and their counsel even as I persist in following an approach rather distant from the formal linguistics they practice.

My ultimate concern in this textbook is with the careful, informed reading of literary Chinese rather than with a full linguistic account of the classical language. My approach, therefore, is driven by a desire to find the best way to instill good habits of reading as quickly as possible. In the end, students should outgrow the framework of this textbook: once their own reading becomes better informed by experience with other texts, they will discover that there remain gray areas of syntax for which this textbook gives no adequate account. But by then, this work will have accomplished its purpose of training the student to pay close attention to the nuances of the language on the page.

The textbook is structured to help students move beyond the safe confines of the classroom and of the textbook itself. It begins with an overview of the syntax of literary Chinese that serves both as an introduction to the terminology I employ and as a handy synopsis for later reference. Then I present the basic syntactic structures through eight introductory lessons with a full complement of explanations and exercises. The vocabulary lists for the lessons use the *pīnyīn* romanization of Mandarin Chinese, a choice that deserves some comment. On the whole, given the great distance between the ancient language and the

---

2. In the meantime, Stimson's own approach has evolved over the years, and we no longer agree on many fine points. I suppose this is my indirect way of saying that Stimson deserves much credit for what is good but should not be blamed for what is bad.

modern dialects, the modern pronunciation of the characters is of little significance. The textbook does assume some knowledge of Chinese characters as used in a modern East Asian language, but it makes no real difference if the language is Mandarin, Cantonese, Japanese, or Korean. Indeed, it is important to remember that the corpus of texts written in "literary Chinese" is more accurately an *East Asian* textual tradition and that the elites of pre-modern Korea, Japan, and Vietnam were both familiar with the authors whose works have been selected for this textbook and used literary Chinese as the primary medium for serious writing. Literary Chinese thus has a much wider audience than just speakers of modern Mandarin.

After introducing the student to the basic structures, the textbook uses a set of readings of intermediate difficulty to increase the student's familiarity with the syntactic and rhetorical patterns of the classical language. These lessons also include simple bibliographic exercises to encourage the reader to begin to explore the many resources available for reading literary Chinese. The student then meets advanced texts that are longer, more sophisticated, and more in need of historical contextualization. The textbook also provides brief comments—along with the usual glossaries—to suggest some of the themes and the cultural background of these works, but the point is to introduce interpretive issues rather than exhaust them. The student should be strongly encouraged to look for annotated editions and other supplementary readings. Finally, I offer a collection of famous writings in various genres from the Tang and Song dynasties. These texts are both wonderful examples of the pleasures of reading literary Chinese and a gateway through which to enter the culture of pre-modern China. Since I do not provide glossaries for these texts, students will have to turn to other editions for help in reading. And when they are through with the final readings, they will be ready to lay this textbook aside altogether and read on their own.

I am grateful for the support of the Chiang Ching-kuo Foundation, whose Institutional Enhancement Grant brought me to the University of California, Irvine, and which provided other assistance in the final preparation of this textbook for publication. Several colleagues have read sections of the textbook, and I have benefited from their comments: I am particularly indebted to Feng Shengli, Terry Kleeman, Vivian Ling, Keith McMahon, William Powell, Stuart Sargent, and Stephen West. I also have been fortunate to have John Ziemer as my editor: he has brought clarity and order to this work. The patches of obscure writing and the errors that remain are of my own making.

An Introduction to Literary Chinese

Introduction: Part One

Problems of Reading and Understanding

This textbook presents one approach to learning to read literary Chinese, the pre-eminent language for writing in China for the past two thousand years. I stress that the goal here is *reading*, not translating. It is important to realize from the beginning that literary Chinese is a *language*—a written, conventionalized language—that has its origins in the spoken vernacular of Warring States (403–255 B.C.) China. As in the learning of any language, our final goal is to learn to think in the language itself rather than to be constantly translating into some other tongue. By carefully working through the selections in this book, one can begin to think in literary Chinese as one reads the text, just as when one reads this introduction, one hears English.

Grammar Is Not Enough

Learning to recognize the basic structures of literary Chinese syntax is a relatively easy matter of acquiring experience with the language. Learning the patterns, however, is just the beginning. After one has mastered the technical aspects of grammar presented in this textbook, one meets a new and unusual problem. Literary Chinese is an uninflected language. That is, its verbs are not conjugated and lack endings that indicate tense or person (as in Spanish, *hablo* "<u>I</u> speak," or *habla-bas* "<u>you were</u> speak<u>ing</u>"). Its nouns have no case endings to describe their number or function in the sentence (as in Latin, *res* "thing" as subject; *rerum* "<u>of</u> things"). Instead, as in English, word order largely determines meaning. In English,

> John hit Mary.

tells a different story from

> Mary hit John.

*[handwritten margin note: * multiple meanings of words.]*

[handwritten margin note: Chinese: modern is less ambiguous than classical]

Many problems arise from the even more complete lack of inflection in literary Chinese. Literary Chinese texts often are syntactically *over-determined*; that is, there may be several perfectly grammatical ways to explain the syntax of a sentence. Skill in reading, then, lies in deciding which alternative is most likely rather than simply whether the alternatives are grammatically possible.

Such judgments of meaning cannot be based on grammar alone. They rely not only on a knowledge of syntax but also on a sense of the larger arguments of the sentence, the paragraph, and the composition as a whole. They also call upon knowledge of the usage of the particular characters in question, in terms of both the author's habits and the contemporary and prior history of the expression. They call, further, upon the text's many intersecting historical contexts and, finally, upon one's own tendencies as a reader—how one wants to push the text, given one's own preconceptions and purposes.

To read literary Chinese, then, one must know more than syntax. Although this textbook begins by focusing on grammar, its approach broadens as the texts get longer and more complex. This chapter, as an introduction, sets out the general issues of reading and meaning that surround even the simplest texts. I present these more abstract issues before introducing the grammar because our approach to the syntax of sentences in any actual text is always circumscribed by the larger processes of understanding.

Parts and Wholes:
The Levels of Structure in Meaning

The act of reading is a constant movement between parts and wholes. We understand what a sentence means by putting words together. But we also figure out how to understand the words from their context in the sentence. For example, "parts" can be a noun or a verb, but we know that "parts" in the first sentence in this paragraph must be a noun because of its position in the phrase "parts and wholes."

Sometimes one can know the meaning and function of every word in a sentence and still not have the slightest idea what the sentence means. In that case one looks for other clues. The sentence is part of a paragraph: perhaps the organization of the paragraph will help. The paragraph is part of a composition, the composition is part an author's extant works, the author's extant works are part of the writings of a particular time, and the writings of a particular time are part of a culture's evolving textual tradition. We read each group of texts in the context of the larger body of material. But the process works both ways. The parts tell us how to read the whole, just as the whole tells us how to read the parts. So, if one discovers something new or raises a compelling question never asked before, the reinterpretation of a single work may require a rereading of the larger oeuvre. The rereading of a single author may compel the re-evaluation of an era, and revising our understanding of one era may reshape our understanding of an entire tradition. This movement—using parts to construct wholes and using wholes to understand parts—is called the *hermeneutic circle*.

Sometimes we go outside generic traditions. If the sentence refers to historical events, we can seek help from other accounts of the same events or even from physical "things" that were part of the events in question. It may help to know how the doors of the Bastille were set in their hinges or what sort of caulking was used on the boat in which Washington crossed the Delaware, or how exactly they made the wine that Li Bai drank. And sometimes we may begin to suspect that an author is not entirely sane, in which case we can attempt to reconstruct the pathology from the author's history and writings and all we know of human nature.

In general, we can look at the layers of organization through which we can make sense of a character, sentence, or text as shown in the chart on p. 4.

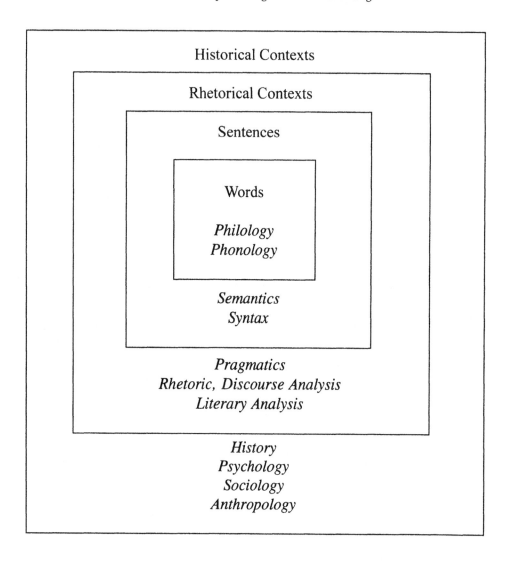

Some Examples

A few examples will serve to clarify the sorts of issues involved in reading.

Fragment One: "John hit the man with the schnogle."

The syntax of this sentence is ambiguous: does the "schnogle" describe what John used to hit the man, that is:

John hit (the man) with a schnogle.

Or does "schnogle" describe an attribute of John's victim?

John hit (the man with the schnogle).

How do we decide?

FIRST STRATEGY: CONTEXT

First we read the larger context (the rest of the paragraph), if we have one. Suppose the story is as follows:

Recollections of John

John was always a mischievous child. I remember when I was young, John and I were playing together: we saw two men—obviously a little tipsy—weaving down the street. John scooped up a handful of the newly fallen snow with a wicked grin. Although he aimed at the man with two good legs, *John hit the man with the schnogle.*

On the basis of this story, we would conclude that "schnogle" seems to mean a bad leg. But, suppose the story is:

John was always a mischievous child. I remember when I was young, John and I were playing together: we saw a man—obviously a little tipsy—weaving down the street. John scooped up a handful of the newly fallen snow with a wicked grin. Having found an old sock into which he loaded the tightly packed ball, *John hit the man with the schnogle.*

In this version, a "schnogle" seems to be a sock filled with snow. In both versions of the story, we can be reasonably—but not absolutely—certain of what a "schnogle" is, since our knowledge comes entirely from context. In the end, we are still guessing.

SECOND STRATEGY: VOCABULARY

Another way to determine what the sentence means is to find out the meaning of the key word from dictionaries and other sources of information about the language of the time. Suppose that we find the following entry in *The American Dictionary of Regional Usage*:

In the language of Detroit, a *schnogle* is a sock into which has been placed a snowball. The origin of the word seems to be Yiddish, but we have no further information.

Suppose, however, that by a strange coincidence, we notice the following passage in *I Survived a Detroit Childhood*, by Ralph J. Smallbread:

When I was a child, there was a Mr. Smith on our street whom we teased for having what we called a *schnogle*, or limp, because of a war injury to his leg.

Both sources, the dictionary and the memoir, give good, though contradictory information about schnogles. You make a decision by judging which source is most trustworthy.

Fragment Two: "Mr. Wentworth, I just cut down that zablena bush." "Oh, that's just great."

The question here is not one of grammar but of tone. How are we to take Mr. Wentworth's reply? Is he being ironic about an action he does not appreciate, or is he in fact grateful for the pruning job? Both readings are possible. Much of our reading of texts is based on knowing cultural assumptions about the statements made in texts and about probable attitudes about objects and events that appear in them. Sometimes we cannot be sure of how to read the attitude in the text because its wording is ambiguous. What can we do to resolve this sort of doubt?

STRATEGY THREE: HISTORICAL DOCUMENTATION

Suppose in our diligent research on the question, we locate the following item in the *Oakdale Daily News*:

Mr. John Wentworth today went to court to sue his neighbor Peter Farthing for having accidentally cut down his rare Peruvian zablena bush.

We would know for sure how to read the dialogue. But suppose, instead, that we searched through the author's personal papers and found a gardener's invoice:

Axel's Garden on Wheels
Invoice no. 00325

Mr. John Wentworth　　　　　　　　　　　May 21, 1992
34 Via Lobos
Catalina, CA

for digging out of one zablena bush:
　　labor:　　　　　　　　　　　　　　　$30.00
　　supplies:　　　　　　　　　　　　　　10.00
　　　　　　　　　　TOTAL:　　　　　　$40.00

The invoice makes it clear that the dialogue is between Mr. Wentworth and the gardener and that Mr. Wentworth is indeed sincere in his thanks for the job.

In Summary

This textbook stresses the bare bones of how to read a literary Chinese text. It introduces the grammar and attempts to give enough experience with simple passages to prepare the way for increasingly more difficult texts. Contextual, hermeneutic issues rarely come to the fore in the material to be presented. Nonetheless, as the texts grow more difficult, the emphasis shifts from simply parsing a sentence to deciding which of several grammatically possible readings for a line is most reasonable in the context of the passage as a whole. That is, informed interpretation plays an ever larger role in reading as one becomes more adept. From the very beginning, one should be aware that grammar provides no sure answer—there is nothing mechanical in the reading of literary Chinese—and that one should bring as much information to the act of interpretation as possible.

Introduction: Part Two

A Sketch of Literary Chinese

This chapter outlines a basic set of analytic categories with which to approach texts written in literary Chinese.[1] It is designed to serve both as an initial overview of the textbook—to be read largely as an introduction to the terminology—and as a reference guide as one proceeds deeper into the textbook itself. This overview is admittedly incomplete and specifically focuses on the needs of beginning students. More advanced students, or those seeking greater detail, can consult the references cited in the footnotes and in the bibliography at the end of the chapter.

The topics follow traditional linguistic categories. *Morphology*—the formation of words, their categories, and the features used to mark

---

1. My approach derives largely from Hugh Stimson, from whom I learned literary Chinese in 1973. His perspective at that time can be found in *55 T'ang Poems* (New Haven: Far Eastern Publications, 1976), a textbook designed to introduce students to poetry written in literary Chinese. For more technical discussions of the details of late Old Chinese, I have found Christoph Harbsmeier's *Aspects of Classical Chinese Syntax*, Scandanavian Institute of Asian Studies Monograph Series, no. 45 (London and Malmö: Curzon Press, 1981), and Edwin G. Pulleyblank's *Outline of Classical Chinese Grammar* (Vancouver: University of British Columbia Press, 1995) extremely useful. For comparison with modern Chinese usage, I have used Charles N. Li and Sandra A. Thompson, *Mandarin Chinese: A Functional Reference Grammar* (Berkeley: University of California Press, 1981). I also have consulted Lisa Cheng and James C. T. Huang of the University of California, Irvine. For a more extensive bibliography, see the end of this chapter.

those categories—comes first. Then the chapter introduces some aspects of *phonology*—the patterns of sounds in the language. *Syntax*—the grammatical rules—comes last.

I. Words

In English, we do not usually worry about what a "word" is. We assume that the white space around a group of letters indicates that the group is a word. In reality, of course, the situation is not this simple. When, for example, can we combine words to form another "word"? We write "someone" but not "somecat." And there are gray areas: how many words is "heavier-than-air"? Moreover, in English, as in most languages, words can be built by adding *affixes*—extra syllables to the beginning of words (*prefixes*), to the end (*suffixes*) and, occasionally, to the middle (an *infix*). Thus we have "play," "*re*play," "play*ing*," and "scrum*diddlyum*ptious."

Although many basic words in modern Mandarin are monosyllabic and written with one character—for example, "come," "go," "eat"—so much of the vocabulary involves compounds of two or more characters that it is considered a polysyllabic language. Mandarin, like the other modern dialects, also has its own set of affixes. For example, there are the *aspect*-marking suffixes, *-le* 了 , *-guò* 過, and *-zhe* 著, the pluralizing suffix *-men* 們, and the *potential* infix *-de-* 得. However, compared with English and many other languages, modern Chinese in its various dialects has relatively few affixes and is considered an "isolating" language.

A. Literary Chinese has even fewer affixes and, in contrast to modern Mandarin, is basically a *monosyllabic* language.

人	man, men, person, people, human
去	depart, leave, go

There are, however, exceptions, words of two or more characters that cannot be broken down into meaningful single-character units:

芙蓉	lotus

B. In other cases, two-character compounds work as single words, that is, as indivisible semantic units.

1. *Reduplication*: sometimes repeating a character creates a word whose meanings extend significantly beyond the meaning of the single character:

> 人 man, person   人人 all people
> 年 year   年年 year after year

2. *Descriptive binomes*: sometimes instead of a reduplication of a word, an intensifying two-character expression consists of words in which either the initial or the final sound is repeated:

> 崢嶸 dzæng-ɣuæng[2]   descriptive of high mountains
> 參差 ts'ɪɪm ts'ɪ   descriptive of uneven, scattered
> 徘徊 buəi-ɣuəi   move back and forth > irresolute

3. *Polar Binomes*: sometimes writers use a pair of words (synonyms or opposites) to refer to an entire set of "things" (either objects or actions):

> 少長 young + old   > people of all ages
> 動靜 move + be still   > all [one's] activities
> 草木 grasses + trees   > all vegetation

[handwritten margin note: opposites: everything included (abstract notion)]

C. Affixation in literary Chinese is relatively late and tends to be associated with more colloquial styles.[3] The major exception are the pluralizing affixes, which were widely used from the Warring States period on. Two common pluralizers are the suffix 等 and the modifier 諸.

2. By convention, Old Chinese romanizations are preceded by an asterisk (*) as a reminder of the provisional nature of the reconstruction. Middle Chinese romanizations are used without such caution. For Middle Chinese, I use the reconstructions in Yú Nǎiyǒng 余迺永, *Hùzhù jiào zhèng Sòng běn Guǎngyùn* 互註校正宋本廣韻 (Taipei: Lian Guan, 1975). I have taken my few examples of Old Chinese from Bernard Karlgren's *Grammata Serica Recensa* (Stockholm: Museum of Far Eastern Antiquities, 1957) simply because of its convenience: other studies have significantly updated his initial work, but the details are beyond the scope of this textbook.

3. I leave aside the important question of affixes in Old Chinese. There is good evidence to suggest that words with similar syntactic features shared *phonological* features and that there were syntactically important suffixes and prefixes in the early language. See the discussion in Appendix A, Part II, "Syntax and Phonology in Old Chinese."

1. *Pluralizers*:

    公等　　　"you all"
    諸賢　　　"all the worthies"[4]

2. *Aspect Markers and Resultatives*: The sorts of function words we find in modern dialects began to appear in their grammaticalized forms during the Táng dynasty.[5]

II. Pronunciation

The history of Chinese as a spoken language often is roughly divided into three main periods: Old Chinese (商 Shāng and 周 Zhōu to 西漢 Western Hàn), Middle Chinese (東漢 Eastern Hàn to 初唐 Early Táng), and Mandarin (Old Mandarin from 晚唐 Late Táng to 明 Ming, Middle Mandarin from mid-Míng to early 清 Qīng). Scholars have researched the sound systems of Chinese for the earlier periods and have proposed various reconstructions of those languages based on the often limited information they can glean from the written texts.

A. Old Chinese *– mor like cantonese*

What we know of the sound of Old Chinese is based largely on an analysis of the rhymes of the *Shī jīng* 詩經, combined with other linguistic data. Among these early data are patterns of phonetic loanwords and comparisons with other languages.

As Chinese scribes developed conventions for writing characters to correspond to spoken words, they used a system of borrowing similar sounding characters and adding a different *radical* to distinguish the new word from the old. For example:

    吉　　　*ki̯ĕt

---

4. See Harbsmeier, *Aspects of Classical Chinese Syntax*, pp. 166–75, for a discussion of distinctions in early usage.

5. Cáo Guǎngshùn, for instance, gives the Táng dynasty poetic couplets below as examples of the development of aspect markers (取) and resultatives (得):

　　待取滿庭蒼翠日，酒尊書案閉門休。
　　會待路寧歸得去，酒樓漁浦重相期。

See Cáo Guǎngshùn 曹廣順, *Jìndài Hànyǔ zhùcí* 近代漢語助詞 (Beijing: Yuwen, 1995).

佶   *g'i̯et
髻   *kied

A more difficult series is:

妥   *t'nwâr
綏   *sni̯wər
諉   *ni̯wər

As the clusters of consonants at the beginning of the words suggest, the sound system for Old Chinese reconstructed by historical phonologists from these data is much more complicated than that of modern Mandarin.

A second sort of additional data used by historical phonologists is comparisons with early Tibetan (for early Old Chinese) and with loanwords from Indo-European languages (for late Old Chinese).[6] These data, combined with the rather complicated sound system derived from loan-character information, suggest that Old Chinese may have been a *very* different language from even Middle Chinese. For example, it may not have had tones. Instead, it may have had other sorts of morphological characteristics (a final -s, or -χ, for example) that disappeared as the affixes transformed in a regular manner into a tonal language, Middle Chinese, after the Hàn dynasty.[7]

A toneless Old Chinese may have been different in another important way. If there was a final -s, it may have carried specific grammatical information. Like Tibetan, Japanese, and European languages, Old Chinese may have been *inflected*, that is, a language in which the endings or beginnings of words show the case of nouns and the de-

6. For a recent example of the use of Tibetan sources for the reconstruction of early Old Chinese, see Randy J. LaPolla, "Variable Finals in Proto-Sino-Tibetan," 歷史語言研究所集刊 65, no. 1 (March 1994): 131–73. For the use of Indo-European languages in the reconstruction of a Hàn dynasty dialect, see W. South Coblin, "BTD Revisited: A Reconsideration of the Han Buddhist Transcriptional Dialect," 歷史語言研究所集刊 63, no. 4 (Sept. 1993): 867–943.

7. For a good discussion of the issue, see Jerry Norman, *Chinese*, Cambridge Language Surveys (Cambridge: Cambridge University Press, 1988), pp. 52–57. For a more technical approach, see, for example, William H. Baxter, *A Handbook of Old Chinese Phonology*, Trends in Linguistics Studies and Monographs 64 (Berlin and New York: Mouton de Gruyter, 1992), pp. 302–25.

clensions of verbs (*amo, amas, amat,* etc.). If Old Chinese *was* inflected, then we need to reconstruct the groups of characters that represent the declensions of the same word.[8] In any case, if the morphological features (sound segments) of words conveyed syntactic information, the Chinese themselves seemed no longer to have been aware of such distinctions by the time of the compilation of the first major dictionary, the *Shuō wén jiě zì* 說文解字, in the Hàn dynasty.

B. Middle Chinese

Our understanding of Middle Chinese is much more complete than our picture of Old Chinese. For one thing, Chinese scholars themselves sought to regularize and codify the accepted pronunciation of words through the production of rhyming dictionaries.[9]

Fǎn qiè

In these dictionaries, scholars used a system of two-character combinations called 反切 *fǎn qiè* to represent the sound of a word. In this approach, the sound of the character in question is found by joining the *initial* sound of the *first* character of the combination with the *final* sound of the *second* character. Thus, for example,

祿盧谷切

That is:

盧	**luo**
谷	**kuk**
祿	**l[uo] + [k]uk = luk**

---

8. Axel Schusler has attempted such a reconstruction in *Affixes in Proto-Chinese* (Wiesbaden: Steiner, 1976), but his work remains controversial. Pulleyblank and others have proposed more modest sets of patterns (see Appendix A).

9. Jerry Norman and W. South Coblin have argued that we have no good reason to accept the simple picture that the rhyming dictionaries present anything like a standard dialect. Moreover, regional dialects have probably existed throughout Chinese history—rather than being later developments—and probably did not derive directly from the northwestern dialect supposedly recorded in the rhyme-books. See Jerry Norman and W. South Coblin, "A New Approach to Chinese Historical Linguistics," *Journal of the American Oriental Society*, 115, no. 4 (Oct.–Dec. 1995): 576–84.

Tones

Middle Chinese had four tones, but these were different from those of modern Mandarin:

1. 平 Level   2. 上 Rising   3. 去 Falling   4. 入 Entering

Entering-tone words end with a **-p**, **-t**, or **-k**. When one repeats a sound in the four tones (as in modern *mā, má, mǎ, mà*), the entering-tone endings **-p**, **-t**, and **-k** correspond to words ending in **-m**, **-n**, and **-ng**, respectively, in the other three tones (e.g., *lim, lǐm, lìm, lip*). When written characters are constructed from a radical + phonetic, we see the same pattern of correspondence. For example:

曠 xuang	廣 kuǎng	曠 k'uàng	擴 ɣuɑk
嬮 ʔiæm	魘 ʔiăm	厭 ʔiæm	壓 ʔap

To give some idea of the manner in which Middle Chinese pronunciations have been reconstructed, consider the following table of apicals, words beginning with a **t-**, **th**, or **d** sound.[10] Note the presence of words beginning in **n-** in the table: the two sounds are produced with the tongue at the same place in the mouth. (This is also why the entering-tone **-t** corresponds to **-n** in the other tones.)

---

10. Jerry Norman explains:

Each of the *shétóu* [apical] sounds corresponds to a distinctive set of *fǎnqiè* upper [first] characters in the *Guǎngyùn*. The only way phonetic substance can be given to these categories is by comparing them to actual pronunciations in modern Chinese dialects and in the Sinoxenic dialects of Japan, Korea, and Vietnam. [The table] gives the readings of several common characters from each of the *shétóu* initials in several Chinese and Sinoxenic dialects. A glance at the table shows that a large majority of the forms are either dental or alveolar stops and nasals. The initial *ní* may be safely reconstructed as a nasal on the basis of the forms given. The initials *duān* and *tòu* are voiceless dental (or alveolar) stops in all the dialects; with the exception of Kanon, which has merged the two series. The remaining dialects have an unaspirated stop for *duān* and an aspirated stop for *tòu*; it is reasonable to suppose that Middle Chinese possessed the same sort of contrast. The only dialect which clearly distinguishes the initial *dìng* from *duān* and *tòu* is Sūzhōu [Wú] in which *dìng* corresponds to a voiced stop contrasting with the voiceless correspondences for *duā* and *tòu*. Provisionally at least, the initial *dìng* can be considered some kind of voiced dental stop in Middle Chinese.

The chart, except for the Middle Chinese reconstructions, derives from Norman, *Chinese*, pp. 34–35.

A Few Comparisons in Reconstructing
Middle Chinese: The Apical Group

(官話 Mandarin; 吳 Wú; 閩 Mǐnnán; 粵 Cantonese; 越南 Sino-Vietnamese; 高麗 Sino-Korean; 漢音 *Kanon*, one form of Japanese pronunciation of Chinese characters; MC, middle Chinese)

	官話	吳	閩	粵	漢音	越南	高麗	MC
duān 端								
多	tuo	təu	to	to	ta	ʔda	ta	tɑ
刀	tau	tæ	to	tou	to	ʔdao	to	tɑu
短	tuan	tø	tuan	tyn	tan	ʔdoan	tān	tuɑn
tòu 透								
他	t'a	t'ɒ	t'a	t'a	ta	tha	t'a	t'ɑ
天	t'ien	t'iɪ	t'ien	t'in	ten	thien	ch'ǒn	t'iɛn
鐵	t'ie	t'iəʔ	t'iet	t'it	tetsu	thiet	ch'ǒl	t'iɛt
dìng 定								
弟	ti	di	ti	tai	tei	ʔde	che	diɛi
頭	t'ou	dɤ	t'ɔ	t'au	tō	ʔdəu	tu	dəu
豆	tou	dɤ	tɔ	tau	tō	ʔdao	tu	dəu
ní 泥								
內	nei	nE	lui	noi	dai	noi	nae	nuəi
年	nien	niɪ	lian	nin	nen	nien	yǒn	niɛn
農	nuŋ	noŋ	loŋ	nuŋ	nō	noŋ	nong	nuong

C. Modern Dialects

There are eight major modern dialects that can be divided into three groups based on the time when the speakers of the dialect split off (see the dialect map):

1. 官話 Mandarin (subdivided into Northern Mandarin, Northwest Mandarin, Southern Mandarin, and Southwest Mandarin)
2. 吳 Wú
   贛 Gàn
   湘 Xiāng
3. 閩 Mǐn
   客家 Kèjiā
   粵 Yuè
   徽州 Huīzhōu

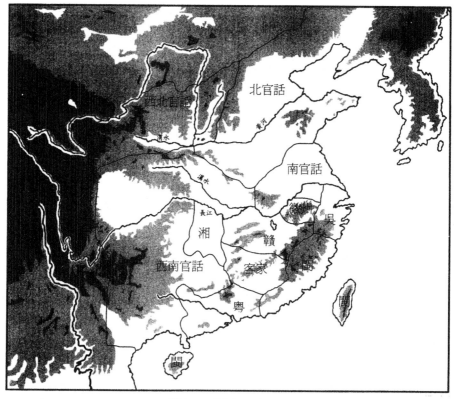

Chinese Dialect Areas

(based on Jerry Norman, *Chinese* [Cambridge: Cambridge University Press, 1988], p. 184)

A Time Line

1800 B.C.	Proto-Chinese	
1200 B.C.	early Old Chinese	甲骨文 (oracle bones)
		language of 尚書, 詩經
		大篆 (seal-script, 籀)
600 B.C.	Old Chinese	Austronesian influence(?)[11]
		language of 左傳, 國語

11. See, for example, Jerry Norman and Mei Tsu-lin, "The Austroasiatics in Ancient South China: Some Lexical Evidence," *Monumenta Serica* 32 (1976): 274–301; and Laurent Sagart, "Chinese and Austronesian: Evidence for a Genetic Relationship," *Journal of Chinese Linguistics* 21, no. 1 (1996): 1–62.

300 B.C.	late Old Chinese	language of 孟子, 莊子, 戰國策, etc., Qin unification of script (小篆 and 隸書); written and spoken forms are similar(?)
0 A.D.	early Middle Chinese	significant syntactic and phonological change; written and spoken languages begin to diverge
		説文解字 written tones replace final consonants(?)
600 A.D.	Middle Chinese	切韻 written by committee to standardize readings; Mǐn develops as a dialect[12]
800 A.D.	Old Mandarin	Other southern dialects split off from northern; "modern" aspect markers, resultatives, 把, begin to appear
1000 A.D.		廣韻 written; entering tones start to fuse, then disappear
1200 A.D.		中原音韻 written 1300 A.D.
	Middle Mandarin	central dialects (Wú, Gàn, Xiāng)
1600 A.D.	Modern Mandarin	final **-m** disappears
2000 A.D.		

D. Inflection

In European languages we are used to talking about the case, number, and gender of nouns and the mood, voice, and tense of verbs. The endings of nouns and verbs contain this information, and we call these languages *inflected*. The words of literary Chinese—the individual characters—contain no similar markers to indicate tense and the like. Instead, literary Chinese relies strictly on *word order*—to tell us who did (or is doing, or will be doing) what to whom—and on *function*

---

12. Mei Zulin and Yang Xiufang's discussion of the stages in the development of the Min dialect may serve as a model for future analyses of the origins and development of the various southern dialects. See Méi Zǔlín 梅祖麟 and Yáng Xiùfāng 楊秀芳, "Jǐge Mǐnnányǔ yǔfǎ chéngfèn de shíjiān céngcì" [The temporal strata of several components of the grammar of the Mǐnnán dialect] 〈幾個閩語語法成份的時間層次〉, 歷史語言研究所集刊66, no. 1 (March 1995): 1–21.

words (also called *particles*) to convey all the other types of information we derive from word endings in Western languages.

III. The Syntax of Literary Chinese

A. A Preliminary Discussion of Strategy

The version of grammar presented in this textbook has two major goals. First, it provides a flexible framework for approaching literary Chinese, Second, using the syntactic categories discussed below, it attempts to break students of habits of reading appropriate to modern English and modern Chinese that are not helpful—or are even misleading—in the reading of literary Chinese.

The version of syntax presented in this textbook will disappoint linguists for several reasons. First, by "literary Chinese," I mean the standard written language of pre-modern China and *not* the spoken language—Late Old Chinese—from which it derives. Late Old Chinese is a transitional language with features remaining from an earlier period and with intriguing variations that suggest regional dialects. Writers of literary Chinese in the later tradition recognized the idiosyncracies of Warring States and early Han prose and imitated them to give their styles an "ancient" feel, but I suspect that the syntactic logic behind Warring States texts had long since been lost. Thus I shall not dwell on the syntactic features of Late Old Chinese itself but only on those aspects of literary Chinese that remained largely constant throughout the written tradition.

Another reason that the syntactic analysis presented here diverges from a fully adequate account is that I try to adhere to the principle of "make no unnecessary distinctions." I include only those syntactic elements for which literary Chinese itself has function words that explicitly indicate the syntax in cases of ambiguity or rhetorical emphasis. I try to be true to the syntactic relations marked by those function words. For example, I do not use the category "preposition" because literary Chinese has no set of words that behaves sufficiently closely to how prepositions behave in English for this to be a useful category. The two closest candidates—coverbs and locative objects—behave according to rules appropriate for verbs and objects, respectively (see below). In contrast, modern Mandarin *does* have prepositions: for instance, one can say both

跟著他回家

and

跟他回家

but not

*由著這條路回家[13]

That is, in modern Mandarin not all coverbs are alike. Some are more grammaticalized—reduced from a verb to the status of a function word—than others, and usage clearly distinguishes them. The most grammaticalized have indeed become prepositions, whereas the newer coverbs, like 跟, are still in some middle state. The distinctions in usage of coverbs in literary Chinese do not appear strong enough to warrant the introduction of a grammatical term to mark the difference. I use a similar approach to other syntactic categories that are shared by both modern Chinese and English but that are better treated as special cases of broader categories within literary Chinese. (See Appendix A for a discussion of the question of *complements*, in particular.)

B. Parts of Speech: Nouns and Verbs

On the whole, one can rely on dictionaries to determine "what part of speech" a character is. Nonetheless, words in literary Chinese shift word-classes sufficiently easily that the word's *actual function* in any particular sentence should take precedence over its *usual* classification. How, then, does one know when syntax demands a particular word class? There are a few rather safe rules:

1. Nouns are negated by 非, 無
   Verbs are negated by 未, 不, 勿, 莫

Note, however, that *direct objects* are occasionally placed *between* the negating function word and the verb itself:

歲不吾與 The years do not give us [respite].

---

13. By convention, ungrammatical sentences are marked with an asterisk (*).

nyator, word, object

莫之知 None knew it.

未之信也 He did not yet believe it.

2. The character 所 is used to represent the direct or locative objects of verbs, as in

    吾食之 I eat it.

    吾所食 That which I eat. . . .

That which follows the 所 must be a *verbal* expression.

3. The character 之 is often used to mark explicit *subordination* (see below, section C.4). Placing 之 between the subject and verb of a complete sentence turns that sentence into a *nominal* phrase:

    神來 The spirits come.

    神之來 The coming of the spirits. . . .

4. Similarly, when a *verbal* phrase appears within the *topic* of an explicit topic-comment construction A B 也 (see below, section C.1), it becomes *nominalized*:

    不私其父，非孝子也 [One who] is not partial to his father is not a filial son.

5. Almost every word we think of as an adjective in English—"tall," "short," "red," "green"—can serve as a *stative verb*, a verb describing the state of some object:

    嵩山高 Mount Sōng *is tall*.

6. Finally, some verbs that ordinarily are *intransitive*, that is, they have no direct object, will occasionally be used *with* a direct object. The effect of this syntax is to make the verb *causative*:

    敬神鬼而遠之 Respect the spirits but keep them at a distance [cause them to be distant]

Sometimes this "causing" is of a more abstract nature, where "causing X to become Y" means to "put X in category Y," as in

    叟不遠千里 Elder Sir, you do not *consider* a thousand *lǐ* too far.

C. Grammatical Relations

There are only five types of grammatical relationships: *topic-comment*, *verb-object*, *coordination*, *subordination*, and *number complement*. And "elements"—whether words, phrases, or entire sentences—"that stand in grammatical relationship to each other are always *adjacent*."[14] This rule that the two halves of a syntactic unit are always next to each other strongly affects our understanding of literary Chinese syntax. In particular, it shifts our focus from the linear sequence of individual words to a more complex view of their role in the construction of the sets of relationships that determine the actual syntax of the sentence. How a top-down, sentence-oriented analysis of syntax works in practice is the substance of this book. The following section introduces the five types of grammatical relationships that are the basic tools of our analysis.

☆ 1. Topic-Comment

Literary Chinese, like all other languages, can be described as having sentences of the form:

Subject + Predicate

However, the concept of "subject" in more recent linguistic theories is an abstract entity that can perhaps be most simply described as the "external argument" for the predicate. That is, "subject" is an element of syntactic structure rather than our usual notion of the "subject" as filling the thematic role of "agent," the person or thing that carries out the action of a verb.[15] For example, in

John bought the book.

"John" is both the *subject* (the external argument to "bought the book") and the *agent* (the person who bought the book). In the passive construction

14. Stimson, *55 T'ang Poems*, p. 9.
15. Randy J. LaPolla argues that by current linguistic theory, modern Mandarin has neither "subjects" nor even "direct objects." See Randy J. LaPolla, "Arguments Against 'Subject' and 'Direct Object' as Viable Concepts in Chinese," 歷史語言研究所集刊 63, no. 4 (Sept. 1993): 759–813.

The book was bought by John.

"Book" is now the *subject*, but its thematic role is the *patient* (the object that receives the action of "bought").

In subsequent discussions, I refer to "the simplest form" of a sentence, by which I mean an "original" version in which the *subject*, the *topic*, and the *agent* all coincide. The *topic-comment* structure used as the basis for analysis in fact derives from the more fundamental concepts of subject and predicate. But in practice since *topic-comment* proves more useful and flexible for describing the actual organization of sentences in literary Chinese, I use it rather than *subject-predicate*. (For more on this question, see the discussion in Appendix A.)

The topic-comment structure used in this textbook is a mixture of three separate categories used in the discussion of texts. First, a "topic," by itself, is what a sentence "is about," and the comment is what the sentence says about the topic. Second, sentences in literary Chinese—as in English and modern Chinese—have two *focal points*, at the beginning and at the end. The "theme" is the element at the front of the sentence, and an element that has been brought to the front to receive focus has been *thematized*. The third descriptive category blended into the terms "topic" and "comment" is that of "old information / new information." That is, the topic *usually* corresponds to the *old information*, and the comment is *new information*.[16] These three separate meanings largely coincide in practice, except for the rare rhetorical inversion. To summarize:

---

16. These categories are somewhat fuzzy, and *topic-comment* as used in the textbook is correspondingly broad. For example, the usual test to identify a "topic" (in the stricter usage) is to ask, "If this sentence is the answer to a question, what would that question be?" Yet

China is a very ancient culture.

could be the answer to two different questions:

(1) What is a very ancient culture?
(2) Why is China interesting?

As an answer to (1), the topic (strictly conceived) is "is a very ancient culture," which is the "old information," and the comment (and new information) is "China." In contrast, as the answer to (2), "China" becomes both the topic and the old information, and "is a very ancient culture" becomes the comment and the new material. I am indebted to the discussion in Keith Brown and Jim Miller, *Syntax: A Linguistic*

Topic | Comment
what the sentence is about | what is said about the topic
the (usually unstressed) | focal point at the end of
  beginning | sentence
old information | new information

a. The simplest type of topic-comment construction is a *nominal sentence* that identifies one noun with another:

慎道趙人 Shèn Dào was a man from Zhào.
詩者志之所之也 Poetry is where the resolve goes.

The second example makes the topic-comment structure explicit through the use of the function words 者 and 也, but these markers are not *required*.

Nominal sentences in the form **A B** 也 usually state that **A** is a *type* of **B**, or that **A** is of the category **B**. That is, since there were many people from Zhào, the statement does not *uniquely* define Shèn Dào, but at least we know that he fits the category "man of Zhào." Similarly, resolve usually leads to action, and thus there are many places where it might "go," but the above sentence states that poetry is one such place, one member of the set.

Pulleyblank points out that sentences of the form **A** 猶 **B** 也 should also be viewed as nominal sentences since they are a form of a statement of identity: **A** is *of an analogous type* to **B**.[17]

性猶湍水也 The nature is like quickly flowing water.

b. One common use of the topic-comment structure is to move the time or location to the beginning of the sentence to set the scene for the event to be described:

丁酉祿山陷東京 On the Dīngyǒu day Ān Lùshān captured the Eastern Capital.

If the topic and the comment were reversed, the effect would be to stress the day, as if the date were in question or part of some reckoning:

Introduction to Sentence Structure, 2nd ed. (Hammersmith, Eng.: HarperCollins, 1991), pp. 343–68.

17. See Pulleyblank, *Outline of Classical Chinese Grammar*, pp. 18–19.

祿山陷東京者丁酉也 It was on the Dīngyǒu day that Ān Lùshān captured the Eastern Capital.

c. The transformation of the "normal" order of a sentence to change the element that is being stressed is called *topicalization*. This process of shifting parts of the sentence to the topic position in order to *de-emphasize* them is a major tool of literary Chinese rhetoric and an important element in the creation of complex sentences. Consider the following famous sentence from *Zhuāng Zǐ*:

臣之所好者道也 (i) What I, your servant, like is the Way.

which is a transformation of a "base" sentence:

臣好道 (ii) I, your servant, like the Way.

It is unclear in (ii) what the central point of the sentence is: is the speaker stressing that *he* in particular likes the Way, or that, contrary to previous evidence, he really *likes* the Way, or that, finally, *what* he likes is the Way. In sentence (i), both the "I" and the "like" have been moved to the topic, and the speaker reduces what he wants to stress to one word, 道, the Way. He likes *the Way*.

Consider a second example, and notice in particular that the topicalized element here is *not* the subject:

先生，不知何許人也 (iii) The Master's place of origin is not known.

This sentence can be more cumbersomely but more accurately translated as "As for the Master, he is a man of whom we do not know his place of origin." Approximately the same information is conveyed by the non-topicalized sentence,

不知先生爲何許人 (iv)

By moving 先生 to the beginning of the sentence as a topic, the writer emphasizes in particular the information or lack of it. As noted above, in sentence (iii), the topic is neither the *subject* nor the *agent* for the main verb of the sentence. Always remember: *topics are not the same as subjects*.

d. Topicalization is one aspect of a broader type of movement of parts of a sentence to the front called *exposure*. Sometimes, the movement is for rhetorical emphasis, as in

善哉問也 What a *good* question!

Sometimes, the point is to mark a contrast:

冷風則小和，飄風則大和 The *breeze* is the small harmonizing, and the *whirlwind* the great harmonizing.

Note that 則 is here an explicit marker of topic-comment rather than simply the sign of an "if . . . , then" sentence.

Sometimes, especially if the topic is a long phrase, it is marked off as a unit, then resumed with a 是, ". . . , as for this, ..."[18]

旣不能令，又不受令，是絕物也 Not being able to command and also not accepting command, this is a "cut-off thing."

e. Many sorts of relations that are expressed in English as subordinate clauses are structured in literary Chinese as topic-comment relations. The most common are *conditional expressions*: "if . . . , then" or "when . . . , then":

王如知此，則無望民之多於鄰國也 If you, the King, know this, then do not expect [your] populace to become greater than [that of] the neighboring countries

2. *Verb-Object*

Although *verb-object* seems a familiar category, literary Chinese syntax includes some verb-object relationships that are treated quite differently from those we encounter in English.

a. Locative Objects

Time and place information that is expressed through prepositional phrases in English is the *object of a verb* in literary Chinese:[19]

先生居山林 The Master lives [in] the mountain forest.

18. For a detailed discussion of exposure, see Pulleyblank, *Outline of Classical Chinese Grammar*, pp. 69–75.

19. For a more detailed explanation of why locative expressions are treated as objects, see the discussion of complements in Appendix A.

Sometimes a *locative particle* like 於 or 于 precedes the locative object and makes the function of the word very clear.

Note that one can substitute 中 for 林 to arrive at the sentence:

> 先生居山中 The Master lives [in a place] among the mountains.

The handful of words that function like prepositions in English, specifically 上, 下, 前, 後, 中, and 間 are all nouns.

b. Direct Objects

The simplest case is a verb and a noun:

> 飲酒 drink wine
> 開門 open the gate

Sometimes the direct object of a verb is *another verb* or verb phrase. There are three major variations of this structure:

i. Verbs that take *event objects*

> 不知說生 [He] does not know *to delight in life*.

This is a perfectly normal usage in which the only difference is that the object of the verb happens to be an event, that is, a nominalized verb.

ii. Verbs that take *pivots*

> 請歸 requested to return
> 使歸 caused to return
> 使漁夫歸 caused the fisherman (*pivot*) to return
> 使之歸 caused him (*pivot*) to return

Some verbs—those making requests or commands—often take an entire sentence (the content of the command itself) as their object. The *subject* of the embedded sentence becomes attached to the verb of command as an *indirect object,* and the *verb* in the embedded sentence—the main verb of the sentence—becomes a *direct object.* In fact this is the same basic pattern as in English:

> I ordered that *he* be shot.   ["he" is subject of "be shot"]
> I ordered *him* shot.   ["him" is indirect object of "ordered"]

Because the subject of an embedded sentence becomes bound to both verbs, it is called the *pivot*. This type of "subject raising" occurs only with a small group of verbs called *pivot verbs*.

iii. Auxiliary Verbs

應歸 ought to return
能歸 can return

Some verbs (必, 肯, 須, etc.), usually expressing *modality* (that is, the probability, desirability, or possibility of an event) are called auxiliary verbs. They require a second verb (the direct object of the first), which becomes the main verb.[20] These main verbs, moreover, cannot have a different topic from the auxiliary:

漁夫能歸 the fisherman can return

but not:

*能漁夫歸 ~~can cause the fisherman to return~~

c. Indirect Objects
Like both modern Mandarin and English, literary Chinese has verbs that take an *indirect object–direct object* construction.

爲之君 [The sage] made rulers for them (i.o.).
俗謂之小人 The populace call him (i.o.) a small person.

3. *Coordinate Relationships* – *same level*

In a *coordinate relationship* the two elements are of the same type and stand as equals. The units may be nouns, verbs, adjectives, or adverbs, or larger groupings of phrases or even sentences:

by importance 1st = 1 imp.

Nouns: 仲由、冉求可謂大臣與 Can Zhòngyóu and Rǎnqiú be called great officials?
Verbs: 君子不憂不懼 The noble man is neither worried nor alarmed.

---

20. Lin Jo-wang and Jane Chih-chen Tang argue that even in modern Mandarin auxiliary verbs serve as the verb (head) in a verb phrase and thus differ from auxiliaries in English. See Lin Jo-wang and Jane Chih-chen Tang, "Modals as Verbs in Chinese: A GB Perspective," 歷史語言研究所集刊 66, no. 1 (March 1995): 53–105.

Sentences: 君子懷德。小人懷土。 The noble man cherishes virtue; the small man cherishes [his] land.

a. Sometimes grammatical function words make the coordinate relationship explicit:

Nouns:唯我與爾有是夫。 Is it not that you **and** I alone share this?
Verbs: 富且貴焉恥也。 I would be ashamed to be wealthy **and** esteemed under these [circumstances].
Verbs: 王笑而不言。 The king smiled **but** did not speak.

b. Sometimes coordination defines *alternative* possibilities, and in English translation, an "or" is required:

安危在晷刻 Safety or danger were in the moment.

Sometimes the character 或 or 將 is used to make the presentation of alternatives explicit:

守令或開門出迎或棄城竄匿 Some of the magistrates opened the gates and went out to greet [him], some abandoned the city walls and fled into hiding.

c. Very often when two verbs stand in coordinate relation, the first action becomes the *antecedent condition* for the possibility of the second action. This implied connection can be translated as "in order to" or "with the result that." Thus:

咸來問訊 They all came [in order to] enquire [of him].
恥之逃隱 He was ashamed of it [with the result that he] fled and hid.

d. Sometimes, in order to stress the causal relationship between coordinate verbs, authors will use 以 to mark their coordination:

脩身以俟之 He cultivates his person to await it [whatever comes].

Originally, 以 in such cases perhaps represented the fusion of 以之, "and using this, . . ." where "this" refers back the first verb. (See section 3.e below.)

e. The function word 而 between coordinate verbal expressions has a rhetorical effect analogous to 則 as an explicit marker of exposed nouns: by moving one verb group further to the front, it serves as a point of focus that highlights the question of the actual relationship between the two groups. In a sentence like *wang xiao er bu*

王笑而不言。 The king smiled [and? but?] did not speak.

we must ask ourselves what in fact is implied. Did the king consider his smile sufficient? Was the king using a smile to hide his embarrassed silence? Was Mèng Zǐ expecting speech, so that the 而 registers his dismay? Or is the 而 simply used to fill out a four-character rhythm?

f. A special class of coordinate verbal expressions is the *coverb*. As the language developed, some very common verb-object phrases came to be used regularly as the first verb phrase of a coordinate verb pair (thus suggesting antecedent condition) and lost their independent status. They came to be seen as bound to, and auxiliary to the second verb of the pair. For example:

與汝遊 wander with you
方以類聚 types [of creatures] gather by their categories

The verb of the verb-object pair (here, the 與 and the 以) is called a *coverb*. In other situations, both verbs, 與 "to give, (and by extension) to accompany" and 以 "to grasp," attain full verbal status. They speak of action on their own. As coverbs, however, they simply describe an antecedent condition.

g. Some types of coordinate verb constructions in literary Chinese express relations that are treated in English as subordinate clauses. One major group is time constructions: "After . . . , then . . . ," "When . . . , then . . . ," etc:

既得人爵而棄其天爵，則惑之甚者也。 Having obtained man's ennoblement, to then reject Heaven's ennoblement is [an act] of extreme confusion.

h. Another major group of coordinate verb constructions treated differently from English are *concessives*, "Even though . . . ," "Even if not . . . ," etc.:[21]

雖直而不病 Even though he is direct, he is not faulted.

4. Subordinate Relations

The first element modifies the second. The second element, to which the first is attached, is called the *head*. Thus:

青草 green (modifier) + grass (head)

There are many different types of grass—blue grass, sere grass, dense grass, short grass—and "green grass" delimits one particular subgroup of all possible grasses.

In subordinate relations—as in coordinate—the elements can be nouns, verbs, or longer phrases, but since the first element modifies the second, it functions grammatically as an English adjective or adverb.

a. The marker for explicit subordination to a noun is the character 之. Consider the two meanings for

草青 (1) The grass is green. (2) the green of the grass (or "the greening of the grass")

That is, the two words could be either (1) a sentence or (2) a modifier-head noun phrase. But the syntax of

草之青 (3) the green(ing) of the grass

is clear. In this reading, 之 has been inserted between the topic and verb comment pair of sentence (1). The result is to turn the *verbal* sentence into a *nominal* phrase (that is, the verb becomes its noun counterpart that describes either an action—*turning* green—or a state, *being* green.)

b. One commonly used character for marking modification of verbs is 然, which is equivalent to 如是 ("like this"):

泠然善也 In a 泠 (light and wonderful) manner, it was good.

21. For Pulleyblank's discussion, see *Outline of Classical Chinese Syntax*, pp. 156–58.

c. As noted above, the characters 上, 下, 前, 後, 中, and 間 are nouns. Therefore in phrases these characters are often the *head*, modified by what comes before them, rather than the other way around. In

山前 [the place] in front of the mountain

"Mountain" *modifies* "[the place] in front." Similarly, the sentence

草上之風必偃 > (((草)之上)之風) Topic (必偃) Comment

can be translated awkwardly but in keeping with the sense of the original Chinese as "[As for] the wind (of the above part (of the grass)), [the grass] must bend [to it]." What one sees when reading 上, 下, 前, 後, 中, and 間 is a *place*, that is, a noun.

5. Number Complements

One final type of relationship between syntactic units is the use of a *number + measure* after the noun or verb:

閑居三月 He lived at ease [to the extent of] three months.
遣大夫二人 He sent two ministers.

In these sentences, the *number + measure* constructions do not modify the words to which they are attached because they do not actually restrict the domain of reference for those words. Rather, they simply add further information. Compare the following:

有士二人 There were noblemen [to the extent of] two men.
此二士之節 This was the virtue of the two noblemen.

The usual rule is that elements in a sentence that are moved closer to the front of a sentence are de-emphasized, but here we have the opposite. In the first sentence, the 二人 is not crucial to the identity of the noblemen; it merely gives us incidental information. In contrast, when 二 (without the measure 人) modifies 士 in the second sentence, the information is no longer incidental: the sentence points to the "virtue" of *two* specific noblemen. The importance of this difference is perhaps difficult to see, but examples in the texts should help clarify the usage. In any case, this relationship is common and easily identifiable, and poses no particular problems.

III. Sentences

This brief sketch of the components of literary Chinese as a language is not an arbitrary taxonomy. Although the preceding account of the grammar is by no means complete, it is, I hope, sufficient to provide a certain perspective on the syntax of literary Chinese and a set of tools for its analysis. The four relations—topic-comment, verb-object, coordination, and subordination—offer a way to approach and make sense of even the most complex sentences. A syntactic analysis based on this handful of relations is *sentence-oriented* rather than word-oriented. The sentence as a whole, rather than the individual words, is the basic unit of analysis. Sentences are divided into subunits related to one another in one of the four ways described above, and these subunits can be further divided into elements that also relate to one another in one of four ways. The final elements are, of course, the individual characters themselves. After one has sorted out the basic questions—What is the topic? What is the verb? What modifies what?—even convoluted sentences begin to fall into place. Or if they do not, then one can at least state quite precisely wherein the ambiguities lie.

IV. Suggestions for Further Reading

The following list of books and articles is intended to point to some of the major works in the history of the modern study of the linguistics of Old Chinese as well as give the student a sense of the current approaches and issues in the field both in English and in Chinese.

Baxter, William H. *A Handbook of Old Chinese Phonology.* Trends in Linguistics Studies and Monographs, no. 64. Berlin and New York: Mouton de Gruyter, 1992.

Cáo Guǎngshùn 曹廣順. 近代漢語助詞. 北京:語文, 1995.

Coblin, W. South. "BTD Revisited: A Reconsideration of the Han Buddhist Transcriptional Dialect." 歷史語言研究所集刊 63, no. 4 (Sept. 1993): 867–943.

Downer, G. B. "Derivation by Tone-Change in Classical Chinese." *Bulletin of the School of Oriental and African Studies* 22 (1959): 258–90.

Gāo Shùfán 高樹藩, ed. 文言文虛詞大詞典. 武漢: 湖北教育, 1991.

Graham, Angus C. "The Final Particle *Fwu* 夫." *Bulletin of the School of Oriental and African Studies* 17 (1955): 120–32.

———. "The Relation Between the Final Particles *Yu* 與 and *Yee* 也." *Bulletin of the School of Oriental and African Studies* 19 (1957): 105–23.

———. "*Yún* 云 and *Yuē* 曰 as Verbs and Particles." *Acta Orientalia Havniensia* 44 (1983): 33–71.

Harbsmeier, Christoph. *Aspects of Classical Chinese Syntax*. Scandinavian Institute of Asian Studies Monograph Series, no. 45. London and Malmö: Curzon Press, 1981.

———. *Science and Civilisation in China*, vol. 7, pt. I, *Language and Logic*. Cambridge: Cambridge University Press, 1988.

Hé Lèshì 何樂士. 〈《左傳》、《史記》介賓短語位置的比較〉. 語文研究 8 (1985): 57–65.

———. 〈《左傳》的單句和複句初探〉. In 程湘清, ed., 先秦漢語研究. 濟南: 山東教育 1992: 143–271.

Her, One-soon. "Historical Development of *Ba* and *Jiang* in the Tang Dynasty." *Language Variation and Change* 2 (1990): 279–96.

Karlgren, Bernhard. "The Early History of the *Chou Li* and *Tso Chuan* Texts." *Bulletin of the Museum of Far Eastern Antiquities* 3 (1931): 1–59.

———. *Grammata Serica Recensa. Bulletin of the Museum of Far Eastern Antiquities* 29 (1957): 1–332.

Kennedy, George A. "A Study of the Particle *Yen*." *Journal of the American Oriental Society* 60 (1940): 1–22, 193–207.

———. "Another Note on *Yen*." *Harvard Journal of Asiatic Studies* 16 (1953): 226–36.

LaPolla, Randy J. "Arguments Against 'Subject' and 'Direct Object' as Viable Concepts in Chinese." 歷史語言研究所集刊 63, no. 4 (Sept. 1993): 759–813.

Li, Charles N., and Thompson, Sandra A. *Mandarin Chinese: A Functional Reference Grammar*. Berkeley: University of California Press, 1981.

Lǐ Fānggui. "Archaic Chinese." In David N. Keightley, ed., *The Origins of Chinese Civilization*. Berkeley: University of California Press, 1983, pp. 393–408.

Lǐ Zuǒfēng 李佐豐〈先秦漢語的自動詞及其使動用法〉. 語言學報 10 (1983): 117–44.

Lin Jo-wang and Jane Chih-chen Tang. "Modals as Verbs in Chinese: A GB Perspective." 歷史語言研究所集刊 66, no. 1 (March 1995): 53–105.

Liú Qí 劉淇. 助字辨略. Reprinted—Kyoto: Chūbun, 1983.

Lǔ Guóyáo 魯國堯.〈《孟子》" 以羊易之 " " 易之以羊 " 兩種結構類型的對比研究〉. In 程湘清 ed., 先秦漢語研究. 濟南: 山東教育, 1992, pp. 272–90.

Méi Zǔlín 梅祖麟.〈從漢代的「動、殺」「動、死」來看動補結構的發展兼論中古時期的起詞的施受關係的中立化〉. 語言學論叢 16 (1991): 112–36.

——— and 楊秀芳,〈幾個閩語語法成份的時間層次〉. 歷史語言研究所集刊 66, no. 1 (March 1995): 1–21.

Norman, Jerry. *Chinese*. Cambridge Language Surveys. Cambridge: Cambridge University Press, 1988.

——— and W. South Coblin. "A New Approach to Chinese Historical Linguistics." *Journal of the American Oriental Society* 115, no. 4 (Oct.–Dec. 1995): 576–84.

Pān Yǔnzhōng 潘允中.〈漢語動補結構的發展〉. 中國語文 1980, no. 1: 53–60.

Peyraube, Alain. "History of the Passive Constructions in Chinese Until the 10th Century." *Journal of Chinese Linguistics* 17, no. 2 (1989): 335–71.

———. "On the History of Chinese Locative Prepositions." 中國境內語言暨語言學 2 (1994): 361–87.

———. "Recent Issues in Chinese Historical Syntax." In James C. T. Huang and Y. H. Li, eds., *New Horizons in Chinese Linguistics*. Dordrecht: Kluwer Academic Publishers, 1995, pp. 161–213.

———.〈早期‧把，字句的幾個問題〉. 語文研究 30 (1989): 1–9.

Pulleyblank, Edwin G. "The Locative Particles *Yü* 於, *Yü* 于, and *Hu* 乎." *Journal of the American Oriental Society* 106 (1986): 1–12.

————. *Outline of Classical Chinese Grammar*. Vancouver: University of British Columbia Press, 1995.

————. "Some Notes on Morphology and Syntax in Classical Chinese." In Henry Rosemont, ed., *Chinese Texts and Philosophical Contexts: Essays Dedicated to Angus C. Graham*. LaSalle, Ill.: Open Court, 1991, pp. 21–45.

————. "Some Embedding Constructions in Classical Chinese." In Chinese Language Society of Hong Kong, ed., *Wang Li Memorial Volumes: English Volume*. Hong Kong: Joint Publishing, 1987, pp. 349–56.

Sagart, Laurent. "Chinese and Austronesian: Evidence for a Genetic Relationship." *Journal of Chinese Linguistics* 21, no. 1 (1993): 1–62.

Sun, Chaofen. *Word-Order Change and Grammaticalization in the History of Chinese*. Stanford: Stanford University Press, 1996.

Wei Peiquan 魏培泉.〈古漢語介詞「於」的演變略史〉. 中央研究院歷史語言研究所集刊 62, no. 4 (1993): 317–86.

Yáng Bójùn 楊伯峻 and Hé Lèshì 何樂士. 古漢語語法及其發展. 北京: 語文, 1992.

Yú Nǎiyǒng 余迺永. 互註校正宋本廣韻. 臺北: 聯關, 1975.

Zhōu Fǎgāo 周法高. 中國古代語法: 稱代編. 臺北: 中央研究所, 1959.

————. 中國古代語法: 造句編(上). 臺北: 中央研究所, 1961.

————. 中國古代語法: 構詞編. 臺北: 中央研究所, 1962.

Zhū Zìqīng 朱自清, Yè Shèngtáo 葉聖陶, and Lǚ Shúxiāng 呂叔湘. 文言讀本. 上海: 上海教育, 1980.

Part One

Texts to Introduce Basic Grammar

Lesson 1

Nominal and Verbal Sentences

The most basic structure of literary Chinese to be studied in this textbook is the *topic-comment* sentence. Sentences can be extremely complicated, with elaborate noun phrases and elegant coordinate clauses. Yet, no matter how daunting the text, one can always begin the analysis with the basic questions: "What is the topic? What is being said about the topic?"

Topics and Comments

The **topic**, as the name suggests, is *what you want to write about*, and the **comment** is *what it is that you want to say* about the topic. The comment is *new information*; it is usually the stressed element in the sentence. Every sentence has a comment, but it does not necessarily have an *explicit* topic. If the topic is missing, one always needs to ask oneself what is being talked about. Topics often switch in mid-paragraph or even mid-sentence without an explicit indication that the topic has changed.

Literary Chinese has two types of comments and two corresponding types sentences: the **nominal** and the **verbal**. In terms of syntax, the distinction is quite simple:

- A nominal sentence has a noun phrase as its comment.

- A verbal sentence has a verb phrase as its comment.

Nominal Sentences

Nominal sentences are fundamentally **statements of identity**. The sentence **A, B** 也 asserts that **A** is a type of **B**:

宋，小國也 Sòng **is** a small state.

仲子，齊之世家也 [Chén] Zhòngzǐ **is** of an eminent clan of Qí.

物之不齊，物之情也 Things being unequal **is** their nature.

無父無君，是禽獸也 [One] without a father and without a ruler—this **is** a wild animal.

In these identity statements, the second category—the noun phrase in the comment —tends to be more general than the first category—the noun phrase in the topic. There are many small states: Sòng is one of them. Qí has many men from clans with a tradition of service to the state: Chén Zhòngzǐ is one of them. "Things" have many aspects to their nature, and inequality is one of them. These assertions of identity place an object (the topic) into a larger context and situate it.

Simple identity statements, however, constitute only a small fraction of all nominal sentences. The comment in a nominal sentence is frequently **verb +** 也. Verbs serving as topics are nominalized, since topics are nouns. As nouns, they refer to a repeating action or a specific event. When verbs serve as nominal comments, they refer to a general category of action that defines the identity of the topic:

上好禮則民易使也 If the ruler delights in ritual, then the populace is **tractable**.

That is, "tractable" (more literally, "easy to direct") is a general situation that typifies the populace.

王之不王，不為也 Your Majesty's not ruling as a true king is **a case of not trying**.

Here, the "not ruling as a true king" is defined as an instance of the more general category of "not trying."

Writers often extend the **verb +** 也 construction that provides categories to describe actions and use it to **offer an explanation** for an action:

桀紂之失天下也，失其民也。失其民者，失其心也。Jié and Zhòu's losing the realm was **a matter of losing the populace**. Losing the populace was **a matter of losing their hearts and minds**.

Since neither modern Chinese nor modern English has a structure similar to the explanatory **verb** + 也 nominal sentence, it is not easy to grasp when one first encounters it. However, because the structure is an important feature of literary Chinese, it reappears throughout this textbook. Repeated encounters will help clarify its nuances.

Verbal Sentences

Verbal sentences are the familiar type: they are those in which the comment has a verb. Beginning students of literary Chinese, however, often have problems recognizing verbs. Transitive and intransitive verbs present few difficulties, but **stative verbs** do not behave in the same way they do in modern Mandarin, and they are entirely lacking in English.

As the name suggests, a stative verb in the comment describes a continuing state of the topic:

嵩山高 Mount Sōng **is high**.
德不孤 The virtuous **are not alone**.
風雨瀟瀟 The wind and rain **are chill and forlorn**.

Stative verbs can also mark a *transition* into a state or an *intensification* of a state:

哀情多 Sorrowful feelings **grow ever more**.
去爾日遙遠 [My] separating from you is daily more distant.

On occasion a noun can be forced to serve as a verb, but just as the *persisting of a state* of a "thing" is a form of action, so too asserting, acquiring, or simply *maintaining an identity* can be a form of action:

齊景公問政於孔子。孔子對曰君君臣臣父父子子。公曰善哉，信如君不君，臣不臣，父不父，子不子，雖有粟，吾得而食諸。 Duke Jǐng of Qí asked Confucius about governing. Confucius replied, "The ruler **acts as the ruler**, and the minister **acts as minister**; the father **acts as the**

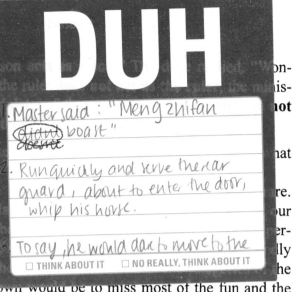

42

father, and the ~~son~~ ... ~~... rul~~ ... ... ~~... the ~~minis-ter **not act as** ~~...~~ ... **not act as son**, even ...

Identity here is not inna... ... ...at the identity demands. ... ...

These variations on ... ...re. Most of the time, the ... ...our own. Still, we need to ... ...er-spectives on identity an ... ...lly different from those of t ... ...he classical texts into our own would be to miss most of the fun and the challenge.

Text 1: 困學 (論語 16.9)

1. 孔子曰，生而知之者，上也。
2. 學而知之者，次也。
3. 困而學之，又次也。
4. 困而不學，民斯爲下矣。

Text 2: 馬不進也 (論語 6.15)

1. 子曰，孟之反不伐。
2. 奔而殿，將入門，策其馬，
3. 曰，非敢後也，馬不進也。

Vocabulary

困　　*kùn* (v), to be blocked, oppressed, in difficulties

●學　　*xué* (v), to learn

不 *always negates a verb.*
非 *negates sentences.*

- 論語   *Lún yǔ*, the *Analects*, the sayings of Confucius recorded by his disciples. The numbers 16.9 are to be read the "ninth passage in the sixteenth book."

- 孔子   *Kǒng Zǐ*, "Master Kǒng," i.e., Confucius (ca. 551–479 B.C.)

- 子   *Zǐ* (n), "master," a polite form of address

- 生   *shēng* (v), to be born

- 而   *ér* (fw: marker of verb coordination)

- 知   *zhī* (v), to know

- 之   *zhī* (n), him, her, it, them

- 者   *zhě* (a bound-form abstract noun that requires a modifier) *nominalizer.*

- 上   *shàng* (n), the top

- 也   *yě* (fw: phrase-final, marker of nominal phrases)

- 次   *cì* (n), place > specified place > next in specified order

- 又   *yòu* (adv), again

- 不   *bù* (adv), not

- 民   *mín* (n), the populace

- 斯   *sī* (n), this > (fw: "this being so, then/thus . . .")

- 爲   *wéi* (v), to act > to become > to be reckoned as *to be considered as.*

- 下   *xià* (n), the bottom

- 矣   *yǐ* (fw: sentence-final marker of change of state)

- 馬   *mǎ* (n), horse

- 進   *jìn* (v), to advance

- 曰   *yuē* (v), to say

- 孟之反   Mèng Zhīfǎn, an official in the state of Lǔ

- *伐   *fā* (v), (here) to boast, claim unearned merit *normally = attack.*

- 奔   *bēn* (v), to run > to flee > to be routed (said of an army)

- 殿   *diàn* (n), the rear guard (that protects a withdrawing army) > (v) to serve in the rear guard

- 將   *jiāng* (adv), to be about to *N.= general*

- 入   *rù* (v), to enter

- 門   *mén* (n), two-leafed gate

- 策   *cè* (n), horse-whip > (v) to whip

困 *stranded / hard pressed*

奔 *bēn run quickly*
奔 *bèn go straight towards.*

✦其   *qí* (adj), his, her, its,   敢   *gǎn* (av), to dare to
            their
                                            • 後   *hòu* (n), the rear > (v) to
• 非   *fēi* (fw: marker of nega-   be at or move to the rear
            tion for nominal sen-
            tences)

* of identity

Notes

1. 生而知之 The two verbs 生 and 知 are *coordinate*, and the 生 serves as a strong **antecedent condition** for the 知: "Knowing it *simply under the condition of* having been born" is best. The other three sets of verbs all follow the same pattern in which the first verb in each pair **sets the condition** under which the second verb occurs:

> 學而知之 to learn *and then* know it
> 困而學之 to be perplexed *and then* learn it
> 困而不學 to be perplexed *but then* not learn

2. 生而知之者 The character 者 simply indicates a "thing," often to be treated as a general category. It is a **bound form**; that is, it cannot appear by itself and must always be modified by either a noun or verb. The verb phrase that modifies it here specifies what sort of thing: a "being born and knowing it" thing. Such an entity can be *a person* who is born knowing it, or it can refer to the *state* of being born and knowing it. Since a person may be born knowing one thing but not another, the phrase here is best taken as the state.

3. 上 In general, position words like 上, 後, and 中 are **nouns**: "the place on top," "the place behind," "the place in the middle," and so on.

4. 生而知之者，上也 This is a nominal sentence that makes a **categorical judgment**. That is, it says the topic—生而知之者—belongs in the category 上, "the highest." The next two lines repeat this pattern:

> 學而知之者，次也 to learn and then know it *is the next rank*
> 困而學之，又次也 to be perplexed and then learn it *is again the next*

5. 民斯爲下 The character 斯 usually means "this." The sentence here, however, illustrates an important extension. 斯 comes to serve as **a marker of exposure**: it highlights the (normally) unstressed topic as a focal point in the sentence. At the same time, 斯 also retains some of its meaning as "this" by continuing to refer back to an earlier reference: ". . . , this being the case / for this reason / under these circumstances . . . ." In this sentence, the "this" refers to the "being perplexed but not learning."

6. 爲 is a difficult word. It can mean either "to enact," that is, to be something by virtue of one's actions, or, "to be deemed," to be taken by others to be something. Both possibilities work here.

7. 矣 is also a difficult word. Its usual role is as a **perfective** marker, the marker of a completed change of state. Sometimes, as in this sentence, however, it serves as an emphatic marker with a sense of finality: "That's it completely!"

8. 非敢後也，馬不進也 This pair of nominal clauses provides an answer to the implied question, "What was the matter? Why were you the last person back?" Mèng's first comment explains what was *not* the matter: "It isn't the case that I dared to remain at the rear." The second comment finishes Mèng's elegantly modest (and untrue) explanation: "[The problem] was that my horse wouldn't advance." Mèng uses nominal constructions to lay out **the facts of the matter** and to declare the meaning of the action (his lagging behind) seen as an event, a "thing" with a definite shape (a beginning, a middle, and an end).

It is perhaps worthwhile to note that in 馬不進也, the structure is *not*

> 馬 (Topic) + [不進] 也 (不進 as verb phrase nominalized by 也)

but

> [Arriving last] (Implied Topic) + [馬不進] 也 (whole verbal sentence as comment)

The statement is not about the horse but about Mèng's action.

Exercises

1. Pattern Completion: Please complete the following sentences. For each one, explain what is the new information. (That is, what sort of question does the statement answer?)

吾父之名，＿＿＿＿＿＿＿＿＿也。

吾母之名，＿＿＿＿＿＿＿＿＿也。

＿＿＿＿＿＿＿＿＿，吾生日也。

＿＿＿＿＿＿＿＿＿，唐代詩人也。

2. Answer the following questions: Note: 與 = *yǔ*, "and," 孰 = *shú*, "which?" For other expressions, please use a dictionary.

   Example: Question: 生而知之與學而知之，孰上也。
   Answer: 生而知之，上也。

   養狗與養貓，孰上也。

   學習與遊樂，孰上也。

   道教與儒禮，孰上也。

   處家與出仕，孰上也。

Lesson 2

Parts of Speech

Readers of literary Chinese must always be aware of the flexibility of word-classes. Depending on context, verbs become nouns, nouns become verbs, and intransitive verbs (verbs without direct objects) become transitive.

In general we have two major ways of determining what part of speech—what role—a character has in a sentence. A character's *regular usage* is an important initial guide for deciding its word-class. However, classical usage often is different from modern. For example, the character 言 frequently is a *verb*, "to say," in literary Chinese, whereas in modern Mandarin it usually is a noun, "word." Therefore, for beginning students of literary Chinese, **concordances** can be very useful for establishing how a character was used in a particular period or by a particular author.

Context provides the second major guide to a character's word-class. The overall structure of the sentence usually tells you the role of a particular word (see Introduction). In the end, *a character's position in the sentence is more important than its usual usage.*

Dictionaries for Reading Literary Chinese

Most small dictionaries, whether Chinese-Chinese or Chinese-English, are woefully inadequate for the study of pre-modern texts. Luckily, scholars in China and Japan have produced large but usable dictionar-

ies. One should become familiar with them as quickly as possible. The
two best dictionaries are:

Morohashi Tetsuji 諸橋轍次, *Daikanwa jiten* 大漢和辭典
(Tokyo: Taishukan shoten, 1955–1960), 12 vols.

and

Hànyǔ dàcídiǎn 漢語大詞典 (Hong Kong: Sanlian, 1987), 12
vols.

These dictionaries are organized in the traditional **radical + stroke-
count** format. That is, each character is constructed of a general clas-
sifying element (the radical) and, unless the character is itself a radical, some other elements, often used to indicate the sound. For example:

桂 "cassia tree" (*guì*, **kiweg*) = 木 (radical #75) + 圭 (*guī*,
*kiweg), 6 strokes

江 "river" (*jiāng*, **kǔng*) = 水 (radical #85) + 工 (*gōng*,
*kung), 3 strokes

In other cases, the character as a whole portrays a meaning, but the
traditional classification system selects one part of the character as the
radical, as in

上 = 一 (radical #1) + two strokes (the *upper* part)

Consider the entries in the 漢語大詞典 that are relevant to reading
雨 as *yù* in the text for this lesson. First is the entry for 雨 itself.

雨²   [yù 《广韵》王遇切,去遇,云] ①降雨。《诗·小
雅·大田》:"雨我公田遂及我私。"唐韩愈《袁
州祭神文》之一:"以久不雨苗且盡死。"

This is the *second* pronunciation listed for 雨 in the dictionary. The
entry uses a standard format. First it gives a *fǎnqiè* reading from one of
the early rhyming dictionaries, in this case the *Guǎngyùn* 廣韻.
Shown here is the first definition, which consists of two sections: a
definition in modern Chinese (written in simplified characters), followed by citations from early texts as examples of actual uses.

The next example is for the phrase 天雨. The phrase is under "天"
and listed according to the stroke-count of 雨 (8 strokes).

Handwritten top notes:
1. There once was a wealthy man in Sorg, when show rain was falling, the wall of his house broke down. (heavenly)
2. His son says, not repairing/building the wall, necessarily then there will be theirves. (certainly) "if you don't"

【天雨】天降雨。战国宋玉《高唐赋》:"遇天雨之新霽兮，觀百谷之俱集"《史记·老子韩非列传》:"宋有富人，天雨牆壞。"

Once again, the dictionary first gives a definition and then offers examples. (The second example occurs in the lesson below, even though the dictionary cites the 史記 rather than 韓非子.)

Text: 宋國富人(韓非子)

Handwritten: song you fu ren, tian yu qiang huai
1. 宋有富人，天雨牆壞。

Handwritten: qi zi yue
2. 其子曰：不築，必將有盜。

Handwritten: qi lin ren zhi fu yi yún
3. 其鄰人之父亦云。

Handwritten: mù er guo da wang qi cai   ci xi dao zhi gù da wang ye   V · · · V · O
4. 暮而果大亡其財。此夕盜至故大亡也。

Handwritten: qi jia shen zhi qi zi   er yi lin ren zhi fu
5. 其家甚智其子，而疑鄰人之父。

Vocabulary

富	*fù* (v), to be wealthy	築	*zhù* (n), a ram > (v), to ram earth for a wall
韓非子	Hán Fēi Zǐ, Warring States Legalist/Taoist philosopher	必	*bì* (v), to be necessarily so
天	*tiān* (n), sky, heaven	將	*jiāng* (adv) [future marker]
雨	*yǔ* (n), rain > *yù* (v), to rain	盜	*dào* (n), thief
牆	*qiáng* (n), wall	鄰	*lín* (n), neighbor
壞	*huài* (v), to break	之	*zhī* (fw) [marker of explicit subordination]
其	*qí* (adj), his, hers, its, their	父	*fù* (n), father
子	*zǐ* (n), son	亦	*yì* (adv), also
曰	*yuē* (v), to say	云	*yún* (v), "to say [it]"

Handwritten bottom notes:
3. The neighbour also said the same.
4. When the men set, consequently alot of wealth left. That evening, a thief arrived, and therefore alot of wealth was lost.
5. The household strongly considered their son to be wise, and suspected the neighbours father.

• 暮   *mù* (n), sunset > (v), the sun sets

夕   *xì* (n), evening

• 而   *ér* (fw) [explicit verb co-ordinator]

• 至   *zhì* (v), arrive

• 故   *gù* (adv), therefore

果   *guǒ* (adv), as anticipated
as a result, in consequence

• 也   *yě* (fw), [final: nominal phrase]

大   *dà* (v), great > (adv) greatly

家   *jiā* (n), household

亡   *wáng* (v), leave, flee

• 甚   *shèn* (adv), extremely

• 財   *cái* (n), wealth

智   *zhì* (v), to be wise

• 此   *cǐ* (n), this

疑   *yí* (v), to doubt, suspect

Grammar Notes

1. 天雨 In sentence 1, the second half of the line could be read as a **topic-comment**: "As for the sky's rain: the wall broke." However, the more natural reading is simply as a pair of topics with verbal comments: "The sky: rained; the wall: broke." In this second reading, however, 雨 changes from a *noun* into a *verb*. This possibility is well established in classical usage.

2. 不築 Although there is no doubt that 築 is a verb (it is negated by 不), the character initially referred to a rod used to ram earth; only later was the meaning transferred from the tool to the action of using that tool. Such transferences were common.

3. 鄰人 In literary Chinese, nouns (鄰) easily modify other nouns (人). Since not all characters that modify nouns are adjectives, and most of what we consider adjectives in English also are stative verbs (赤 "red", 小 "small"), it is best initially to use "modifier" rather than "adjective."

4. 暮 usually is a noun meaning "sunset," but the use of 而, a marker of coordination between verbs, forces us to treat it as a verb, "the sun sets."

5. 果 The character 果 essentially means "fruit" (a noun), but very early it came to refer to results that arise from an action, "the fruit"

and "to bear fruit" (a verb), as it were. Then by extension, 果 and 果然 took on the adverbial meaning "as we might expect from such circumstances," or more simply "in fact."

6. 大亡 Ordinarily 大 is a verb, "to be big." Here, however, since it clearly modifies 亡, it becomes an adverb meaning "greatly."

7. 亡其財 The verb 亡 usually means "to go, depart, leave." It does not take a direct object. Here, however, 其財 clearly serves as a direct object. When an intransitive verb takes a direct object, the verb acquires a *causative* meaning: here 亡其財 becomes "causes his wealth to go."

8. 故大亡也 This comment illustrates the **nominalization** of a verbal sentence with the function word 也. The sentence ends an *explanation* of a situation: "Thus it was *a case of* (or *a matter of*) 大亡."

9. 甚智其子 The verb 智 usually means "to be wise" (often in a crafty way) and is intransitive. Here 其子 is its direct object. This is another example of the rule explained in (7), and the phrase means "cause (or take) his son to be wise."

Exercises

1. Translate the following pairs of phrases to reflect the changes in word-class. Look up any character you do not understand.

Nouns > Verbs

a. 時雨降。

天雨。

b. 天有春秋冬夏旦暮之期。

暮而果大亡其財。

Intransitive Verbs > Transitive Verbs

c. 其子不智。

其家甚智其子。

Verbs > Adverbs

d. 其財之亡大。

大亡其財。

2. Note that some verbs in both English and literary Chinese can be either transitive or intransitive in normal usage:

  The plate broke.
  John broke the plate.

Translate:

  牆壞。

  大雨壞牆。

3. Translate the following and indicate what shifts in word-class have occurred. (If you do not know a character or expression, use a dictionary.)

  其子能赤其面而白其睛

  過客駐征軒

4. Write the **radical** for each of the following characters; explain what it means and why the radical is used in that character; then indicate the number of strokes in the remainder of the character.

    a. 鄰

    b. 盜

    c. 智

    d. 牆

    e. 壞

5. Look up the following characters and copy the entries that explain their usage in the story "宋國富人."

    a. 果

    b. 亡

Reference: This is the context for《宋國富人》in 韓非子:

昔者鄭武公欲伐胡。故先以其女妻胡君以娛其意。因問於群臣，吾欲用兵。誰可伐者。大夫關其思對曰，胡可伐。武公怒而戮之曰，胡，兄弟之國也。子言伐之，何也。胡君聞之。以鄭爲親己。遂不備鄭。鄭人襲胡，取之。宋有富人。天雨牆壞。其子曰，不築，必將有盜。其鄰人之父亦云。暮而果大亡其財。其家甚智其子而疑鄰人之父。二人說者皆當矣。厚者爲戮，薄者見疑。則非知之難也。處之則難也。(韓非子，說難)

Lesson 3

Coordinate Verbs

In literary Chinese, as in any language, one must create sequences of actions if one wants to tell a story or make an argument. In *persuasive* writing, the connections between actions often are hypothetical:

1. If we do not hang together, we shall surely hang separately.

The first action is offered as a possibility whose consequences are to be explored. In literary Chinese, such a sequence of actions therefore takes the form of a **topic-comment** structure.

Narrative description, in contrast, sets out a series of actions that unfold in time. They do not necessarily follow as a logical progression:

2. There were rose bushes in front of the house. I went up the walk. I listened before I pushed the bell.[1]

The relationship between the actions can be quite complex. In the small scene above, all the actions occur sequentially. They also can be simultaneous:

3. I sat there and listened to it and thought long careful thoughts. (p. 48)

---

1. Raymond Chandler, *Farewell, My Lovely* (New York: Vintage, 1976), p. 155. Sentences 3–5 are also from *Farewell, My Lovely*; page numbers cited in parentheses.

The actions can also be a cause followed by its effect:

> 4. I had nightmares and woke out of them sweating. (p. 161)

or a means followed by its purpose:

> 5. I got up and locked the doors. (p. 189)

Moreover, a second action can occur despite the first or as a reaction: the list of possible relationships gets quite long.

In literary Chinese the most abbreviated form of a sequence of actions is the use of **coordinate verbs** in the comment of a single sentence. Even this seemingly simple structure, however, retains all the complex possibilities for relationship implicit in parallel action in general. Are the two events of the same sort, or are they opposites? Does the second event occur as the result of the first, or despite it? Do the two actions occur simultaneously or in succession? All these are possible interpretations of verbal parallelism in literary Chinese. Indeed, unlike in English, verb coordination in literary Chinese tends to suggest that the first verb is the **antecedent condition** for the second. That is, the first action strongly influences how the second action occurs or whether it occurs at all.

Literary Chinese can be explicit about the precise nature of the relationship between two actions, but writers usually leave the connections implicit and trust to the reader's acumen. Modern readers therefore must develop the habit of reflecting on how the actions presented in a pair of coordinate verbs relate to one another. Indeed, these implicit relations form an important part of how Chinese authors organized their texts not only at the level of verbs in sentences but also at the level of sequences of actions out of which the larger arguments are built.

Text: 守株待兔(韓非子)

1. 宋人有耕者，田中有株，兔走觸株，折頸而死。
2. 因釋其耒而守株，冀復得兔。
3. 兔不可復得，而身為宋國笑。
4. 今欲以先王之政治當世之民皆守株之類也。

Vocabulary

守 *shǒu* (v), to maintain, guard

株 *zhū* (n), tree trunk, stump

待 *dài* (v), to await

兔 *tù* (n), rabbit

宋 *Sòng* (n), name of a state

人 *rén* (n), person

有 *yǒu* (v), there is

耕 *gēng* (v), to plow

者 *zhě* (n), abstract noun (bound form)

田 *tián* (n), cultivated field

中 *zhōng* (n), the middle part

走 *zǒu* (v), to run

觸 *chù* (v), to knock against

折 *zhé* (v), to break

頸 *jǐng* (n), neck

死 *sǐ* (v), to die

因 *yīn* (cv), to rely on > (fw) thereupon

釋 *shì* (v), to release

耒 *lěi* (n), plow

冀 *jì* (v), to hope

復 *fù* (adv), again

得 *dé* (v), to obtain

不 *bù* (adv), not

可 *kě* (av), can + [verb]

身 *shēn* (n), body > one's person

爲 *wéi* (v), to enact, become > [passive marker]

國 *guó* (n), state, kingdom

笑 *xiào* (v), to laugh

今 *jīn* (n), now, the present

欲 *yù* (v), to desire

以 *yǐ* (v), to take > (cv) taking . . .

先 *xiān* (n), former part

王 *wáng* (n), king

先王 *xiān wáng*, the Former Kings (周文王武王, Kings Wén and Wǔ of Zhōu)

政 *zhèng* (n), governance

治 *zhì* (v), to govern

當 *dāng* (v), to be at > (adj), contemporary

世 *shì* (n), generation (~30 years)

民 *mín* (n), the populace

皆 *jiē* (adv), in every case

類 *lèi* (n), category

Grammar Notes

1. 宋人有耕者，田中有株　Here 有 is the verb of "existential predication": that is, it says that its object exists. "*There is* a plower." "*There was* a stump." When 有 has a **topic**, it usually indicates a *time* or *place*. Here we have "*Among the people of Song* there is a plower" and "*In the field* there was a stump."

2. 兔走觸株，折頸而死　In both cases, the coordinate verb phrases indicate that the second action occurred *as the result* of the first: "The rabbit ran, *with the result that* [it] hit the stump." "[It] broke its neck, and *as a result* [it] died. Note that in the second sentence, 而 explicitly indicated the verbal coordination. Since the syntax is rather unambiguous, the character's function probably is to fill out the *four-count* rhythm that dominates this story and most literary Chinese prose.

3. 因　When 因 takes a *direct object*, it is a **coverb** and means "relying on . . . ." Here, however, it appears alone at the beginning of the sentence and takes *the previous sentence* as its assumed object: "relying on [the previous situation], ..."

4. 釋其耒　Note that the last **topic** of the first sentence is the rabbit. Yet it is not the rabbit but the farmer who lets go of the plow. The second sentence, which has **no explicit topic**, does not indicate this change of topic; the author simply assumes that readers are paying attention.

5. 可復得　The construction 可 + **verb** is a **passive** construction, "can be *verb*ed."

6. 而身為 . . .　Notice that 而 here marks coordination not of verbs but of complete **verbal sentences**. Larger units—phrases, clauses, sentences—all behave according to the same rules as single characters. The basic rules can be applied to even very long sentences: the art lies in recognizing the "larger units" as verbs, nouns, and other parts of speech.

7. 身為宋國 [所] 笑　This is another type of **passive** construction: "his person *became* (為) that at which [the people of] the state of Song

laughed." The character 所 often is used to make the construction clearer. (See Lesson 4.)

8. 今   Here 今 serves as a **time topic**: "Now [under these circumstances] . . . ."

9. 以 . . . 治 . . .   This sentence is long and complex, but its organization follows simple rules. The first step in analyzing it it to see that 以 and 治 form a **coverb / main verb** pair with their respective objects.

10. 守株之類   Note the use of 之 here to mark **explicit subordination**. We have 類 "a category": what sort of category? The phrase says a "guard the stump" sort of category. Notice that when the **verb-object** compound is used to modify 類, it effectively becomes nominalized to "[the category of] guarding the stump."

Questions

1. What are the relationships between the four parts of the first sentence? Is the second a comment on the first, the third a comment on the second, and so on? Are they all coordinate?

2. What about the two parts of the second sentence?

3. What is the topic in the fourth sentence?

Exercises

1. Topic and Comments

Note the various transformations of the sentences below. Translate each in a way that reflects the change in emphasis with the different topics:

   a. 宋人耕田。

      宋人有耕田者。

   b. 耕田者宋人也。

耕田者有宋人。

c.　兔觸株。

觸株者兔也。

兔有觸株者。

2.　Passive Constructions

In the following examples, note how *active verbs* are changed into *passive verb* constructions. Translate:

a.　宋人笑之。

身爲宋人笑。

b.　耕者得兔。

兔爲耕者得。

Note that 可 is a **passive** construction: "can be . . . ," "cannot be . . . ." (Sometimes there is the further implication of "*should* be" or "*should* not be.")

a.　兔觸株。

株不可觸。

b. 耕者守株。

株者不可守。

c. 耕者得兔。

兔不可得。

3. Coordinate Verbs and Antecedent Conditions

The following sentences test whether the first verb in a pair of coordinate verbs is truly independent or if it serves as an antecedent condition. Translate to see if the sentences make sense:

a. 兔走而觸株。

兔觸株而走。

b. 兔折頸而死。

兔死而折頸。

c. 釋其耒而守株。

守株而釋其耒。

4. How to Build a Complex Sentence

Notice how each sentence builds upon the one above it. Translate each of them.

治民。

欲治民。

欲以政治民。

欲以先王之政治民。

欲以先王之政治當世之民。

欲以先王之政治當世之民此類也。

欲以先王之政治當世之民皆此類也。

今欲以先王之政治當世之民皆守株之類也。

Lesson 4

The Modifier 所 and
Nominalized Verbs

Consider an action:

> John went to the store.

Where is the emphasis in this sentence? What is the most important information being conveyed? Consider the various ways to change the
stress:

> *John* (not Robert) went to the store.
> John *went* to the store (but they didn't have what you wanted).
> John went to the *store* (not to the movies).

All languages need ways of controlling the placement of emphasis in
telling a story. Literary Chinese has several direct and powerful grammatical structures that allow very precise control of how one talks
about an action. One of these is the important modifier 所, which refers to the objects of verbs. Another structure is **nominalization,**
which allows one to *talk about actions*.

The Character 所

that which.

suŏ

Perhaps the greatest obstacle to understanding how 所 works is our
"commonsense" view of how words refer to things. What, for example,
does the English word "tree" bring to mind? The shape, smell, and
growing pattern of pine trees differ from those of apple trees and ma-

62

ples. Given the many different types of trees, how does "tree" mean anything at all? Yet we know what a tree is when we see one. "Tree" refers both to a set of attributes we associate with trees and to a set of "things" we have seen and have learned to think of as trees. Based on these two sets of information, if we encounter a plant we have never seen before, we can make a judgment—"Yes, this is a tree," or "No, it is not." The judgment may not be right from a biologist's perspective, and we may be forced to revise our sense of what plants belong to the category "tree." As this example shows, understanding even a seemingly simple word like "tree" involves complex processes of abstraction and comparison. Words are labels for what we might call "differential sets": sets of objects and attributes marked by their difference from other sets of objects and attributes. *All* words are complex, even if most of the time the inner machinery of human language processing hides this complexity from us.

所, like all other words, is a label. It is the label that allows us to refer to *a set of objects selected simply for their role as objects of verbs.* Why would one want to refer to such a "thing." Consider the following examples:

1. 李子往市。 Master Lǐ went to the market.
2. 李子所往，市也。 Where Master Lǐ went was the market.
3. 李子所往，何也。 Where was it that Master Lǐ went?
4. 吾不知李子所往。 I do not know where Master Lǐ went.

In the first version of the sentence, we cannot know where the emphasis should be placed. In the second sentence, however, the V-O pair has been split apart, and the **verb**, the action of going, has been *shifted into the topic.* All that remains in the comment is what **had been the object**—"market." The character 所 makes possible this shift to talking about the object of a verb. Notice that in the third and fourth sentences one can refer to an object of a verb even when one does not know what the actual object is. Consider another sentence of the general form:

5. 我食 X。 I eat *X*. (*X* is the **object**)

6. X，我所食也。 *X* = "what I eat" (*X* is moved to the **topic position**)

Anywhere you might want to use the variable **X** (Object_{Eat}), you can use 所食:

> 7. 我所食使我肚疾。   ***Something I ate*** upset my stomach.
> 8. 我不知我所食者何物。   I don't know ***what I ate***.
> 9. 人無所食也。   People were without ***anything to eat***.

Nominalization of Verbs

Sometimes, instead of wishing to refer to an ***object*** of the verb, one wants to point to an ***action*** in its entirety:

> 10. 往市已晚矣   It is already late for ***going to the market***.
> 11. 忘往市   He forgot ***to go to the market***.
> 12. 往市者吾弟也   ***The one who went to the market*** was my brother.

The simplest way to nominalize a verb is to use it as the topic of a sentence (10) or the object of another verb (11). Such a change in function can be implicit, unmarked by any grammatical particle, or one can use the explicit **nominalizing function word** 者, to clearly mark the nominal usage, as in (12). Note that verb + 者 can refer to the action of the verb, the fact of that action, or to the person who performs the action.

Text: 刻舟求劍 (呂氏春秋)

1. 楚人有涉江者，
2. 其劍自舟中墜於水。
3. 遽契其舟，曰是吾劍之所從墜。
4. 舟止，從其所契者入水求之。
5. 舟已行矣，而劍不行。
6. 求劍若此，不亦惑乎。

(handwritten pinyin glosses above characters; handwritten notes: "introduces rhetorical Q." and "acts rhetorical Q")

(handwritten translation:)

1. Among the people of Chu, there was one crossing the river
2. His sword fell from the boat into the water.
3. While he was carrying his boat, he swiftly said "this was the place/spot from which my sword fell"
4. The boat stopped, he entered the water from this point to search for his sword.
5. The boat had already moved, and yet the sword hadn't moved
6. To seek the sword like this, isn't that a deluded idea?

Vocabulary

刻　　*kè* (v), to cut

舟　　*zhōu* (n), boat

求　　*qiú* (v), to seek

劍　　*jiàn* (n), sword

呂氏春秋 *Lǔ shì Chūnqiū* (n), a
book written by Lǔ
Bùwéi 呂不韋 in the late
Warring States period.

楚　　*Chǔ* (n), an early Chinese
state

涉　　*shè* (v), to cross

江　　*jiāng* (n), river

自　　*zì* (cv), to come from

墜　　*zhuì* (v), to fall

於　　*yú* (fw) [locative marker]

*遽　　*jù* (v), to be swift >
swiftly

契　　*qì* (v), to cut, carve

是　　*shì* (n), this

吾　　*wú* (n), I, me

所　　*suǒ* (adj), [points to ob-
ject]

從　　*cóng* (cv), to follow

止　　*zhǐ* (v), to stop

入　　*rù* (v), to enter

水　　*shuǐ* (n), water

之　　*zhī* (n), him, her, them, it *(de)*

已　　*yǐ* (v), to bring to an
end > (adv), already *2, zhi*

行　　*xíng* (v), to travel */to move /to act*

矣　　*yǐ* (fw), [final: change of
state] *marker of completion.*

若　　*ruò* (v), to resemble

此　　*cǐ* (n), this

不亦 **X** 乎　*bú yì* X *hū*, "Is it not
X!"

惑　　*huò* (v), to be confused,
deluded, misguided

乎　　*hū* (fw) [final: "!" or "?"]

[handwritten margin notes: "marker of subordination", "replacement object."]

Grammatical Notes

1. 有涉江者　The character 者 nominalizes the phrase 涉江. It is
perhaps best to take 者 in the way suggested by its usual translation
into Japanese, that is, as *mono*, or "thing." That is, 者 is a **noun** that is
modified by the phrase 涉江 and functions as the **object** of 有.

2. 自舟中   Here the character 自 is a **coverb**. Its object is 舟中, "[the place] in the boat." Remember that 中 is a **noun**. The main verb here is 墜.

3. 墜於水   The character 於 explicitly marks **locative objects** (or, more generally, **locative case**) in literary Chinese. Like 而, the explicit marker of verb coordination, 於 is not *required*: in 入水 (line 4), for example, 水 "water" is the locative object of 入 "enter." Authors use 於 (or 于 or 乎) either to avoid ambiguity or for stylistic or rhetorical reasons.

4. 所從墜   Coverbs take objects. A variation on the usual pattern for 所 + verb allows one to talk about the *object of a coverb*. That is, if we have an initial phrase:

   　　　從 **X** 墜。   [It] fell from **X**.

Then we can talk about the object **X**:

   　　　X 者，所從墜也 。   **X** is the place from which [it] fell.

The traveler, then, is explaining what is so important about the place he has just marked: "This is the place from which my sword fell." This pattern of 所 + coverb + main verb is in fact common. See the exercises below.

5. 求劍若此   The structure here is *topic* (求劍)–*comment* (若此). In turn, the whole four-character phrase is the topic of the comment 不亦惑乎. Note that the **verb-object** pair 求劍 becomes implicitly nominalized.

Questions

1. What is the function of 之 in (3)?

2. What is the relation of 入水 to 求之 in (4)?

3. What is the function of 而 in (5)? How would you translate it?

4. What is the larger point of this parable? One account describes the river crosser as 固執不知變通. Does this description seem appropriate? What are the political implications of this story?

Exercises

A. Diagram the following sentences. In each case, explain the relationship between the sentences in the group. For example,

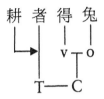

In this sentence, 兔 is the **object** of the verb 得. (耕 modifies 者, and the phrase 耕者 is the topic, about which 得兔 is the comment.)

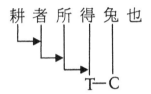

The **object** of the verb has now become the ***comment***. Instead of the verb-object pair sharing the stress, the single word 兔 is now alone in the comment position.

1. For *direct objects*

   a. 涉江者求劍。

      劍者，涉江者所求也。

      求者已行而所求不行。

   b. 耕者守株。

      耕者之所守，株也。

    c. 宋人笑守株之耕者。

        守株之耕者，宋人所笑也。

    d. 其子言盜必至。

        鄰人之父亦言盜必至。

        以其子所言爲可貴。[Note: 以 **A** 爲 **B** = "takes **A** to be **B**."]

        以鄰人之父所言爲可疑。

        其家疑鄰人之父。

        鄰人之父，其家所疑也。

2. For *locative objects*

    a. 兔行田中。

兔所行，富人之田也。

b. 盜至。

盜至於壞牆。

盜所至者，壞牆也。

盜所至之牆，已壞矣。

3. **With** *coverbs*

a. 劍從舟墜於水。

劍之所從墜於水者，舟也。

楚人刻舟。

楚人刻其劍之所從墜於水者。

b. 宋人以耒耕田。

宋人所以耕田者，耒也。

B. Change the following sentences so that the **object of the verb** becomes the **comment**:

Example: 其家疑鄰人之父 ➤ 其家所疑，鄰人之父也

a. 富人亡其財 。

b. 耕者待兔。

c. 宋人笑其守株待兔。

d. 盜出於窗。

C. Change the following sentences so that the **object of the coverb**
becomes the **comment**:

Example: 盜以劍殺人 ➤ 盜所以殺人，劍也

1. 盜從山中至。

2. 王以政殺民。

3. 以其所言疑之。

Lesson 5

Negatives

There are many ways to say "no." We must learn not only to acknowledge them but also to see the real differences among the various modes of negation. Each of the many different negatives in literary Chinese has a discrete meaning. The basic vocabulary of negatives is:

不 *bù* modifies and negates *verbs*: the action does not occur. A noun following *bù* becomes a verb.

未 *wèi* negates *the occurrence of actions*: the action designated by the verb has *not yet* occurred but still may. Sometimes, in terms of rhetorical force, *wèi* suggests that since the action has never happened, it therefore will not and cannot.[1]

無 *wú* is a **verb** that *negates existence*: "there is no . . . ." It is the opposite of 有. Since 無 is a verb, it takes a **noun** as its object; a verb following *wú* becomes a noun.

非 *fēi* may reflect early Old Chinese syntax and is the "negative copula" that *negates the identity* of a topic with a **nominal predicate: "A is not a case of B."** Later usage occasionally treats 非 as a verb, but it should be seen as modifying noun phrases, and a verb following *fēi* becomes a noun.

弗 *fú* is a special *fusion* character derived from 不 + 之. The placement of the 之 reflects a characteristic of early Old Chi-

---

1. Pulleyblank (*Outline of Classical Chinese Grammar*, p. 114) suggests that 未 is a fusion of a negative root ***m-** with 既 , "to complete."

71

nese: 之 here is the *transposed object of a negated verb*. (See below.)

勿 *wù* is another fusion, derived from 毋 + 之. It usually appears as a *negative imperative*: "Don't . . . ."

莫 *muò* is the *negative distributive*: "in no case . . . ." It is the opposite of 或. [pronounced *mò*]

The sense of each of these characters is distinct, and the particular usage of each must be taken into account.

One special aspect of early literary Chinese that disappears in later writing is the **transposition of objects** of negated verbs.[2] This insertion of the **object** of the verb **between the negating modifier and the verb** does not occur with all objects—in fact, it occurs primarily with pronouns:

歲不吾與　The years do not give us [respite].
莫之知　　None knew it.
未之信也　He did not yet believe it.

Text: 矛盾(韓非子)

1. 楚人有鬻盾與矛者，譽之曰吾盾之堅，物莫能陷也。

2. 又譽其矛曰吾矛之利，於物無不陷也。

3. 或曰以子之矛陷子之盾，何如。

4. 其人弗能應也。

5. 夫不可陷之盾與無不陷之矛不可同世而立。

Vocabulary

矛　*máo* (n), spear　　　*鬻　*yù* (v), to sell

盾　*dùn* (n), shield

2. When such constructions appear in later writing, they are usually self-conscious **archaisms**, a stylistic technique designed to give the writing an "ancient" quality.

矛盾 → contradiction
máo dùn

⊛A students Dictionary
of Classical & Medeival ≈$30.
Chinese. (mostmodern)
☆Mathews Dictionary
73

"function word" *Lesson 5*

與	*yǔ* (v), to give > (fw), "and"]	以	*yǐ* (v), to grasp > (cv) us-ing . . . "use by means of"	

與 *yǔ* (v), to give > (fw), "and"]

譽 *yù* (v), to praise

堅 *jiān* (v), to be sturdy

物 *wù* (n), [phenomenal] thing / *kind of thing.*

莫 *mò* (adv), in no case / *no single person / nothing*

能 *néng* (av), to be able to

陷 *xiàn* (v), to fall into > to sink into

利 *lì* (v), to be sharp / *profit*

無 *wú* (v), there is not

或 *huò* (fw), some > (n) someone

以 *yǐ* (v), to grasp > (cv) us-ing . . . "use by means of"

何如 *hé rú*, "What about it?" *what is that like*

何 *hé* (n), what?

如 *rú* (v), to resemble

弗 *fú* (fw) [fusion of 不之] *[not it], then verb*

應 *yìng* (v), to respond

夫 *fū* (fw), "now . . ." *fū As a matter of fact*

同 *tóng* (v), to partake of > be of the same . . .

立 *lì* (v), to stand / *to establish / to erect.*

以子之矛，攻子之盾
= set a persons own spear against
his own shield (attack opponent
with own devices)

Grammar Notes

1. 楚人有鬻盾與矛者   By now the classical usage of 有 should begin to be clear. 楚人 is the topic: "Among the people of Chǔ, *there was* (verb of "existential predication") one who . . . ."

2. 譽之曰   Here 譽 and 曰 are *coordinate verbs*: "in order to praise it, he said . . . ."

3. 吾盾之堅，物莫能陷也   The nominalizing character 也 has an important function here. Rather than simply making the observation that "As for objects, in no case can they penetrate it," the sentence be-comes "As for the hardness of my shield (*topic*), well, it is so hard that nothing can penetrate the shield." That is, the addition of the 也 makes the sentence nominal; it sets up a definition: **shield's hardness** = the **state** in which nothing can penetrate it. This is an unalterable fact, true under all circumstances and defines precisely what sort of hardness the spear seller attributes to his shield.

4. 於物無不陷也   It is clear *what* this phrase means: "There are no objects into which [my spear] does not sink." The question is *how* the

phrase says this. In English, we use an empty subject "there" and a relative clause beginning with a preposition, "into which," to modify "objects." Literary Chinese uses a different strategy. To understand this strategy, we need to ask two questions: Why does the topic begin with the locative marker 於? And what happened to the object of the verb 陷? These questions can be answered in two different but related ways. First, the phrase can be viewed as a ***topicalized*** construction. The normal word order would be: 不陷於 **X**, "it does not sink into **X**." Here, however, the spear seller wants to emphasize that there **is no X** such that "it does not sink into **X**." Thus he raises as the topic the general category "*things taken as possible locations*, that is, targets" and uses the locative marker 於 to indicate the relation explicitly. Often, however, sentences that topicalize a locative object leave the ***resumptive pronoun*** 焉 (equivalent to 於之) as a "trace" to mark the locative object position. For example,

萬取千焉 As for ten thousand, take one thousand *from it.*

The second approach emphasizes that the construction 無不陷 is equivalent to 無所不陷, "There does not exist that into which it does not penetrate," much as the common expression 無不爲 means 無所不爲, "There does not exist that which [they] will not do." Because the object of 不陷 is already represented by the 所, the 於物 is not the verb's topicalized object. Instead, the seller uses the phrase to make the most general possible statement: "Let's consider *any* object taken as a location." Thus, the end result of the two accounts is the same: the seller makes clear that he is talking about "any object as target," and that "there aren't any" that can resist his spear.

The distinction between 莫 in the preceding sentence and the 無 in this sentence is a question of scope: with 莫, the sentence refers to *all* objects and makes a statement about them collectively. 無, in contrast, stresses that the second sentence is talking about *no* object: the thing to which it points does not exist.

5. 何如   The word 何 basically is an ***interrogative noun***, and 何如 is equivalent to 如何, "What does [it] resemble?" which, in turn, is an idiomatic way of saying "What do you make of that?" This **inversion of verb-object** with question words (and the character 是) is another lingering feature of Early Archaic Chinese. There are several similar inversions:

何以 ＝ 以何 "by means of what"
是以 ＝ 以是 "by means of this"
誰與 ＝ 與誰 "with whom"

6. 其人弗能應　The use of 弗 here is very typical. One starts with a "base" sentence:

其人不能應之 The man cannot respond to it.

Since the object of the main verb 應 in the negated verb phrase is the pronoun 之, it is moved (transposed) to a position **between the negating word 不 and the verb phrase**:

其人不之能應

Finally, the two words 不之 fuse to become 弗: 其人弗能應.

7. 其人弗能應也　This sentence finishes the author's story, a self-contained vignette that illustrates thoughtless self-contradiction. He uses 也 to indicate this **completion of the account**. In English, we might say, "And it was the case that the man could not respond to [the question]." The 也 used here at the end of a verbal sentence *frames* the action and turns it into a "thing," a situation that can be analyzed and commented on, with patterns and implications to be explored. This use of 也 to signal the completion of an account occurs frequently in literary Chinese.

8. 不可同世而立　Remember that 可+verb is a **passive** construction: "*cannot be established* in the same generation." Notice also that the full verbal expression that is the object of 可 is 同世而立. 同 and 立 are *coordinate verbs* where 同 sets up the **antecedent condition** for 立. Also note, however, the syntactically as well as semantically unbalanced quality of the verb pair: 同 already has its own object, 世, and cannot serve as an independent object of 可. That is, transitive verbs should not have objects when used in passive constructions:

$$\text{Subject}_{agent} + \text{verb} + \text{object}_{patient} > \text{Subject}_{patient} + 可 + \text{verb}$$

立 is the actual object of 可, and 同世 is reduced almost to the status of a modifier of 立.

Questions

1. What part of speech is 堅 in 吾盾之堅 in (1)? Why?

2. What is the main verb for the coverb 以 in (3)?

3. What does the phrase 其人 mean? Why is it used in (4)?

4. Given the explanation of 弗 above, what does 弗能應 mean?

5. Explain the use of 也 in (4).

6. What is the function of 與 in (5)?

7. What is the object of 無 in (5)?

Exercises

1. *Basic patterns*. Diagram and translate:

舟中之人莫知其劍之利。

The person in the boat, nobody knew the sharpness of his sword.

觸株之兔莫不折頸而死。

If a rabbit hits a tree, it will never not break its neck, and then die.

宋人莫之能得。

As to the people of Song, nobody was able to obtain it.

此非吾家。

This is not my home.

兔走田中而耕者莫之能止。

and as of all the ploughers, nobody is able to stop it.

至今宋國無兔。

Up to today, the state of Song doesn't have any rabbits

孟之反曰非敢後也、馬不進也。 (Note: 孟之反 is a man's name.)

Ma Zhe Fan said, it's not that I (chose) to stay in the back, my horse wouldn't advance.

至 classical meaning of 到

'no 不 before 敢後 because the 非 makes it → nominalism not because of A but B.

我未之見也。
(zhī)
I have not yet seen him.

2. 莫 *and* 無. Translate the sentences below to make the differences clear:

吾盾之堅，物無能陷也。
The shield is sturdy, Nothing exist which can penetrate it.

吾盾之堅，物莫能陷也。

3. 不 *and* 非. Translate the sentences to clarify the distinction:

我不求利劍。
I do not seek a sharp sword

利劍非我所求也。
It is not the sharp sword which I am looking for.

齊王不能好先王之樂。(樂 = "music")
(hào) (to like)
He was not able to like the music of the former kings.

齊王非能好先王之樂也。
As to Qi Wang he didn't like it

A 非 B 也

4. 弗. Translate the following sentences to reflect the presence of a "hidden" 之:

耕者待兔而弗得。

楚王弗信。

矛弗能陷。

5. *Negations*. Change the following into negative sentences and translate:

宋人有走於水之上者。

耕者皆亡。

吾有利劍。

舟中之兔或墜於水。

其子求之。

盜所至者富人之家也。

牆有雨所壞者。

利民之政，楚王皆用之。

欲以其政利其民。

Lesson 6

Pivot Verbs, Auxiliary Verbs,
and
Classical Commentary

Pivot Verbs

In English, asking, urging, or ordering someone to do an action has two basic forms. We can say either:

    1. I asked that he give you this.

or, more commonly:

    2. I asked him to give you this.

In (1), the request ("he give you this") is a form of indirect discourse, a reporting of speech at secondhand, but because the quoted speech is a request, the verb is in the subjunctive mood. In (2), the *subject* in the quoted speech who is to perform the requested action ("he give you this") has become the *indirect object* ("him") of the verb "ask." This change is called "subject raising."

Asking, urging, ordering, and—more abstractly—causing in literary Chinese also use subject raising; the person who is to perform the requested action appears in the sentence as the indirect object of the request:

3. 亞父勸項羽擊沛公 Yǎfù urged Xiàng Yǔ to strike the Lord of Pèi.

4. 五色令人目盲 The five colors cause people's eyes to go blind.

5. 使之聞之 [Confucius] caused [the messenger] to hear it.

Sentences 3–5 all use a *pivotal construction*, where the pivots are 項 羽, 人目, and 之, respectively. That is, Xiàng Yǔ is both the person being urged and the person who is to strike. The eyes in (4) are what are affected by the colors, and they are what goes blind; and in (5), Confucius is subjecting the messenger to an action, the action of hearing him (play his zither). It is particularly clear in Sentence (5) that the pivot is the *indirect object* of the pivot verb because 之 can be used only as an object, and not as a topic or modifier. Moreover, since the pivot is the indirect object, the action to be performed by the pivot is the *direct object* of the pivot verb.

Many verbs can be used in pivotal constructions, but a few—like 使, 令, and 勸—almost always appear in pivotal constructions and thus this textbook refers to them as pivot verbs.[1]

Auxiliary Verbs

In literary Chinese an auxiliary verb changes the sense of the main verb in terms of its possibility, probability, or desirability. The most important auxiliary verbs are:

能 *néng,* able to . . .
可 *kě,* can be . . .
可以 *kěyǐ,* can . . .
必 *bì,* must . . .
應 *yīng,* ought to . . .
肯 *kěn,* willing to . . .
敢 *gǎn,* dare to . . .
難 *nán,* hard to . . . > impossible to . . .

---

1. See Yáng Bójùn 楊伯峻 and Hé Lèshì 何樂士, *Gǔ Hànyǔ yǔfǎ jí qí fāzhǎn* 古漢語語法及其發展 (Beijing; Yuwen, 1992), pp. 589–616, for an exhaustive analysis.

An auxiliary verb requires a main verb as its *object*. Like many transitive verbs, however, an auxiliary verb's object may be omitted if it is
obvious and therefore considered unnecessary. The main verb may be
implicit. That is, the reader can infer from context what the elided
main verb must be.

Although an auxiliary is like a pivot verb in taking a main verb as
its object, unlike a pivot verb, an auxiliary *cannot* be followed immediately by an indirect object preceding the main verb:

    肯之去   [She] is willing that he leave.

This sort of intention must be expressed in other ways, perhaps most
simply as a auxiliary with a pivot construction: 肯令之去.

Commentaries

Most texts written in literary Chinese do not have glossaries, or even
punctuation. And few have been translated into a modern language.
But occasionally texts do have commentaries, fortunately for us. A
commentary may tell the referent of a particular expression, the historical context of the text, or the pronunciation of a word. It often provides paraphrases of especially difficult passages, as well as stylistic
analyses of the organization of the text and at least one opinion about
the quality of argumentation and writing in the text. Moreover, the
commentator's choices of what to gloss indicates his (in premodern
China, commentators were male) perceptions of the passages that
readers are likely to find problematic. The very fact of a gloss can be
reassuring; it is a sign that the modern reader is not alone, that for
centuries Chinese readers have struggled over the same passage. However, there is an art to reading commentary. Commentaries have a specialized vocabulary of technical terms and particular stylistic qualities.

Some important terms used to explain the meaning of a phrase are:

    猶 *yóu*, "to resemble" > [the meaning] is similar to . . .
    貌 *mào*, "appearance" > [the phrase] is descriptive of . . .
    借 字 "loan character" > [this character] is used for [the
        homophone] . . .
    一 作 "one makes" > one [version of this text] has [the char-
        acter(s)] . . .

On occasion, the editors of a text will indicate that they are offering their own opinion:

案 *àn*, "case" > in the editor's opinion . . .

The text for this lesson includes a line of commentary as an introduction to the topic.

Text: 楊布 (列子)

1. 楊朱之弟曰布。衣素衣而出。

    釋文云衣素衣之衣於既切。下衣緇衣同。素衣之衣依字。

2. 天雨，解素衣。衣緇衣而反。

3. 其狗不知，迎而吠之。

4. 楊布怒將扑之。

5. 楊朱曰子無扑矣。子亦猶是也。

6. 嚮者使汝狗白而往，黑而來，豈能無怪哉。

Vocabulary

楊布	Yáng Bù
列子	*Liè Zǐ*, a text supposedly written by the Daoist philosopher
楊朱	Yáng Zhū, "hedonist" philosopher
弟	*dì* (n), younger brother
衣	*yī* (n), clothes > *yì* (v), to wear clothes
素	*sù* (n), undyed (white) silk
出	*chū* (v), to go out

釋文	*Shì wén*, short for 經典釋文, written by 陸德明 Lù Démíng (556–627): an important philological text
云	*yún* (v), to say, "open quote"
於既切	*yú jì qiè*, a notation of sound: 衣 ʔièi = 於 ʔi[ō] + 既 [ki]èi
下	*xià* (n), [the text] below
緇	*zī* (n), black silk
依	*yī* (v), to rely on

字	*zì* (n), written character	猶	*yóu* (fw > v), to resemble
依字	*yī zì*, according to the regular meaning	嚮	*xiàng* (n?), formerly > just now
雨	*yǔ* (n), rain > *yù* (v), to rain	使	*shǐ* (v), to cause > (v) let us suppose . . .
解	*jiě* (v), to cut, remove	汝	*rǔ* (n), you [informal]
反	*fǎn* (v), to return	白	*bái* (v), to be white
狗	*gǒu* (n), dog	黑	*hēi* (v), to be black
知	*zhī* (v), to know	來	*lái* (v), to come
迎	*yíng* (v), to greet, meet	豈	*qǐ* [rhetorical question: "How . . . ?"]. The implied answer is almost always negative.
吠	*fèi* (v), to bark at		
怒	*nù* (v), to be angry		
將	*jiāng* (adv), about to	怪	*guài* (v), to consider strange > to blame
扑	*pū* (v), to beat		
無	*wú* > don't [an imperative]	哉	*zāi* [final: exclamation]

Notes on the Text

1. 釋文云 The 經典釋文 is one of the most important collection of glosses in the Chinese tradition. Lù Démíng in his citations preserves many Southern Dynasties interpretations and commentaries that otherwise would have been lost.

2. 衣素衣之衣 The annotation discusses the reading (and hence the meaning) of the character 衣. This phrase is a way of referring to the *first* 衣, i.e. <u>衣</u>素衣之衣. In constrast, the simpler, unambiguous phrase 素衣之衣 refers to the *second* 衣 (素衣之<u>衣</u>).

3. 於旣切 This form is a *fǎn qiè*, a style of notation used by Chinese scholars since the end of the Hàn dynasty to indicate the pronunciation of a word. In a *fǎn qiè*, one takes the initial of the first word and the final of the second word: the two pieces added together give

the pronunciation of the word being glossed. In this example, the sound ʔiəi for the character 衣 is derived as follows:

> initial (beginning sound) of 於 ([ʔ]iō) = ʔ
> final (ending sound) of 既 (k[iəi]) = iəi
> sound of 衣 = ʔiəi

There are two common reasons for indicating a pronunciation. (1) The character is obscure, and the annotator thinks that the reader may not know how to read it. (2) For more common characters, the annotation indicates a special reading and a special meaning. *Pay attention to these*. In this case, the commentary notes that 衣 is to be read in the 去聲, that is, as a *verb*.

4. 下...同   This is commentary shorthand meaning that in the "text below" (下), the situation is the "same" (同) as that just described.

5. 子 Here 子 is a status pronoun, the name of a rank or a status within a group, that is used as a pronoun to refer to oneself (first person), to one's listener (second person), or on occasion to a third person. Here 子 , loosely translated as "master" is an informal but still polite form of address.

6. 無扑矣   This is a mildly negative imperative. Although 無 usually means "there is no . . . ," it also frequently serves as a mildly negative command, "Don't." The 矣 at the end of the sentence behaves in ways strikingly similar to 了 in modern Mandarin Chinese. Most frequently it is a sentence final particle that indicates completed action, but it also can point to a change of status or to new information that the recipients might not know and to which they should pay attention.

7. 嚮者   This is a time topic.

8. 使汝狗白而往   This sentence is a pivot construction, and 使 is perhaps the most common of all pivot verbs. 使 expresses the important act of *causation*: one has or lets (causes) someone do something. The person or thing doing the action appears in the sentence as the pivot. Here, Yang Zhu proposes a situation: "Suppose we have your dog go out white and come back black." 汝狗 is the pivot. As this sentence illustrates, this causative construction with 使 is a standard

way of making a counterfactual proposition. Yang Zhu does not expect this change of color to happen. Indeed, he probably does not even believe it is possible, but he raises this *hypothetical situation* to make his point.

9. 能 無 怪 哉   Here 能 is an auxiliary. The verb that is its object (what we call the "main verb") is 無. The object of 無 is also a verb—怪 "to consider strange or blame"—that is nominalized: "there is no considering strange/blaming" Yet whereas 無 *can* have verbs as its object, 能 *must* have a verb as its object.

Questions

1. What is the function of 而 in (1)?

2. Is the relation between 雨 and 解 in (2) topic-comment or verb$_1$-verb$_2$? Why?

3. Does 知 have a direct object in (3)? If it does, what is it?

4. What is the grammatical function of 怒 in (4)?

5. What is the function of 也 in (5)?

6. What is the direct object of 使 in (6)?

7. What part of speech is 白 in (6)? Why?

Exercises

1. Diagram and translate the following sentences:

   a. 農夫不肯耕田

   b. 農夫不應待兔之觸株

   possessive.
   wait
   The farmer shouldn't ~~rely on~~ for the rabbits to run into the stump.
   rabbits to run into tree stumps

   c. 吾豈敢扑其狗

   How could I dn hit his dog

   d. 子能入水而得其矛乎

   Q word
   – Yes/No Q
   [Are you able to go into the water and obtain the sword.]

"It is not the case"

e. 其言不可疑也

this words cannot be doubted.

2. For the following 反切, what does the character mean? (You may need to use a dictionary.)

    a. 爲喻睡反

    b. 使史吏切

    c. 應於證反

    d. 易羊益切 [This represents a distinction preserved in Cantonese.]

Lesson 7

Coverbs

In literary Chinese, coverbs play the function served by *prepositions* in English. However, coverbs are *not* prepositions and do not behave in the same way. Coverbs are a type of *transitive verb*. That is, they take objects, can be modified by 所, negated by 不, and marked for coordination by 而. And perhaps most fundamentally, they describe an action. The type of action they describe, however, is an *attendant action*, something done in order to bring about the action of the *main verb*. Although this quality of being the *antecedent condition* for the action of the main verb is a possibility in *all* examples of coordination of verbs, several verbs came regularly to play this subordinate function:

> 從 *cóng*, "to follow"
> 自 *zì*, "to start from"
> 由 *yóu*, "to follow along"
> 與 *yǔ*, "to give to" > "to accompany"
> 因 *yīn*, "to rely on"
> 以 *yǐ*, "to grasp" > "to use"
> 爲 *wèi*, "to act for the sake of"

Because these verbs were used with such frequency in coordinate pairs, they acquired a special function and behavior.

Perhaps the most conspicuous sort of irregularity displayed by coverbs is the way in which 所 constructions are made:

> 以刀殺狗 > 所以殺狗者，刀也。
> 義從貴且富出 > 義之所從出，貴且富也。

or, in general $CV + O_{CV} + MV > $ 所 $+ CV + MV, O_{CV}$ 也.

Note the following conventions concerning particular coverbs:

1. The character 因 , like all other coverbs, usually takes an object. On occasion, however, 因 by itself *without an object* is used at the beginning of a sentence to mean "relying on the entire situation recounted in the text above . . . ."

2. The common construction 以 X 爲 Y, means "to take X to be Y." From this expression grew the compound verb 以爲, which means "takes [it] to be . . . " > "believes that . . . ."

3. There are two major possibilities for the construction

$$V_1 \text{ 以 } V_2$$

    a. The two verbs should be taken as $MV+CV+O_{CV}$, where the usual order has been reversed in order to stress that V_2 is the object of the coverb 以: "V_1 by means of V_2." Consider

    告之以有過 informed him *with* [the fact of] *his having erred*

    b. The verbs should be taken as V_1 而 V_2, "V_1 and, by means of it, V_2" That is, 以 often is used to *make clear* the fact that the first verb is the *antecedent condition* for the second. With 而, we cannot know for sure what the fact of coordination implies; 以 removes that doubt, as in

    脩身以俟之 cultivate oneself *to await him*

4. 因 and 以 often appear together. Consider:

    或因枝以振葉 Some rely on the branch to shake the leaves.

This is essentially equivalent to:

    或因枝而振葉

That is, 因 here returns to its fully verbal usage as the first of a pair of coordinate verbs. Note, however, that 以 replaces 而 as a marker of coordination and, as in (3) above, strongly stresses the idea that 因枝 defines the conditions under which the second action (振葉) occurs.

Once Again:
The Function Word 也 *in Verbal Phrases*

In the selection below, 也 appears four times at the end of sentences with verbal comments. The function of this important and difficult structure merits repeated explanation. In all four cases, the function is the same: *to turn an action into a general condition, a state of affairs.* For example:

> 以爲畏狐也 [He] took [it] to be that [the animals] feared the fox.

What the tiger believed is a *categorical statement, a general proposition*: the animals fear the fox not just this one time but always, and such is simply the way things are.[1] Thus, in an important sense, the sentence remains an *identity statement*, like any other nominal sentence ending in 也. Hence when the fox proclaims:

> 今子食我，是逆天帝命也。Now for you to eat me would be a violation of the Heavenly Emperor's command.

he says this as a generally valid truth: "Not only is it a violation this one time; it always has been and always will be a violation." The sentence, being categorical, is far stronger than the verbal sentence without the 也.

Text: 狐假虎威 (戰國策)

1. 虎求百獸而食之，得狐。

2. 狐曰子無敢食我也。

3. 天帝使我長百獸，今子食我，是逆天帝命也。

4. 子以我爲不信，吾爲子先行，子隨我後，觀百獸之見我而敢不走乎。

---

1. Pulleyblank (*Outline of Classical Chinese Grammar*, p. 118) explains this usage as a type of continuative aspect marker.

5. 虎以爲然，故遂與之行，獸見之皆走。

6. 虎不知獸畏己而走也，以爲畏狐也。

Vocabulary

狐   *hú* (n), fox

假   *jiǎ* (v), to borrow

虎   *hǔ* (n), tiger

威   *wēi* (n), majesty, prestige

戰國策   *Zhàn guó cè, Strategies of the Warring States*, a quasi-historical collection of stories about Warring States persuaders 遊說者

求   *qiú* (v), to seek

百   *bǎi*, hundred > all types of

獸   *shòu* (n), animal

食   *shí* (v), to eat

子   *zǐ* (n), master > you [polite]

敢   *gǎn* (av), to dare

帝   *dì* (n), emperor

長   *zhǎng* (v), to grow > (v) be an elder (leader) to

逆   *nì* (v), to go against

命   *mìng* (n), decree, command

信   *xìn* (v), to be trustworthy

先   *xiān* (n), former [part]

隨   *suí* (v), to follow

後   *hòu* (n), latter [part]

觀   *guān* (v), to observe

見   *jiàn* (v), to see

故   *gù* (fw), [for this] reason

遂   *suì* (v), to follow > (adv) accordingly

皆   *jiē* (adv), in all cases

畏   *wèi* (v), to fear

己   *jǐ* (n), oneself, third-person reflexive pronoun

Notes on the Text

1. 百獸   The number 百 is used to represent "all of the many . . . ." For example, 百姓 "all of the many surnames" (i.e., everyone) and 諸子百家 "the many philosophers [of the Warring States period]."

2. 子無敢食我也　無 can be a mild negative imperative. Here it retains this quality: "You most certainly don't dare eat me." Note also the final 也, which makes the sentence a statement of fact. This is a strong assertion that borders on an order.

3. 是逆天帝命也　The character 是 means "this," but it often is used at the beginning of a comment construction to refer to a much longer topic, or a phrase that needs to be marked off as a topic: "as for what I have just mentioned, it . . . ." In such cases, the comment is itself an abbreviated topic (是)–comment (逆天帝命) construction.

4. 吾爲子先行　The problem here is with 爲: is it *fourth* tone, meaning "for your sake" or *second* tone, meaning "I will enact . . . ."? The two readings tell the same story about who goes first:

> 爲[Coverb] 子[Object] + 先[Modifier] 行[Main verb] for your sake, [I'll] travel in front
> 爲[Verb] + 子[Modifier]先 [Modifier]行[Object]　enact a "traveling in front of you"

The commentaries seem to agree that it should be in *second* tone, but that the usage here is slightly unusual.

5. 觀百獸之見我而敢不走乎　The object of 觀 is a complex *embedded sentence* (see Lesson 8). Its free, unbound sentence form is:

> 百獸見我而敢不走乎 The animals see me, and dare they not run away?

That is, the first half of the sentence (百獸見我) is a normal declarative sentence that sets up the conditions for the rhetorical question in the second half (敢不走乎). The sentence is embedded, that is, it *acts like a noun* (here, the direct object of 觀); this is accomplished by *placing a 之 between the* topic *and the* comment.

6. 然　Here 然 is a one-word sentence: "[It] is like this." Moreover, it is a verbal sentence rather than nominal.

7. 與之行　This is a *coverb* construction. That is, in this case 與 does not serve to mark coordination of the two nouns 虎 and 之. First, the 虎 is too far away for this to be simple coordination. Moreover, 與 has a specificity of meaning here. Try substituting 從: the sentence

gives a very different picture of the relationship of the two animals. Now, instead of "traveling with" the fox, the tiger would be "following him."

8. 虎不知獸畏己也   As this sentence shows, 己 differs from 自 in an important way. 自 is a modifier, and 自畏 would mean "The animals feared *themselves*." Or "They feared *of their own accord*." The author says instead that the animals fear the *tiger*. The 己 often is used in situations like this, in which the pronoun refers back to the *speaker* in the framing sentence (in this case, the tiger who 不知) rather than to the actors (獸) of the embedded action.

Questions

1. What is the function of 而 in (1)? What is the relationship between the two actions?

2. What type of object is 百獸 in (3)? Why?

3. What is the grammatical function of 後 in (4)? How can you tell?

4. What is the relationship between 見 and 走 in (5)?

5. What two verbs does 而 connect as coordinate in (6)?

6. What phrase does the first 也 in (6) mark as nominal? What is its function?

Exercises

1. Translate

    從其父還家

    與其弟還家

    自佛寺還家

    由其向所往路還家

爲其弟不樂還家

2. Change the following from a 所 construction to a V-O sentence and translate the sentence:

Example: 所從還家者其父也→ 從其父還家

王所以殺民者政也

所與相樂者同心之人也

列子所因而遊者順風也

3. Change the following to a 所 construction and translate the sentence.

Example: 與弟還家 → 所與還家者弟也

以心聽其言外之意

從其事之跡得其情

Lesson 8

Embedded Sentences

The goal of the introductory chapters of this textbook is to stress how authors writing in literary Chinese create ever more complex sentences from the simple building blocks of *topic-comment*, *verb-object*, *modifier-modified* (subordinate), and *coordinate* grammatical pairings. We have seen the importance of the technique of controlling emphasis through topicalization. We also have seen the various sorts of nominalizations that allow one to create larger, nested grammatical units.

A final key feature in the creation of complex sentences in literary Chinese is the *embedded sentence*. What is an embedded sentence? A sentence is *embedded* when a sentence replaces a noun in a grammatical structure. For example:

1. "Mary has the measles."
2. "I know that."
3. "I know Mary has the measles."

In the second sentence, "that", a noun, is the object of "know." The third sentence then replaces the "that" with the *entire first sentence*, which is now the object of "know." Therefore, in the third sentence, "Mary has the measles" is an *embedded sentence* and the object of "know." If one wanted to mark the sentence explicitly as embedded, one could rewrite (3) as:

4. "I know *that* Mary has the measles."

The phrase "that Mary has the measles" is the "completed form" of the embedded sentence: this *completed form* can be used in many situations:

> 5. "That Mary has the measles is a shame."

but not

> *6. ~~"Mary has the measles is a shame."~~

The point is that there are specific rules in English for indicating and using embedded sentences. The same is true in literary Chinese, but the rules are different.

> 7. 劍入水。
> 8. 見之。
> 9. 見劍入水。

and, to use the completed form:

> 10. 見劍之入水。

The most common form of embedded sentence in literary Chinese is illustrated in sentence (10):

> *topic 之 *comment

The asterisks serve as a reminder that in the completed form, what had been the topic of the sentence is now a *modifier* and the comment is now the *head* of the noun phrase. Note that

a. the 之 is optional; and
b. if the topic is well understood, then *topic + 之 is replaced by 其.

Text: 揠苗(孟子)

敢問何謂浩然之氣。
曰難言也。其爲氣也，至大至剛。以直養而無害，則塞於天地之間。其爲氣也，配義與道。無是，餒也。是集義所生者，非義襲而取之也。行有不慊於心，則餒矣。我故曰告子未嘗知義，以其外之也。必有事焉而勿正，心勿忘，勿助長也。無若宋人然。

1. 宋人有閔其苗之不長而揠之者。

2. 芒芒然歸，謂其人曰，今日病矣。予助苗長矣。

3. 其子趨而往視之。苗則槁矣。

4. 天下之不助苗長者寡矣。

5. 以爲無益而舍之者，不耘苗者也。

6. 助之長者，揠苗者也。　　A者，B者（＋也）

7. 非徒無益，而又害之。

Vocabulary

揠	*yà* (v), to pull		養	*yǎng* (v), to nourish
苗	*miáo* (n), sprouts		塞	*sè* (v), to block, fill up
孟子	Mèng Zǐ, the Confucian philosopher Mencius		配	*pèi* (v), to be a match for, equal
敢	*gǎn* (v), to dare to		義	*yì* (n), righteousness
謂	*wèi* (v), to refer to		道	*dào* (n), road > the Way
浩然	*hàorán* (v), to be vast, expansive		餒	*něi* (v), to be famished
氣	*qì* (n), breath, pneuma		集	*jí* (v), to gather together
難	*nán* (v), to be difficult > to be difficult to . . .		襲	*xí* (v), to win by luck (military term)
至	*zhì* (v), to arrive > (adv) the most		取	*qǔ* (v), to take, grasp in hand
剛	*gāng* (v), to be hard		行	*xìng* (n), deportment, what one does
直	*zhí* (v), to be direct, straight > (n) direct straightness		慊	*qiàn* (v), to resent; 不慊 > to be dissatisfied
			心	*xīn* (n), heart/mind

告子 Gào Zǐ, a Confucian philosopher, rival to Mencius

嘗 *cháng* (v), to try out > (adv), once (had the experience of)

未嘗 *wèi cháng* (adv), not yet once

外 *wài* (n), the outside > (v), take to be outside

勿 *wù*, thought to be a *fusion* of 毋之, "Don't . . . it."

正 *zhèng* (v), to stand straight > to set straight

若 *ruò* (v), to resemble, be like

閔 *mǐn* (v), to pity

長 *cháng* (v), to be long > *zhǎng* (v), grow long

芒芒然 *máng máng rán* (v), to be weary

然 *rán* (v), to be like this > (fw), in a . . . manner

歸 *guī* (v), to return

謂 *wèi* (v), to address, to speak to

今 *jīn* (n), now

日 *rì* (n), sun > day

病 *bìng* (v), to be sick, weary

予 *yú* (n), I, me

助 *zhù* (v), to help

趨 *qū* (v), to rush

往 *wǎng* (v), to go to

視 *shì* (v), to see, look at

槁 *gǎo* (v), to wither, dry out

天下 *tiān xià*, all under heaven > the realm

寡 *guǎ* (v), to be few

以 . . . 爲 *yǐ wéi* (v), to take to be, make

益 *yì* (v), to increase > to benefit

舍 *shě* (v), to set aside, reject 捨

耘 *yún* (v), to weed

非徒 *fēi tú*, not only

非 *fēi* (v), not [of the class . . .]

徒 *tú* (v), to be in vain > (fw), only

又 *yòu* (adv), again

害 *hài* (v), to harm

Notes on the Text

1. 敢問.... The initial, unnumbered text is the context in 孟子 in which this well-known story appears. This discussion of 浩然之氣 in fact is *more* famous than the story of the pulling on the sprouts.

2. 閔其苗之不長而揠之 The entire section is a long nominalized phrase (see note 8 below) that serves as the object of 有. Moreover, within this nominalized phrase is an embedded sentence of the form *topic* 之 *comment*:

其苗之不長 his sprouts' not growing

The original form of the sentence is:

其苗不長 His sprouts do not grow.

3. 芒芒然 This is a typical descriptive adverbial construction: *X* 然 + *verb*.

4. 今日病矣 Note the use of 矣 here. As we have seen before, it conveys the sense that the preceding statement is new information to which the listener ought to pay attention. It has both the sense of a change of state and a slight emphatic quality.

5. 助苗長 This is a *pivoting verb* construction. *He* helps the sprouts, but it is the *sprouts* themselves that grow. 苗 is a *pivot*, which grammatically remains an *object*. Note the phrase 助之長 in (6), where the pronoun 之 has replaced 苗.

6. 趨而往視之 There are three coordinate verbs in this phrase: 趨, 往, and 視. The question, then, is why is the 而 between 趨 and 往? How does the sentence differ from

6'. 趨往而視之

The emphasis in both sentences is on the half *after* the 而. In the first version, Mencius stresses that the sons *went to see*, whereas in (6') the emphasis is focused more narrowly on the final result, their looking at the sprouts. The *fronting* of the verb 趨 *de-emphasizes* it—indeed it becomes all but reduced to a simple modifier—and is the verbal parallel to topicalization.

7. 苗則槁矣 The particle 則 is a strong rhetorical *marker of the topic* as an *exposed* element. There is no real doubt that "sprouts" is the topic here, but the 則, by separating the topic off in an exposed position, marks it for emphasis: "As for the *sprouts* . . . ." Yes, what about them? "Well, they *had already dried out.*"

8. 天下之不助苗長者寡矣 All embedded verbal sentences are necessarily *nominalized* because they replace a noun and therefore occupy a noun slot, but not all nominalized verbs are parts of embedded sentences. Although the phrase 天下之不助苗長 in this example *looks* like an embedded sentence, "All-under-heaven's not helping the sprouts grow," the sentence refers to a complete situation—an actor doing an action—that would be too restrictive in its reference. Instead, the nominalized verb construction allows one to refer either to any *person* who performs the action (anyone who doesn't help) or to the *action* itself ([instances of] not helping). Moreover, it is relatively rare for complete sentences to modify the abstract noun 者.

9. 舍 In the development of Chinese characters, radicals were frequently added at some later point to distinguish different uses of the same character, which often had different pronunciations that reflected the difference in meaning. 舍 is one such character. Among frequently occurring characters, other examples are:

> 說 can be *shuō*, "to explain," *shuì*, "to persuade", or *yuè*, 悅 , "to please"
> 知 can be *zhī*, "to know", or *zhì*, 智, "to be wise or shrewd"

A particularly difficult problem arises in the phrase 養生 "nourish life." It can also mean 養性 "to nourish one's nature." In early writings, it is not easy to tell from the text which alternative is meant.

10. 非徒...而又 This is a standard construction: when you see the first half, you should expect to find some variant of the second half soon.

Questions

1. What is the rhetorical function of the 而 in sentence (1)?

2. What is the grammatical relationship between 謂 and 曰 in (2)?

3. What is the grammatical function of 今日 in (2)?

4. What is the relationship between the two "sentences" in (2)? Are they coordinate?

5. Where is the division between topic and comment in (4)? What is the rhetorical effect?

6. What two verbs does 而 mark as coordinate in (5)?

7. Is (5) a verbal or nominal sentence? What about (6)?

8. To what does the 之 refer in (5)? in (6)? in (7)?

Exercises

1. Rewrite the following pairs of sentences as single sentences.

    獸皆畏虎。虎不知之。

    白獸見我。請觀之。

    楚人之矛甚利。楚人譽之。

2. Find *two* embedded sentences in the previous lessons. Rewrite them as pairs of separate sentences.

    a.

    b.

Part Two

Intermediate Texts

Lesson 9

Your servant says, to be young and fond of learning is like the sunrise

晉平公問於師曠 説苑

Text

晉平公問於師曠曰吾年七十，欲學恐已暮矣。師曠
曰何不炳燭乎。平公曰安有爲人臣而戲其君乎。師
曠曰盲臣安敢戲其君乎。臣聞之，

　少而好學，如日出之陽。

　壯而好學，如日中之光。

　老而好學，如炳燭之明。

炳燭之明，孰與昧行乎。平公曰善哉。

Talks in 3rd person - arrogance
tries to depersonalise situation
shows fear of situation and consequence
munselling = metaphor for brain/vitality
exclamation
action

Vocabulary

晉平公 *Jìn Píng Gōng*, Duke Píng of Jìn (r. 557–32 B.C.)

公　*gōng* (n), duke

師曠　Shī Kuàng, music master to Duke Píng

説苑　*Shuō yuàn*, book of exemplary tales written by Liú Xiàng 劉向

年　*nián* (n), year

七　*qī*, seven

十　*shí*, ten

而 - connects 2 verbs - indicator of connection.

To be in the prime of life and fond of learning is like the sun at noon.
To be old and fond of learning resembles the light of the candle. The light of the lightened candle, how can it be compared to acting in the dark. Well said!

103

欲　*yù* (v), to desire

學　*xué* (v), to learn

恐　*kǒng* (v), to fear

何不　*hé bù* why not . . . ?　*retorical*

炳　*bǐng* (v), to gleam > light up

燭　*zhú* (n), candle

安　*ān* (n), where? why? how?　*interrogotive.*

臣　*chén* (n), servant, *I your humble servant*

戲　*xì* (v), to jest, make fun of

君　*jūn* (n), lord

盲　*máng* (v), to be blind

聞　*wén* (v), to hear

少　*shào* (v), to be young (*shǎo* = few)

好　*hào* (v), to be fond of (*hǎo* = good)

日出　*rì chū*, sun rises > sunrise

陽　*yáng* (*dịang) (n), radiance

壯　*zhuàng* (v), to be hale, in one's prime

日中　*rì zhōng*, noon

光　*guāng* (*kwâng) (n), gleam

老　*lǎo* (v), to be old

明　*míng* (*mịang) (v), to be bright > (n) brightness

孰　*shú* (fw), which? > [modal: how would?]

孰與　*shú yǔ*, "how can it be compared to . . . ?"

昧　*mèi* (v), to be dark

善　*shàn* (v), to be good

Notes

1. This story is a "persuasion" and has some of the features typical of this type of anecdote. A ruler asks a question of an adviser. The adviser's reply is startling. The ruler then asks for an explanation of the remarkable reply. The adviser, having gotten the ruler's attention, then delivers his message.

2. Notice that 問 takes a locative object. One asks a question (direct object) to someone (locative object).

3. The object of 有 is the entire phrase 爲人臣而戲其君.

4. Shī Kuàng, like many music masters in antiquity, is literally blind.

5. Notice that in the phrase 臣聞之, the 之 refers not to an antecedent but forward to the poem Shī Kuàng is about to recite. This sort of forward reference is common.

6. Notice that the three words at the ends of the parallel phrases—陽, 光, and 明—all rhyme in Old Chinese (as in 詩經 poem 96, 雞鳴).

7. Shī Kuàng's final question is rather elliptical: "How would [you not choose it when compared] with walking in the dark?" 孰 often is used when given a pair of choices.

Questions

1. Why did Duke Píng think Shī Kuàng was making fun of him? What does Duke Píng mean by 暮? How does Shī Kuàng interpret it?

2. Explain the comparisons that Shī Kuàng makes in the poem.

Review

1. Does 吾 modify 年, or is it a topic? Discuss.

2. Discuss the coordination of verbs in 欲學恐已暮. Does the wording imply "and" or "but?" What about 爲人臣而戲其君?

3. Is 與 used as a coverb here?

Sentence Patterns

1. 何不

    何不炳燭乎

    君何不更乎 (更 here means "change [it]")

    汝何不早言 *why didn't you speak earlier*

    王何不聽乎 *why did the kiy not listen*

2. 安⋯乎

   盲臣安敢戲其君乎

   齊安得救天下乎 *How could they succeed in saving the world.*

   君安得長有寵乎 *How can the Lord have long lasting grace.*

   安敢不對乎
      to answer.

3. 孰與

   炳燭之明孰與昧行乎

   趙孰與秦大

   wúshúyǔ xú nei
   吾孰與徐公美
      who/grant rhomy beauty.
   way zhishì xizhòn weiiwas.
   王上者孰與周文王
   How can the king be compared to the king of Zhou.
      of any ruler king

Bibliographic Exercises

1. Locate the account of 晉平公 in 史記 39. In what part of the 史記 is this chapter? Does 師曠 play a role?

2. Find out more about 師曠. Use one of the large dictionaries: 漢語大詞典 or 大漢和辭典.

The one who sees the double headed snake will die. I saw one, and now I am afraid, I am (more) dying, leaving behind my mother.

I was afraid that other people would see it and die, therefore I killed it and buried it.

Lesson 10

兩頭蛇 新序

Text

孫叔敖爲嬰兒之時，出遊，見兩頭蛇，殺而埋
之，歸而泣。其母問其故。叔敖對曰，聞見兩頭之
蛇者死。嚮者吾見之，恐去母而死也。其母曰，
蛇今安在。曰，恐他人又見，殺而埋之矣。其母
曰，吾聞有陰德者天報以福，汝不死也。及長爲
楚令尹，未治而國人信其仁也。

Vocabulary

兩	*liǎng*, two, a pair of
頭	*tóu* (n), head
蛇	*shé* (n), snake
新序	*Xīn xù*, another book by Liú Xiàng
孫叔敖	Sūn Shú'ào, a minister to Chǔ Zhuāng Wáng during the Chūnqiū

period, created a policy of enriching the people.

嬰兒	*yīng ér* (n), infant
遊	*yóu* (v), to wander > play
殺	*shā* (v), to kill
埋	*mái* (v), to bury
泣	*qì* (v), to weep

107

母　*mǔ* (n), mother

故　*gù* (n), reason

對　*dùi* (v), to face > reply

死　*sǐ* (v), to die

嚮　*xiàng* (n), formerly > just now

安　*ān* (n), where?

在　*zài* (v), to be at

他　*tuō* (n), other

陰德　*yīn dé*, hidden act of goodness

陰　*yīn* (n), shade, darkness

德　*dé* (n), virtue/power

報　*bào* (v), to repay

福　*fú* (n), good fortune

及　*jí* (v), to reach > (cv) by the time when . . .

令尹　*lìng yǐn*, chief minister

未　*wèi* (adv), not yet

仁　*rén* (v), to be humane > (n), benevolence

Notes

1.　爲 is a difficult verb. Although it usually is translated as "to be," it often has the sense of "to enact the role of" or "to be taken to be." That is, something *is* through the agency of some human action. Here, however, 爲 clearly means "is" in its simplest form, and no action is implied.

2.　Note the embedded clauses in

聞ᵥₑᵣᵦ [[見ᵥₑᵣᵦ [兩頭之蛇] ₒᵦⱼₑꜜₜ 者] ₜₒₚᵢꜛ 死 ꜜₒₘₘₑₙₜ] ₒᵦⱼₑꜜₜ

3.　The nominalizing function word 也 is extremely important and changes the tenor of sentences in ways that must be accounted for. In 嚮者吾見之，恐去母而死也, the phrase becomes a statement of fact rather than a narrative account of action. In particular, it is an *explanation*, an answer to his mother's question, "Why [are you crying]?"

4.　吾聞有陰德者天報以福 is another sentence with complex embedding. In the phrase that is the object of 聞, the topic—有陰德者—clearly is *not* the "subject" of the verb (the agent, 天, is). Notice also that in this sentence the main verb 報 comes before the coverb 以.

Questions

1. Why does Sūn add the 又 in 恐他人又見?

2. What is the function of the 也 in 汝不死也? *It is the case that you must die* → *underlines authoritative nature*

3. What is the function of the 也 in 未治而國人信其仁(也)? *statement of truth (gives authority)* *"and then it was the case that"*

Review

1. What is the relationship between the verbs in 出遊? Explain.

2. What is the relationship of 恐 to 他人又見之 in 恐他人又見之?

3. Why does the coverb come after the main verb in the expression 報以福?

Sentence Patterns

1. 聞...

   聞見兩頭之蛇者死。 *jiàn tóu zhī shé sǐ*

   吾聞有陰德者天報以福。 *wú yīn dé zhě bào yǐ fú*

   吾聞輔主者名顯。 *fú zhǔ zhě xiǎn* *I asked host   name obvious/famous*

   吾聞食其祿者死其事。 *shí eat* *someone who is minded*

   吾聞好諫者思其君。 *jiàn sī qí jūn think monarch*

   食其食

   I heard that someone who eats someone else foods, will die for his affairs (completely loyal)

2. 安

   安往而不可。 *ān zhù*

   安往而不得其志乎。 *qí zhì ideal.*

   國危甚矣若將安適。 [Note: 若 = "you"]

Bibliographic Exercises

1. Look up the entry for 新序 in Michael Loewe, ed., *Early Chinese Texts: A Bibliographical Guide*. What are its sources? What modern Chinese edition does the entry give?

2. Use a large dictionary to find out more about 孫叔敖. What other sources does the dictionary entry cite?

Lesson 11

曾參殺人 戰國策

Text

昔者曾子處費。魯邑，屬東海。費人有與曾子同名族者，名，
字。族，姓。而殺人。人告曾子母曰曾參殺人。曾子之母曰
吾子不殺人。織自若。若，如故也。有頃焉，人又曰曾參殺
人。其母尚織自若也。頃之，一人又告之曰曾參殺人。
其母懼，投杼逾牆而走。逾牆逃走也。夫以曾參之賢與母之
信也，而三人疑之，使其母疑。則慈母不能信也。信，猶保也。

Vocabulary

曾參	Zēng Shēn, a disciple of Confucius, known for his filiality, 字子輿	屬	*shǔ* (v), to be in the jurisdiction of
昔	*xí* (n), long ago	東海	Dōnghǎi ("Eastern Ocean")
處	*chǔ* (v), to reside	同	*tóng* (v), to be together > to share [the same]
費	Bì, a city in Lǔ		
魯	Lǔ, a state in early China	名	*míng* (n), personal name
邑	*yì* (n), city	族	*zú* (n), clan

字   *zì* (n), capping name

姓   *xìng* (n), family name

告   *gào* (v), to inform, announce

織   *zhī* (v), to weave

自若   *zì ruò*, to be self-composed

自   *zì* [reflexive pronoun]

故   *gù* (n), the past

頃   *qǐng* (v), lean > (v) a short time passes (measured by the increasing shadow of a sundial)

焉   *yān* (n), equivalent to 於 之 = "therein"

尚   *shàng* (adv), still

懼   *jù* (v), to fear

投   *tóu* (v), to throw

杼   *zhù* (n), shuttle

逾   *yú* (v), to leap over

逃   *táo* (v), to flee

賢   *xián* (v), to be worthy

三   *sān*, three

則   *zé* (fw) [explicit topicalization]

慈   *cí* (v), to be gracious, loving

猶   *yóu* (fw), [marks approximate identity]

保   *bǎo* (v), to protect, safeguard

Notes

1. The short annotation 魯邑 is a comment whose topic is 費.

2. In the phrase 織自若, the topic is 織 and the comment 自若.

3. From the phrases 有頃焉 and 頃之, we know that 頃 is a **verb** that takes a **locative** object.

4. Notice the fairly complicated embedding in 以曾參之賢與母之信也. Two independent sentences—曾參賢 and 母信也—are nominalized and put into a coordinate relationship using 與. The pair becomes the object of the coverb 以.

5. Annotators often gloss usages that they find troublesome. In particular, the commentary here glosses 使其母疑 for 三人疑之. That is, the difficulty is with 之, which we might assume refers to 曾參; instead, the annotator proposes a causative construction in which 之 refers to his mother.

6. In 信猶保也, 猶 seems to mark a **nominal sentence** stating *approximate* identity: "'Trust' is *like* 'protect.'"[1]

Questions

1. Why might a persuader in the 戰國策 use this story? What is its relevance to the art of governing?

2. Is 逾牆逃走也 a good gloss? Is it accurate? Why would an annotator write such a comment?

Review

1. Is 與 a coverb or marker of coordination of nouns in the first line?

2. Why does the author add the 也 to 尚織自若 in the third line?

3. What is the function of the 以 in the fifth line?

4. If the 而 in the fifth line is a marker of coordination of verbs, what are the two verbs?

Sentence Patterns

1. 同

  費人有與曾子同名族者

  飲食衣裘與之同之

  燕王弔死問生與百姓同其甘苦。

Bibliographic Exercises

1. Use the 中國歷史地圖集 to locate 費.

2. Compare this account with that recorded in the 甘茂傳 of the 史記.

3. How would you verify the gloss 信猶保也? What resources could you use?

---

[1] See Pulleyblank, *Outline of Classical Chinese Grammar*, p. 18.

Lesson 12

趙簡子問子貢 說苑

Text

趙簡子問子貢曰，孔子為人何如。子貢對曰，賜不能識
也。簡子不說曰，夫子事孔子數十年終業而去之。寡人
問子，子曰不能識，何也。子貢曰賜譬渴者之飲江海。
知足而已。孔子猶江海也，賜則奚足以識之。簡子曰善
哉子貢之言也。

Vocabulary

趙簡子　Zhào Jiǎn Zǐ, i.e., Zhào
Yǎng 鞅, minister to the
duke of Jìn 晉 during late
Chūnqiū.

子貢　Zǐ Gòng, disciple of Confucius, originally named
端木賜, Duānmù Cì,
served as minister to the
states of Wèi 衛 and Lǔ

孔子　Kǒng Zǐ, i.e., Confucius

賜　Cì, Zǐ Gòng's name

識　*shì* (v), to know, recognize

說　*yuè* (v), to delight, same
as 悅

事　*shì* (n), matter > (v) to
serve

數　*shǔ* (v), to count > (adj)
numerous

114

終	*zhōng* (v), to end	江	*jiāng* (n), river
業	*yè* (n), training	海	*hǎi* (n), sea
終業	to complete one's training	江海	rivers and sea > all waterways
寡人	*guǎ rén*, "the lone one" = ruler's way of refering to himself	足	*zú* (v), to suffice, be sufficient
譬	*pì* (v), to use as metaphor	奚	*xī*, here equivalent to 何以, "by what . . . ?"
渴	*kě* (v), to be thirsty		
飲	*yǐn* (v), to drink	足以	*zú yǐ* (v), to be adequate to , to suffice to

Notes

1. 孔子為人 is the topic; the comment is 何如.

2. 數十年 is a number complement. The 之 in 去之 is a locative object.

3. The verb 譬 takes an embedded sentence (渴者之飲江海) as its object.

4. In 賜則奚足以識之, 則 is an explicit topic marker that creates an implicit *contrastive focus*. That is, Zǐ Gòng contrasts Confucius to himself: "Confucius is like the vast waterways; *as for me* [in contrast], by what means would I be adequate to know him?" The author here uses just one 則, but often the contrasting alternatives are paired topics marked by a pair of 則: see the example in Lesson 13.

5. 足 + **Verb** ("adequate **to be Verb**ed") is like 可 + **Verb** in being a *passive* construction. Similarly, 足以 ("adequate to be used to ") is like the partially grammaticalized version of 可以 ("can be used to "): each refers to what ordinarily would serve as the object of the coverb 以.

Questions

1. Do you think Zǐ Gòng intended his initial reply to surprise Zhào Jiǎn Zǐ? Explain.

2. Paraphrase Zǐ Gòng's explanation why he cannot know Confucius.

Review

1. What is the difference *in meaning* between 賜不能識 and 賜不能
   識也?

2. Why is the 之 in 去之 a locative object?

3. Why is 渴者之飲江海 an embedded sentence?

4. What is the difference *in meaning* between 孔子猶江海 and 孔子
   猶江海也?

5. What is the effect of the rhetorical inversion in 善哉子貢之言也?

Sentence Patterns

1. 為 + Noun as a Topic

   孔子為人何如。

   其為人疾賢妒功臣。

   為臣不忠不信。

2. 足以

   賜則奚足以識之。

   人衆不足以為強。

   重利不足以變其心。

3. 哉 in rhetorical inversions

   鍾子期曰善哉鼓琴。

   孔子曰勇哉士乎憤憤者乎。

Bibliographic Exercises

1. Use a large dictionary to verify the meaning of 終業.

2. *Shuō* 說 and *yuè* 悅 share the same phonetic 兌 *duì* yet seem to
   have very different pronunciations. Look in Bernard Karlgren,
   Grammata Serica Recensa entry 324 to explore this phonetic
   series.

Lesson 13

趙簡子舉兵攻齊 說苑

Text

趙簡子舉兵而攻齊，令軍中有敢諫者罪至死。被甲之士，名曰公盧，望見簡子大笑。簡子曰，子何笑。對曰，臣有宿笑。簡子曰有以解之則可，無以解之則死。對曰當桑之時，臣鄰家夫與婦俱之田。見桑中女，因往追之，不能得之。還反，其妻怒而去之。臣笑其曠也。簡子曰今吾伐國失國，是吾曠也。於是罷師而歸。

Vocabulary

舉 *jǔ* (v), to lift, raise [an army]

兵 *bīng* (n), weapon > soldiers

攻 *gōng* (v), to attack

齊 Qí, a state in early China

令 *lìng* (pv), to order, cause

軍 *jūn* (n), army

諫 *jiàn* (v), to remonstrate

罪 *zuì* (v), to blame > (n) crime

至 *zhì* (v), to reach [as far as]

被 *pī* (v), to wear

117

甲   *jiǎ* (n), armor

士   *shì* (n), officer

公盧   Gōnglú, a man's name

望   *wàng* (v), look afar, look for

宿   *sù* (v), to pass the night > remain from prior time

解   *jiě* (v), to explain

當   *dāng* (v), to be directly at

桑   *sāng* (n), mulberries

夫   *fū* (n), man > husband

婦   *fù* (n), wife

俱   *jū* (adv), together

之   *zhī* (v), to go to

女   *nǚ* (n), woman

追   *zhuī* (v), to chase

還   *huán* (v), to return

反   *fǎn* (v), to go back

妻   *qī* (n), wife

怒   *nù* (v), to be angry

曠   *kuàng* (v), to be pointless (based on empty plans)

伐   *fá* (v), to attack [a state of equal status]

失   *shī* (v), to fail in > lose

於是   *yú shì* (n), "at this [point]"

罷師   *bà shī* (v+o), to stop a military campaign

罷   *bà* (v), to stop, leave off

師   *shī* (n), multitude > army

歸   *guī* (v), to return

Notes

1. The object of the verb 令 is a form of indirect discourse. That is, the object conveys the contents of the order that Zhào Jiǎn Zǐ issued. The syntactic structure of that object is complex:

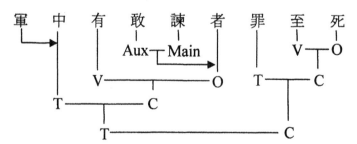

2. The expression 何笑 is an inversion of 笑何.

3. 有以+**verb** is equivalent to 有所以+**verb,** "There is that by means of which ," just as 無以 is equal to 無所以, "There is not that by means of which ."

4. 有…則可，無…則死, is a good example of *contrastive focus*: a way of setting up *alternative* propositions to be discussed: "As for (or "If) there being , then OK; as for (if) there not being , then you die." The idea of *focus* here changes the usual rule about topics being less important than comments: 則, by setting the topic off, serves as a marker of *exposure*, which in effect returns stress to the exposed element (the topic) and thus serves to focus attention on the topic. (Cf. Pulleyblank, *Outline of Classical Chinese Grammar*, pp. 71-71.)

5. In the expression 夫與婦俱之田, 與 seems to be a marker of coordination between nouns. In such a situation, both nouns are part of the topic. However, in the next line, 見桑中女, it is clear that the husband alone is the topic. So, in fact 與 functions as a coverb and is therefore part of the comment.

6. In the final sentence of his account, Gōnglú concludes 臣笑其曠也. As before, the 也 indicates that "And so it is the case that ." is in answer to Zhào's question of why he laughed.

7. Notice how 是 is used to resume a long topic (吾伐國失國) in line five to create a more emphatic short statement, 是吾曠也.

8. The phrase 不能得之 can also be written as 弗能得. However, the personal name of 漢昭帝 (r. 87 74 B.C.) was 劉弗陵, so the character 弗 became taboo. This taboo may account for the wording, or the wording may simply reflect the significant shifts in the Han dynasty spoken language.

9. The phrase 於是 is very commonly used in stories as a marker of sequence. It often implies both a temporal and a logical development: "Now that the above mentioned events have occurred . . . ."

Questions

1. How does this story fulfill the generic features of a "persuasion?"

2. How do we know that 笑 is *coordinate* with 望 and 見 in 望見 簡子大笑? Why is it not the object of 見?

3. Is 之 the *locative* or *direct* object of 去? Discuss the two possibilities and the difference in meaning.

4. Zhào realizes how Gōnglú's story applies to his situation. Paraphrase his comment and explain the comparison.

Review

1. Explain the coordination of 望見. How does it differ from modern usage?

2. Explain the use of 因 when it appears by itself, that is, without an object.

3. Are the two phrases 伐國失國 coordinate or topic-comment? Explain.

Sentence Patterns

1. 有 V 者 V

令軍中有敢諫者罪至死。

命其家臣有敢從者死。

宗廟有不順者為不孝。

2. 有以

簡子曰有以解之則可。

吾未有以言之也。

王未有以應。

有以知君之狂也以其言之當也。

Bibliographic Exercises

1. In a large dictionary, look up the phrase 桑中 (桑中之約, 桑中之喜, etc.).

2. Use the 説苑 concordance to see if 弗 is used as a contraction for 不之.

Lesson 14

鵷鶵 莊子

Text

惠子相梁。莊子往見之。或謂惠子曰，莊子來欲代子相。於是惠子恐。搜於國中三日三夜。莊子往見之，曰，南方有鳥，其名鵷鶵，子知之乎。夫鵷鶵發於南海，而飛於北海，非梧桐不止，非練實不食，成玄英曰練實竹實也。武延緒曰，練楝之借字。非醴泉不飲。於是鴟得腐鼠，鵷鶵過之，仰而視之曰嚇。今子欲以子之梁國而嚇我耶。姚鼐曰，記此語者，莊徒之陋。

Vocabulary

*鵷鶵 *yuān chú*, a fabulous bird

莊子 Zhuāng Zǐ, the philosopher

惠子 Huì Zǐ, a skilled rhetorician and friend/rival of Zhuāng Zǐ.

相 *xiàng* (v), to aid > to be minister to

梁 Liáng, the state of 魏, whose capital was 大梁

代 *dài* (v), to replace

於是 *yú shì*, "at this point, . . ."

搜　　sōu (v), to search for

夜　　yè (n), night

南　　nán (n), south

方　　fāng (n), region

鳥　　niǎo (n), bird

發　　fā (v), to set forth from

飛　　fēi (v), to fly

北　　běi (n), north

梧桐　wútóng (n), pawlonia, a tree

止　　zhǐ (v), to stop

*練實　liàn shí (n), bamboo seeds

實　　shí (n), nut, seed, fruit

*成玄英　Chéng Xuányīng, early Táng scholar

竹　　zhú (n), bamboo

*武延緒　Wǔ Yánxù, a Qīng scholar

*楝　　liàn (n), chinaberry tree

借　　jiè (v), to borrow

*醴　　lí (n), sweet wine > sweet water

泉　　quán (n), spring (of water)

*鴟　　chī (n), owl

腐　　fǔ (v), to rot

鼠　　shǔ (n), rat

過　　guò (v), to cross over

仰　　yǎng (v), to look up

*嚇　　hè hoot (a shout)

耶　　yé [final: interogative version of 也]

*姚鼐　Yáo Nài, important Qīng scholar

記　　jì (v), to record

語　　yǔ (v), to speak > (n) speech

徒　　tú (n), follower

陋　　lòu (v), to be lowly, vulgar

Notes

1. In the sentence 莊子來欲代子相, the verbs 來 and 欲代 can be either topic-comment or coordinate. "As for Zhuāng Zǐ's coming, it is to replace you and be minister," or "Zhuāng Zǐ is coming with the intent to . . . ." In this context, the fact that Zhuāng Zǐ is coming is probably news to Huì Zǐ; hence, 來 should be taken as part of the comment and is therefore coordinate with 欲代.

2. In classical usage, 國 can mean both a state and, on occasion, its capital. It is unclear here whether Huì Zǐ is searching through the countryside or simply within the capital itself.

3. The basic structure of 非梧桐不止 is topic-comment, used to make a propositional statement: "[If] it is not a pawlonia, [then] it does not stop."

4. In the Warring States period, radicals for characters were not yet systematically used to differentiate homonyms. When Wǔ Yánxù notes that 練棟之借字, he implies that when the current text of 莊子 was created, the scribe added the silk radical (糸) rather than the tree (木) radical.

5. Literary Chinese texts often do not indicate a change of the topic when the context makes the change clear. In 鴟得腐鼠，鵷鶵過之，仰而視之曰嚇, the topic of the third clause—the one who looks up—is the *owl*, even though the topic of the clause before it was the *yuān chú*.

6. Notice how the author inserts an 而 between the long coverb phrase (以子之梁國) and its main verb (嚇). The effect is to restore to 以 some of its sense as a full verb, "to grasp."

Questions

1. Does 莊子往見之 in the first line describe Zhuāng Zǐ meeting Huì Zǐ? The phrase is repeated in the second line. Does it mean the same thing? Explain.

2. The phrase 於是 is used twice in the story. Does it mean the same thing in both cases? Explain.

3. Why does the owl hoot at the *yuān chú*? What comparison is Zhuāng Zǐ making here? Why might Yáo Nài consider the story vulgar?

Review

1. What does 或 mean here? What part of speech is it?

2. Notice that the editor does not put a full stop (a period) between 北
    海 and 非: what is the relationship between the two clauses? Are
    they coordinate or topic-comment? Explain.

Pattern Sentences

1. 非 … 不 (or some negative)

    非梧桐不止。

    非練實不食。

    非醴泉不飲。

    取非其道則一簞不可受於人。

    非仁無為也。

    非禮無行也。

2. 或 "Someone"

    或謂惠子曰，莊子來欲代子相。

    或問褅之說。

    或 "Some" (a quantifier contrasting with 皆 "all" and 莫 "none"
    from which the meaning "someone" derives)

    齊人伐燕，勝之。宣王問曰，或謂寡人勿取，或謂寡人取
    之。

Bibliographic Exercises

1. Read A. C. Graham's account of 惠施 Huì Shī in *Disputers of the
    Tao* (La Salle, Ill.: Open Court, 1989). For what was Huì Shī fa-
    mous?

2. What do the dictionaries say about 練實?

Lesson 15

曳尾於塗中 莊子

Text

莊子釣於濮水。楚王使大夫二人往先焉，曰，
願以竟內累矣。莊子持竿不顧，曰，吾聞楚有神
龜，死已三千歲矣。王巾笥而藏之廟堂之上。此
龜者寧其死爲留骨而貴乎，寧其生而曳尾於塗
中。二大夫曰，寧生而曳尾塗中。莊子曰，往
矣，吾將曳尾於塗中。

Vocabulary

曳	*yì* (v), to drag	先	*xiān* (n), former part > (v) to go in advance of
尾	*wěi* (n), tail		
塗	*tú* (n), mud	願	*yuàn* (v), to wish > to request
釣	*diào* (v), to fish (with a hook)		
		竟	*jìng* (n), region (境)
*濮水	Pú River	內	*nèi* (n), area within
大夫	*dàifū*, minister (second level)	累	*lèi* (v), to bind > to burden
二	*èr*, two	持	*chí* (v), to hold in hand

126

竿	*gān* (n), pole	*笥	*sì* (n), a box of woven bamboo
顧	*gù* (v), to look over shoulder > look back	藏	*cáng* (v), to store
神	*shén* (n), spirit, god	廟	*miào* (n), ancestral shrine
龜	*guī* (n), tortoise	堂	*táng* (n), hall
千	*qián*, thousand	寧	*níng* [modal: would rather . . .]
歲	*suì* (n), harvest [festival] > year	留	*liú* (v), to remain
巾	*jīn* (n), a cloth, towel, head cloth	骨	*gǔ* (n), bone
		貴	*guì* (v), to esteem, honor

Notes

1. 楚王使大夫二人往先焉 is a pivot construction. The pivot verb is 使, and the main verb is the coordinate pair 往先. The pivot, 大夫二人, is composed of a noun and a number complement. The number complement does not modify the noun: that is, it does not in fact specify a subset of ministers. It simply says, "and there were two of them." In the alternative construction, 二大夫, the 二 directly modifies 大夫 and the measure 人 disappears.

2. 死已三千歲矣 could conceivably mean "When [the tortoise] died, it already was three thousand years old." 死 would be a time topic. However, the more probable reading is "As for its death, it has already been three thousand years." That is, the death rather than the tortoise is now the topic of the sentence.

3. In the context of the story, the phrase 巾笥 —"cloth and box"— must be a verb. (The verb-coordinator 而 forces this reading.) Thus it must mean "[wrap it in] a cloth and [put it in] a box."

4. 寧 very frequently is used as a question word asking one to choose between two alternatives. Here, the first of the two choices is marked by a 乎 as a question, and the second is not. The 其 following the 寧 may be "modal," that is, it indicates some sense of wishing that what follows it in the sentence may come true.

5. The character 矣 has a set of meanings similar to the modern Mandarin 了. Like 了, it can have an emphatic sense: 往矣, "Go!"

Questions

1. 焉, as a fusion of 于安, is an anaphoric locative pronoun; that is, it is a locative noun that refers to some previously mentioned place. To what does it refer in the first line of the story?

2. In the phrase 死爲留骨, what is the relationship of 死 to the rest? What is the object of 爲? What is the relationship of 留 to 骨?

Review

1. 以 is a coverb in the first line of the story. What is its object? What is the main verb?

2. What is the *rhetorical* function of the 而 in 寧生而曳尾塗中?

3. What is the function of 將 in the final sentence?

Sentence Patterns

1. 寧 … 寧

   a. 此龜者寧其死爲留骨而貴乎，寧其生而曳尾於塗中。

   b. 人之情，寧朝人乎，寧朝於人乎。(於 marks the agent in passive constructions)

   c. 王寧亡十城耶，將亡十國耶。(將 = "or")

2. 矣 in imperative sentences

   a. 莊子曰，往矣，吾將曳尾於塗中。

   b. 公往矣，無污我。

   c. 臣請避矣。

Bibliographic Exercises

1. Locate the 濮水. The first volume of the 中國歷史地圖集 is a good resource. How far is the river from 楚?

2. Look up 矣 in a function word 虛詞 dictionary. Either a traditional work like 劉淇, 助字辨略, or a modern compilation like 高樹藩, ed. 文言文虛詞大詞典 (Wuhan: Hubei Jiaoyu, 1991), will do. Find an entry relevant to the use of 矣 in the final sentence of the text for this lesson.

Lesson 16

石奢 史記

Text

石奢者，楚昭王相也。堅直廉正，無所阿避。行
縣，道有殺人者，相追之，乃其父也。縱其父而
還，自繫焉，使人言之王曰，殺人者臣之父也。
夫以父立政，不孝也。廢法縱罪，非忠也。臣罪
當死。王曰追而不及，不當伏罪。子其治事矣。
石奢曰不私其父，非孝子也，不奉主法，非忠臣
也。王赦其罪，上惠也，伏誅而死，臣職也。遂
不受令，自刎而死。

Vocabulary

*石奢　Shí Shē, a man

*楚昭王　King Zhāo of Chǔ
(r. 515–489 B.C.)

直　*zhí* (v), to be upright and
direct

廉　*lián* (v), to be honest

正　*zhèng* (v), to be impartial

*阿　*ē* (v), to fawn, be obse-
quious

避　*bì* (v), to flee, avoid

縣　*xiàn* (n), county

行縣　*xíng xiàn*, inspect one's
county

道　*dào* (n), road

乃   *nǎi* [strong connector of verbs]

父   *fù* (n), father

縱   *zòng* (v), to release

繫   *xì* (v), to bind

言   *yán* (n), word > (v) to speak

之   *zhī* (n), him, her, it [pronoun used as direct, indirect, or locative object]

立政   *lì zhèng*, establish [principles of] governance

孝   *xiào* (v), to be filial

廢   *fèi* (v), to abandon, discard

法   *fǎ* (n), rules, regulations

忠   *zhōng* (v), to be loyal

當   *dāng* (v), to be appropriate

伏   *fú* (v), to bend down

伏罪   *fú zuì*, to submit to punishment

其   *qí* (fw) [modal: won't you . . . ?]

私   *sī* (n), private [land] > (v) [to protect] as ones own

奉   *fèng* (v), to reverently receive

主   *zhǔ* (n), host, owner, the one in charge

赦   *shè* (v), to absolve, forgive

上   *shàng* (n), the place above > one's superior (usually used to refer to kings and emperors)

惠   *huì* (v), to bestow [kindness]

誅   *zhū* (v), to punish (≅ execute)

職   *zhí* (n), office, post > official duties

遂   *suì* (v), to follow > (adv) subsequently

受   *shòu* (v), to receive

*刎   *wěn* (v), to cut one's throat

Notes

1. This text is the complete biography of Shí Shē that Sīmǎ Qiān 司馬遷 (c. 145 B.C.–86 B.C.) included in Chapter 119 of the 史記. It follows the conventions for a biography established in the 史記. It begins with a simple declarative statement that identifies the subject. The

biography then briefly describes Shí Shē's character and recounts an incident that both reveals that character and shows why Shí Shē's biography belongs in the chapter on obedient officials (循吏列傳).

2. It is difficult to say whether 阿 modifies 避 ("to fawningly avoid") or whether the two are coordinate ("to be fawning and thereby avoid"). The pair of verbs in either case can take 所 as a modifier to point to what one might avoid by fawning.

3. 乃 often serves a strong narrative role: "and it turned out that . . . ." Note that the sentence following the 乃 is a *nominal* sentence (其父也).

4. 夫 at the beginning of a sentence often has the function of introducing a topic into the flow of dialogue or narrative: "Now, ..."

5. The 其 in 子其治事矣 is clearly *modal* : "You just take care of the matter!"

6. Shí Shē's final statement is a formal set speech. Notice the groups of parallel expressions: (1) 不私其父，非孝子也 and 不奉主法，非忠臣也。(2) 王赦其罪，上惠也 and 伏誅而死，臣職也。

7. 遂 is another important term in narratives in literary Chinese. Marking a sequence of actions, it says "and thereupon, he . . . ."

Questions

1. What is the function of 焉 in line 2? To what does it refer? What is the function of the 之 ? To what does it refer?

2. What is the object of the coverb 以 ? What is its main verb? What is the relationship between 以父立政 and 不孝也?

3. Explain the parallelism cited in Note 6 above.

Review

1. If 使 is a pivot verb, what is the pivot? What is the main verb?

2. What is the difference between 非忠 and 不忠?

3. What is the relationship between 臣 and 罪 in 臣罪當死? What is the relationship between 臣罪 and 當死? Explain.

4. What part of speech is the phrase 不私其父 in 不私其父非孝子也? Explain.

Sentence Patterns

1. 乃 in emphatic statements of identity

   相追之，乃其父也。

   善附民者是乃善用兵者也。

   君子明樂(*yuè*)乃其德也。

2. modal 其

   子其治事矣。

   攻之不克，圍之不繼，吾其還也。

   吾子其無廢先君之功。

Bibliographic Exercise

1. Who are the other men whose biographies appear in the 循吏列傳?

Lesson 17

晏子之御_{史記}

Text

晏子爲齊相。出，其御之妻，從門間而窺其夫。
其夫爲相御，擁大蓋，策駟馬，意氣揚揚，甚自
得也。既而歸，其婦請去。夫問其故。妻曰，晏
子長不滿六尺，身相齊國，名顯諸侯。今者妾觀
其出，志念深矣，常有以自下者。今子長八尺，
乃爲人僕御，然子之意自以爲足。妾是以求去
也。其後，夫自損抑。晏子怪而問之，御以實
對，晏子薦以爲大夫。

Vocabulary

晏子	Master Yàn, i.e., 晏嬰, Yàn Yīng	窺	*kuī* (v), to peek at
御	*yù* (n), charioteer	擁	*yǒng* (v), to support, hold
相	*xiàng* (n), high minister	蓋	*gài* (n), a cover > parasol
妻	*qī* (n), principal wife	策	*cè* (n), a whip

駟	*sì* (m), team of four horses	志念	*zhì niàn*, resolute thoughts
意氣	*yì qì*, bearing, spirit	常	*cháng* (adv), always
揚揚	*yáng yáng* (v), to be swelling upward	自下	*zì xià* (v), to humble oneself
甚	*shèn* (adv), extremely	僕	*pú* (n), slave
自得	*zì dé* (v), to be self-satisfied	妾	*qiè* (n), secondary wife > humble status pronoun, "I, your wife"
旣	*jì* (v), to complete, finish		
歸	*guī* (v), to return	損抑	*sǔn yì* (v), to be dispirited
顯	*xiǎn* (v), to manifest, appear	怪	*guài* (v), to consider strange
諸侯	*zhū hóu* (n), the feudal lords	實	*shí* (n), substance
觀	*guān* (v), to observe	薦	*jiàn* (v), to recommend

Notes

1. 晏子爲齊相 and 其夫爲相御 are typical uses of 爲 in the sense of "to enact the role of . . . ."

2. Because of the 而 marking coordination between 從 and 窺, 從 recovers some of its fully verbal meaning. That is, the charioteer's wife *follows behind them to* the gate of the compound in order to peek at her husband.

3. 身 frequently serves as a third-person pronoun without reference to status (in contrast to all the various status pronouns), "in his own person, he . . . ." Here it is used as a contrastive category with 名, "his name."

4. Note the parallelism in 身相齊國，名顯諸侯. That is, 身 and 名 establish the important contrastive pair Name/Substance, and the rest of the sentences develop parallel stories using syntactically parallel language (相 and 顯 are verbs, and 國 and 侯 are nouns modified

by 齊 and 諸 respectively). In each half, Master Yàn flourishes: he, in his person, has high status *within* the state. His name has high status *outside* the state.

5. The "reflexive adverb" 自 has two rather different meanings. One is a true reflexive in which 自 serves as the object of the verb, as in 自 信. The other usage is more difficult and means "of its/his/her own accord," that is, there is nothing else forcing the event to happen. In the text, 自下 is the true reflexive, "to lower himself." The other examples (自以爲足, 自得, 自損抑) probably all mean "of his own accord."

6. 是以 is an inversion of 以是.

7. 以爲 almost always can be considered the same as 以 [之] 爲 , "take [it] to be . . . ." Often this "taking" is a mental act, but here Yàn Zǐ wants to literally take (or use) the driver to "assume the role of" (爲) a minister, that is, to appoint him as a minister.

Questions

1. In 今者妾觀其出, to whom does the 其 refer?

2. What is 有以 equivalent to?

3. What is the function of the 也 in 妾是以求去也?

4. Why did Yàn Zǐ recommend his driver to become a minister?

Review

1. What part of speech is 然? Is it equivalent to 然而 or 然則? Explain the difference.

2. Explain the meaning of 自損抑.

3. Is 怪 an intransitive verb? If transitive, where is its direct object in the text?

4. In 御以實對, what is the object of the coverb? What is the main verb?

Sentence Patterns

1. 從…而

   其御之妻，從門間而窺其夫。

   二三子從夫子而遇此難也。(從 = "to follow")

   必從旁而決之。(從 = "from")

2. 既而

   既而歸，其婦請去。

   子奇年十六，齊君使治阿，既而君悔之。(阿 is a town)

   始無有，既而有生，生俄而死。(有生 = "'Being' is born.")

3. 乃 in sentences with results contrary to expectations

   今子長八尺，乃為人僕御。

   亡國之主反此，乃自賢而少人。

   知德忘知乃大得知也。

Bibliographic Exercises

1. Look up 晏嬰 in a large dictionary. What does the entry say about ·him?

2. What is the 晏子春秋? Michael Loewe, ed., *Early Chinese Texts: A Bibliographic Guide* (Berkeley: Institute for East Asian Studies, 1993), is a good source.

Lesson 18

吳王欲伐荊 _{說苑}

Text

吳王欲伐荊，告其左右曰，有敢諫者死。舍人有少孺子者，欲諫不敢，則懷丸操彈，遊於後園，露沾其衣。如是者三旦。吳王曰，子來。何苦沾衣如此。對曰，園中有樹，其上有蟬。蟬高居悲鳴飲露，不知螳螂在其後也。螳螂委身曲附欲取蟬，而不知黃雀在其旁也。黃雀延頸欲啄螳螂，而不知彈丸在其下也。此三者皆務得其前利，而不顧其後之有患也。吳王曰善哉乃罷其兵。

Vocabulary

伐	*fá* (v), to attack (a state)	懷	*huái* (n), chest > (v) to hold to chest
荊	Jīng (n), the state of Chǔ	丸	*wán* (n), pellet
左右	*zuǒ yòu* (n), [people to] the left and right > retainers and officials	操	*cāo* (v), to hold
		彈	*dàn* (n), slingshot
舍人	*shè rén* (n), palace attendant	露	*lù* (n), dew
*孺子	*rú zǐ* (n), small child	沾	*zhān* (v), to moisten
		旦	*dàn* (n), dawn

138

苦   *kǔ* (v), bitter > grieve bitterly

蟬   *chán* (n), cicada

鳴   *míng* (v), to sing

飲   *yǐn* (v), to drink

居   *jū* (v), to reside

*螳螂   *táng láng* (n), praying mantis

委身   *wěi shēn*, to bend the body

曲   *qū* (v), to bend

曲附   *qū fù* (v), hover over (?)

*黃雀   *huáng què* (n), titmouse, a small bird

旁   *páng* (n), side

延   *yán* (v), to stretch

頸   *jǐng* (n), neck

啄   *zhuó* (v), to peck

務   *wù* (v), to labor at

利   *lì* (n), advantage

顧   *gù* (v), to look over shoulder

患   *huàn* (n), calamity

罷   *bà* (v), to cease, terminate

Notes

1. The situation here is very similar to that in Lesson 13. In both stories, the clever adviser must find a way to circumvent the ruler's prohibition against arguing against his plans.

2. The role of 者 in 舍人有少孺子者 is not entirely clear. Some scholars have suggested that 少孺子者 means "a person called 少孺子." This use of **Name** + 者 to introduce a person (or thing) is in fact very common. Nonetheless, another, perhaps more probable interpretation here is simply "a person who was [no more than] a small child."

3. 則 explicitly marks topics for the sake of clarity or rhetorical emphasis. **Topics** in Classical Chinese, however, function at two levels: **sentence**, and **discourse**. At sentence-level, topics usually are old information, but as parts of discourse, they often serve to introduce initial information the author needs to establish before getting to the interesting part. In 欲諫不敢，則懷丸操彈..., the most natural way to read the text without 則 is as coordinate verb phrases that reveal a strong antecedent condition. However, the author here marks the first phrase as a discourse-level topic on which the second comments.

4. In 何苦沾衣如此, 何苦 (an inversion of 苦何) is most probably coordinate with 沾衣如此: "What troubles you [so that as a result] your wetting your clothes is like this?" However, the pair of verb-object phrases 沾衣如此 are *not* coordinate but topic-comment; that is, "*Your wetting your clothes* is like this," *not* "You wet your clothes and are like this."

5. Notice the use of 之 placed between the topic and comment in creating an embedded sentence in 不顧其後之有患也.

Questions

1. What is the function of the 也 in the situations the boy describes:

> 不知螳螂在其後也
>
> 不知黃雀在其旁也
>
> 不知彈丸在其下也
>
> 不顧其後之有患也

Is the 也 sentence final or phrase final? That is, does it go with the objects of the verbs or with the complete verb phrases?

2. What does the boy's story have to do with the king's plan to attack Jīng?

Review

1. What is the relationship between 欲諫 and 不敢? Explain.

2. In 如是者三旦, what modifies the 者? Explain.

3. Is 高 an adverb, verb, or noun in 蟬高居悲鳴? Explain.

4. What is the relationship between 務 and 得? Explain.

Bibliographic Exercises

1. Compare this story to the anecdote at the end of the 山 木 chapter in 莊子. Is the point of the story the same? (You can use the concordance to locate 螳螂 in 莊子.)

2. Look up 螳螂 in 古今圖書集成 (博物彙編卷174). In the 紀事 section are two more versions of the story. Where are they from?

Lesson 19

和氏之璧 韓非子

Text

楚人和氏得玉璞楚山中，奉而獻之厲王。厲王使
玉人相之，玉人曰石也。王以和爲誑而刖其左
足。及厲王薨，武王即位，和又奉其璞而獻之武
王。武王使玉人相之，又曰石也。王又以和爲誑
而刖其右足。武王薨，文王即位，和乃抱其璞而
哭於楚山之下三日三夜，淚盡而繼以血。王聞之
使人問其故，曰天下之刖者多矣，子奚哭之悲
也。和曰，吾非悲刖也，悲夫，寶玉而題之以
石，貞士而名之以誑，此吾所以悲也。王乃使玉
人理其璞而得寶焉，遂命曰和氏之璧。

Vocabulary

氏	*shì* (n), [of the clan of]	*璞	*pú* (n), uncarved jade
璧	*bì* (n), jade ceremonial disk	奉	*fèng* (v), to hold in both hands to present to a superior

獻	*xiàn* (v), to offer [as tribute]	淚	*lèi* (n), tears
*厲王	Lì Wáng, the king of Chǔ before Wǔ Wáng (r. 740–689 B.C.)	盡	*jìn* (v), to exhaust, use up
		血	*xuě* (n), blood
相	*xiàng* (v), to look at carefully	夫	*fú* (fw), a fusion of 否乎, meaning "is [it] not so?"
誑	*kuáng* (v), to deceive	寶	*bǎo* (v), to treasure
*刖	*yuè* (v), to cut off a foot	題	*tí* (v), to evaluate
薨	*hōng* (v), to die (used for kings)	貞	*zhēn* (v), to be pure, honest
即位	*jí wèi*, to ascend the throne	理	*lǐ* (v), to work jade
		命	*mìng* (v), to call, name

Notes

1. In the phrase 奉而獻之, 之 is the object of both verbs. Since the phrase is short and the meaning clear, the first 之 is simply dropped. Compare it to 奉其璞而獻之.

2. In 使玉人相之, the 使 is fully grammaticalized: its sense as a verb—to send on a mission—has disappeared, and it has become a pivot verb that marks causation. "[He] *had* the jade workers examine it."

3. Once again the order of coverb + object + main verb has been reversed in 繼以血, 題之以石 and 名之以誑.

4. The rhetorical effect of the 而 in 寶玉而題之以石 and 貞士而名之以誑 is to change the nouns in the first half of each phrase, "precious jade" and "honest man," into something like stative verbs: "[It is] a precious jade and yet . . . " and "[I am] an honest man but . . . ."

Questions

1. What is the function of the 之 in 哭之悲?

2. Why does the author write 吾非悲刖也 rather than 吾不悲刖
    也? Explain the difference. What is the function of the 也?

Review

1. What is the significance of reversing the order of coverbs and main
    verbs mentioned in Note 3?

2. What is the relationship between 此 and 吾所以悲也 in 此吾所
    以悲也? Explain.

3. What is the function of the 焉 in 得寶焉?

Sentence Patterns

1. 以 following its main verb

    淚盡而繼以血

    題之以石

    名之以誕

    生事之以禮，死葬之以禮。

2. 夫 as 否乎

    此何木也哉，此必有異材夫。

    用之則行，舍之則藏，唯我與爾有是夫。

    逝者如斯夫，不舍晝夜。

Bibliographic Exercises

1. Locate a picture of a 璧. The volume on jade in the National Pal-
    ace Museum series—*Masterworks of Chinese Jade from the Na-
    tional Palace Museum* 故宮玉器選萃 (Taipei: National Palace
    Museum, 1970)—is a good source. Describe a 璧.

2. Using a large dictionary, find out what 和氏 refers to in later us-
    age. Also find out whether the 璧 remained in 楚.

Lesson 20

施仁政 孟子

Text

梁惠王曰，晉國，天下莫強焉，叟之所知也。及寡
人之身，東敗於齊，長子死焉。西喪地於秦七百
里。南辱於楚。寡人恥之，願比死者一洒之，如
之何則可。孟子對曰，地方百里而可以王。王如
施仁政於民，省刑罰，薄稅斂，深耕易耨，壯者
以暇日修其孝悌忠信，入以事其父兄，出以事其長
上，可使制梃以撻秦楚之堅甲利兵矣。彼奪其民
時，使不得耕耨以養其父母，父母凍餓，兄弟妻
子離散。彼陷溺其民，王往而征之，夫誰與王
敵。故曰，仁者無敵。王請勿疑。

Vocabulary

梁惠王 Liáng Huì Wáng, Marquis Yīng of Wèi 魏, whose funerary title was 惠王. The Wèi capital was 大梁.

晉 Jìn, a state during the Spring and Autumn period, split into Zhào 趙, Wèi, and Hán 韓 (the so-called 三晉).

叟 *sǒu* (n), old person, a term of moderate respect for an elder

寡人 *guǎ rén* (n), "the lone person," used by rulers to refer to themselves.

身 *shen* (n), self (in his own person)

敗 *bài* (v), to defeat, to be defeated

齊 Qí, a state in east China

長子 *zhǎng zǐ* (n), oldest son

喪 *sàng* (v), to be deprived of

秦 Qín, a state in northwest China

辱 *rù* (v), to dishonor, insult

楚 Chǔ, a state in south China

*比 *bì* (cv), to do for the sake of (this is an unusual usage.)

*洒 *xǐ* (v), to wash, same as 洗

方 *fāng* (adj), "on each side"

王 *wàng* (v), to rule as a true king

施 *shī* (v), to apply, put in effect

省 *shěng* (v), to use sparingly

刑罰 *xíng fá* (n), punishments

薄 *bó* (v), to be slight > to make slight

稅歛 *shuì liàn* (n), gathering of taxes

*耨 *nòu* (v), to weed

暇日 *xiá rì* (n), day of rest, of leisure

修 *xiū* (v), to cultivate

悌 *tì* (v), to behave as a proper younger brother

事 *shì* (v), to serve

父兄 *fù xiōng* (n), father and older brother

長上 *zhǎng shàng* (n), elders, superiors

*梃	*tǐng* (n), a club, cudgel	陷溺	*xiàn nì* (n), to entrap and sink > to overwhelm
*撻	*tà* (v), to hit	征	*zhēng* (v), to attack in a punitive campaign
甲	*jiǎ* (n), armor		
彼	*bǐ* (n), those [people]	敵	*dí* (v), to be a match for (an opponent of equal strength)
奪	*duó* (v), to snatch, take by force		
凍餓	*dòng è* (v), to freeze and starve	勿	*wù*, fusion of 毋＋之, a negative imperative: "Don't ...it"

Notes

1. The phrase 晉國天下莫強焉 is a topicalization of the sentence 天下莫強於晉國. This **comparative** structure (強於晉國 "stronger than Jìn") is an important function of 於. This role in comparison is an extension of its normal usage, and one can think of 強於 as "is strong *in relation to . . . .*" Note also how the complete sentence becomes the topic for the phrase 叟之所知也.

2. The phrases 敗於齊, 喪地於秦, and 辱於楚 show another important function of 於. It marks the *agent* in passive constructions: "*was* defeated *by* Qí," "*was* deprived of land *by* Qín," and "*was* shamed *by* Chǔ."

3. In the phrase 喪地於秦七百里, 七百里 is a *number complement*. Notice that it follows the locative object even though it refers (indirectly) to the direct object 地.

4. The 一 in 一洒之 is rhetorically emphatic: he seeks "entirely" and/or "in one decisive action" to cleanse his state of the shame of the defeats.

5. The phrase 如之何 is an idiomatic interrogative construction. Ordinarily 如 takes only a single object, but in questions using 何 (a noun), it can take *two* (here 之 and 何).

6. Note the use of 而 in 地方百里而可以王. This is *not* an "if/then" propositional statement like "If one has land measured 100 *lǐ*

on a side (10,000 square *lǐ*), then one can rule as a true king." Instead, the 而 links two *states of affairs* that might seem in conflict: one can have a mere 10,000 square *lǐ* of land *and yet* rule as a true king.

7. The verb 使 often is a *pivot verb* that is followed by a pivot. However, in 可使制梃 note that the 可 makes 使 passive: "can be caused to. . . ." Following the usual rules of passive construction, 壯者 which had been the object (i.e. the pivot), is now the topic. In contrast, in the sentence 彼奪其民時，使不得耕耨, the pivot for 使 is 其民, but the phrase is simply *deleted* as an unnecessary repetition.

Questions

1. Explain Mèng Zǐ's argument: what is the relationship between military might and Confucian governing as a true king? Why is it true, according to Mèng Zǐ, that 仁者無敵?

2. Note the frequent use of 以 as a connector between *verbs* in this passage:

   入以事其父兄

   出以事其長上

   可使制梃以撻秦楚之堅甲利兵

   使不得耕耨以養其父母

   In each case, explain what the object of the coverb is and why the sentence is structured in this manner.

Review

1. What is the syntactic role of 及 in 及寡人之身?

2. Explain the use of the negative character 勿 in 王請勿疑.

Sentence Patterns

1. 焉 in comparative expressions

   晉國天下莫強焉。

   五帝先道而後德，故德莫盛焉。

2. 於 in passive constructions

> 東敗於齊。
>
> 南辱於楚。
>
> 有備則制人，無備則制於人。
>
> 魏惠王兵數破於齊秦。
>
> 安成君東重於魏而西貴於秦。(安成君 is a person's title)

Bibliographic Exercises

1. In what year was 惠王 defeated by 齊? The 表 in the 史記 (卷 15) will give a traditional date.

Lesson 21

髑髏 莊子

Text

莊子之楚，見空髑髏，髐然有形，撽以馬捶，因
而問之曰，夫子貪生失理而爲此乎。將子有亡國
之事，斧鉞之誅而爲此乎。將子有不善之行，愧
遺父母妻子之醜而爲此乎。將子有凍餒之患而爲
此乎。將子之春秋故及此乎。於是語卒，援髑髏
枕而臥。夜半髑髏見夢曰，子之談者似辯士。諸
子所言皆人生之累也，死則無此矣。子欲聞死之
說乎。莊子曰然。髑髏曰，死，無君於上，無臣於
下，亦無四時之事，從然以天地爲春秋，雖南面
王樂不能過也。莊子不信曰，吾使司命復生子
形，爲子骨肉肌膚，反子父母妻子，閭里知識，
子欲之乎。髑髏深矉蹙頞曰，吾安能棄南面王樂
而復爲人間之勞乎。

Vocabulary

*髑髏 *dú lóu* (n), skull

之 *zhī* (v), to go

空 *kōng* (v), to be empty

*髐然 *xiāo rán* (v), descriptive of bleached bones

撽 *qiào* (v), to hit

捶 *chuí* (v), to whip a horse > (n) a horse-whip

貪 *tān* (v), to covet

失理 *shī lǐ* (v-o), to fail in one's reasoning

將 *jiāng* (fw), or

亡國 *wáng guó* (n), a destroyed kingdom

斧鉞 *fǔ yuè* (n), axes

愧 *kuì* (v), to be ashamed

遺 *yí* (v), to leave behind

醜 *chǒu* (v), to be ugly

凍 *dòng* (v), to freeze

*餒 *něi* (v), to starve

卒 *zú* (v), to end

援 *yuán* (v), to grasp

枕 *zhěn* (n), pillow

臥 *wò* (v), to lie down

見 *xiàn* (v), to appear, 現

談 *tán* (v), to chat

似 *sì* (v), to resemble

辯士 *biàn shì* (n), rhetorician

諸 *zhū* (fw), the assembled > all

累 *lèi* (v), to burden

四時 *sì shí* (n), the four seasons

從然 *zòng rán* (v), in an unbridled manner, 縱然

南面 *nán miàn* (v), to face south (as a ruler)

司命 *sī mìng* (n), Overseer of Destiny

骨肉 *gǔ ròu* (n), bones and muscle

肌膚 *jī fū* (n), skin and flesh

閭里 *lú lǐ* (n), small village

知識 *zhī shì* (n), acquaintances

*矉蹙 *pín cù* (v), to wrinkle (as in frown)

*頞 *è* (n), bridge of nose

安 *ān* (fw), how?

棄 *qì* (v), to abandon

勞 *láo* (v), to toil

Notes

1. Many *adverbs of manner* in literary Chinese have the form X + 然. Here, the compound 髐然 modifies 有形: "in a bleached-bones sort of way, [the skull] had a form."

2. In literary Chinese, 將 is frequently used when one presents a series of possibilities as a question. "Is it perhaps this, or is it perhaps that, or is it . . . ?"

3. In 子之春秋故及此, 子之春秋 probably modifies 故.

4. Several characters in classical usage regularly do not have a radical to clarify their meaning as they do in modern usage. One is 見 (= 現). Other common ones are 舍 (= 捨) and 從 (= 縱).

Questions

1. What is the relationship between 愧 and 遺父母妻子之醜?

2. What part of speech is 枕 as it is used in the text?

3. Is 子之談者 the subject as well as the topic of 似辨士? Explain.

4. What is the function of 則 in 死則無此矣?

5. What is the function of the 也 in 雖南面王樂不能過也?

Review

1. Is 因 a coverb in 因而問之? What does it mean? What about 然 in 莊子曰然?

2. If 使 is a pivot verb in 吾使司命復生子形, what is the main verb?

Sentence Patterns

1. 將 as "or"

> 子貪生失理而爲此乎。將子有亡國之事，斧鉞之誅 而爲此乎。

> 將子有不善之行，愧遺父母妻子之醜而爲此乎。

將子有凍餒之患而爲此乎。

將子之春秋故及此乎。

今欲使勝之邪將安之邪。

傷心哉，秦歟，漢歟，將近代歟。

2. 雖 + Noun phrase

雖南面王樂不能過也。

處人臣之職而欲無壅塞，雖舜不能爲。

富而可求，雖執鞭之士，吾亦爲之。

Bibliographic Exercises

1. Look up 亡國 in a large dictionary. What does it mean?

2. Look up 司命 in a large dictionary. What is the god's role?

3. Look up 醜 in a large dictionary. What else besides "ugly" can it mean? What compounds given in the dictionary explain the meaning of 醜 in the text of this lesson?

Lesson 22

漢高祖 史記

Text

高祖以亭長爲縣送徒驪山，徒多道亡，自度比至
皆亡之。到豐西澤中，止飲。夜乃解縱所送徒
曰，公等皆去，吾亦從此逝矣。徒中壯士願從者
十餘人。高祖被酒，夜徑澤中，令一人行前，行
前者還報曰，前有大蛇當徑，願還。高祖醉曰，
壯士行，何畏，乃前。拔劍擊斬蛇，蛇遂分爲
兩，徑開。行數里，醉因臥。後人來至蛇所，有
一老嫗夜哭，人問何哭，嫗曰，人殺吾子，故哭
之。人曰嫗子何爲見殺。嫗曰，吾子白帝子也，
化爲蛇，當道，今爲赤帝子斬之，故哭。人乃以
嫗爲不誠，欲笞之，嫗因忽不見。後人至，高祖
覺，後人告高祖，高祖乃心獨喜自負。諸從者日
益畏之。

Vocabulary

*漢高祖 Hàn Gāo Zǔ, the "Progenitor on High," founder of the Han dynasty, 劉邦 Liú Bāng (256–195 B.C.)

*亭長 tíng zhǎng (n), head of a 亭, a Qín administrative unit of 10 villages

送 sòng (v), to escort

徒 tú (n), "one on foot" > follower > convict sentenced to labor

*驪山 Lí shān, Mt. Li, to the east of 長安 Chang'an, site of 秦始皇 Qin Shihuang's burial mound

多 duō (v), many > (adv), mostly

亡 wáng (v), to go > to flee

度 duò (v), to calculate

比 bì (cv), by the time that . . .

*豐 Fēng, a city in modern Jiangsu 江蘇

澤 zé (n), a marsh

解縱 jiě zòng (v), to unbind

公 gōng [status pronoun], "you"

等 děng [pluralizing fw]

公等 gōng děng, "you all"

逝 shì (v), to depart

壯 zhuàng (v), to be strong

壯士 zhuàng shì, a sturdy fellow

被酒 bèi jiǔ (v), "under the influence"

徑 jìng (n), path > shortcut > (v), to take a shortcut

當 dāng (v), to be at > to block

願 yuàn (v), to request

拔 bá (v), to pull out

擊 jí (v), to strike

斬 zhǎn (v), to cut in half at the waist

分 fēn (v), to divide

兩 liǎng (n?), two (halves)

數 shù (adj), several

所 suǒ (n), place

*嫗 yù (n), old woman

見 jiàn [fw: passive marker]

白帝 bái dì (n), White Heavenly Emperor (white is associated with the west)

化　　*huà* (v), to transform

赤帝　*chì dì* (n), Red Heavenly Emperor (red is associated with the south)

誠　　*chéng* (v), to be sincere

*笞　　*chī* (v), to flog

忽　　*hū* (adv), suddenly

覺　　*jué* (v), to awaken

獨　　*dú* (v), alone > (adv) privately

自負　*zì fù* (v), to be self-confident

日　　*rì* (n), sun > day > (adv) daily

益　　*yì* (v), to increase > (adv) increasingly

Notes

1. When 多 acts as an adverb, it tends to mean "for the most part," not just "in large numbers."

2. 比 , read *bì*, is a common coverb in literary Chinese that has disappeared in modern usage.

3. In the phrase 亡之, 之 can be either a locative object (behaving almost like an "on" phrase in English: "They all would have fled on him") or a direct object ("He would lose them all"). The problem is that 皆 tends to refer to the agent of the verb (they who *fled*) rather than to the object (they who *were lost*).

4. 見 as used in 何爲見殺 is a common form of passive construction.

5. 爲...故..., as in 爲赤帝子斬之故哭, seems to be a set pattern.

Questions

1. In 高祖以亭長爲縣送徒驪山, if 爲 is read *wèi*, what is the function of 以? What type of object is 驪山?

2. How is 自 used in 自度?

3. In what tone should one read 爲 in 何爲見殺? Explain.

Sentence Patterns

1. 比 "by the time that. . . ."

    自度比至皆亡之。

    王之臣有托其妻子於其友而之楚遊者。比其反也,則凍
    餒其妻子。

    尹玉以殘兵五百人夜戰,比旦皆没。

    明月而宵行,俯見其影,以爲伏鬼也。仰視其髮,以爲
    立魅也。背而走,比至家,失氣而死。

2. 見 as passive marker

    嫗子何爲見殺。

    蔡澤見逐於趙。

    今見破於秦。

    晏子見疑於齊君。

3. 日益

    諸從者日益畏之。

    秦日益大。

Bibliographic Exercises

1. Locate 驪山 and 豐 using the 秦漢 volume of the 中國歷史地圖集.
    How far apart are they?

2. Find out about the 五行 Five Phases (Five Agents). With what materi-
    als are the two elements mentioned in the story associated? Dictionar-
    ies or Wing-tsit Chan, *A Source Book in Chinese Philosophy* (Prince-
    ton: Princeton University Press, 1963), can provide this information.

Lesson 23

熊掌 _{孟子}

Text

孟子曰，魚，我所欲也。熊掌亦我所欲也。二者
不可得兼，舍魚而取熊掌者也。生亦我所欲
也。義亦我所欲也。二者不可得兼，舍生而取義者
也。生亦我所欲，所欲有甚於生者，故不爲苟得
也。死亦我所惡，所惡有甚於死者，故患有所不
辟也。如使人之所欲莫甚於生，則凡可以得生
者，何不用也。使人之所惡莫甚於死者，則凡可
以避患者，何不爲也。由是則生而有所不用也，
由是則可以避患而有不爲也。是故所欲有甚於生
者，所惡有甚於死者，非獨賢者有是心也，人皆有
之，賢能勿喪耳。

　一簞食，一豆羹，得之則生，弗得則死。嘑爾
而與之，行道之人弗受。蹴爾而與之，乞人不屑
也。萬鍾則不辨禮義而受之，萬鍾於我何加焉。
爲宮室之美，妻妾之奉，所識窮乏者得我與。鄉

157

爲身死而不受，今爲宮室之美爲之，鄉爲身死而
不受，今爲妻妾之奉爲之，鄉爲身死而不受，今
爲所識窮乏者得我而爲之，是亦不可以已乎。此
之謂失其本心。

Vocabulary

熊掌 *xióng zhǎng* (n), bear's paws

魚 *yú* (n), fish

欲 *yù* (v), to desire

兼 *jiān* (v), to have at the same time

舍 *shě* (v), to set aside, reject (捨)

義 *yì* (n), right action, often translated as "righteousness"

苟 *gǒu* (adv), in a base, sordid way

惡 *wù* (v), to detest, revile

患 *huàn* (n), calamity

辟 *bì* (v), to avoid, flee (避)

凡 *fán* (adj), any from the class of . . . > "any," "every"

賢 *xián* (v), to be worthy, virtuous

耳 *ěr* (fw), fusion of 而已, "and that's all"

簞 *dān* (n), basket for cooked rice

食 *sì* (n), provisions

豆 *dòu* (n), a footed platter

羹 *gēng* (n), soup, chowder

嘑 *hū* (v), to shout (呼)

爾 *ěr* (fw), in a . . . manner

蹴 *cù* (v), to kick, trample on

乞人 *qǐ rén* (n), beggar

不屑 *bú xiè* (v), not consider worthy

鍾 *zhōng* (m), about 50 liters > 萬鍾 indicates a very large income (granted by the king) measured in grain

辨 *biàn* (v), to make distinctions

禮義 *lǐ yì* (n), proper ceremony and right action

加 *jiā* (v), to add > to benefit

宮室 *gōng shì* (n), home, dwelling (this is an archaic expression)

妻妾 *qī qiè* (n), primary and secondary wives

奉 *fèng* (v), to serve

識 *shì* (v), to be acquainted with

窮乏 *qióng fá* (v), to be straitened, in need

得 *dé* (v), here, equivalent to 德, to acknowledge receipt of virtuous action

與 *yú* (fw), sentence-final question marker (= 歟)

鄉 *xiàng* (n), formerly (= 嚮)

已 *yǐ* (v), to bring to an end

失 *shī* (v), to fail [to maintain]

本心 *běn xīn* (n), "original mind," an important Mencian concept

Notes

1. Mèng Zǐ makes a general argument here. Note the use of 所 constructions to establish initial propositions as nominal sentences. Notice also how the verbal construction 舍魚而取熊掌 is thoroughly nominalized by 者也 to make it a similarly general, abstract statement.

2. The sentence 所欲有甚於生者 and 所惡有甚於死者 are comparative structures, "more extreme than . . . ."

3. In literary Chinese, authors use 使 to express ***counterfactual*** propositions (imagining impossible situations) for which the equivalent in English is "if" + the subjunctive mood. The clause 如使人之所欲莫甚於生 arguably can be translated, "Were one to make it such that . . . ," which is merely an unlikely conjecture. The logic of Mèng Zǐ's argument, however, makes it clear that he intends the conjecture to be not just unlikely but actually impossible.

4. The two phrases 凡可以得生者 and 凡可以避患者 are passivized coverb constructions. That is, one can begin with a sentence like

> 以受飯得生 By receiving rice, one obtains life. (Or, more literally, "One uses receiving rice to obtain life.")

This can be rewritten in a *passive* form, changing "uses" to "can be used" and making the former **object** of "use" into the new **topic**:

受飯，可以得生   Receiving rice can be used to obtain life.

This sentence in turn can be rewritten in a nominal form:

受飯者，可以得生者也 Receiving rice [is what] can be used to obtain life.

The comment 可以得生者, then, is a noun phrase meaning "what can be used to obtain life." Similarly, 可以避患者 means "what can be used to avoid calamity."[1]

5. 則 marks the coverb + object 由是 as a topic, "if [we] follow along this [line of reasoning], then . . . ." Consider how ambiguous the reading would be as 由是生而不用也.

6. The character 爾 often means "like this" and also appears in descriptive phrases in a usage similar to 如 and 然, "in an . . . manner." Here, in 嘑爾 and 蹴爾, it may have a sense of *continuing* action: "while shouting [at him] . . ." and "while trampling [on it] . . . ."

7. In the expression 此之謂失其本心, the 此之謂 seems to be an idiomatic preservation of an older syntactic structure. In earlier Zhou dynasty usage, there was a tendency to move 是 and 之 as the objects to be immediately in front of the verb. Hence 此之謂 means "this, [we] refer to it as . . . ."

Questions

1. Explain the use of 也 in 何不用也.

2. In what tone should one read the 爲 in 鄉爲身死而不受? Explain. What about the two 爲 in 今爲妻妾之奉爲之?

3. Explain Mèng Zǐ's argument here. Does he consider the choice of 義 over 生 as a universal? How does he demonstrate this universality?

---

1. Pulleyblank (p. 24) plausibly explains 可以 as an extension of the usual passive meaning of 可 + 以 (as transitive verb): " . . . may *be used* to . . . ." This instrumental sense then shifted, in most instances, to a way of indicating *who* can do the deed: " . . . may be the agent to . . . ."

4. What does Mèng Zǐ mean by 失其本心 "losing (failing vis-à-vis) one's basic mind?" What *is* one's "basic mind" here?

Review

1. What is the syntax of 何不爲也?

2. Explain the use of 弗 in 弗得則死 and 行道之人弗受.

3. To what does 焉 refer in 萬鍾於我何加焉?

Sentence Patterns

1. 於 in comparisons

   所欲有甚於生者。

   所惡有甚於死者。

   人臣莫難於無妒而進賢。

   苛政猛於虎也。

   福莫長於無禍。

2. 凡

   凡可以得生者，何不用也。

   凡可以避患者，何不爲也。

   凡生於天地之間，其必有死。

   魂曰，凡得道者，形不可得而見，名不可得而揚。

Bibliographic Exercises

1. Look up 熊 in the 古今圖書集成 (博物彙編卷67). Read the introductory account to find out why bears' paws taste so good.

2. Look in a large dictionary to confirm the reading of 得 as 德. Consult Karlgren's *Grammata Serica Recensa*, entries 905 and 919. Do the words sound alike in Karlgren's reconstruction? Do their early graphs look similar?

Lesson 24

淳于髡 史記

Text

孔子曰，六藝於治一也。禮以節人，樂以發和，書以道事，詩以達意，易以神化，春秋以義。太史公曰，天道恢恢，豈不大哉。談言微中，亦可以解紛。淳于髡者，齊之贅壻也，長不滿七尺，滑稽多辨，數使諸侯，未嘗屈辱。齊威王之時，喜隱，好爲淫樂長夜之飲，沉湎不治，委政卿大夫，百官荒亂，諸侯並侵，國且危亡，在於旦暮，左右莫敢諫。淳于髡說之以隱曰，國中有大鳥，止王之庭，三年不蜚又不鳴，王知此鳥何也。王曰，此鳥不蜚則已，一蜚沖天，不鳴則已，一鳴驚人。於是乃朝諸縣令長七十二人，賞一人，誅一人，奮兵而出，諸侯振驚，皆還齊侵地，威行三十六年。語在田完世家中。

　威王八年，楚大發兵加齊。齊王使淳于髡之趙，請救兵，齎金百斤，車馬十駟。淳于髡仰天

162

大笑，冠纓索絕。王曰，先生少之乎。髡曰，何
敢。王曰，笑豈有說乎。髡曰，今者臣從東方
來，見道傍有穰田者，操一豚蹄，酒一盂，祝
曰，甌窶滿篝，污邪滿車，五穀蕃熟，穰穰滿
家。臣見其所持者狹，而所欲者奢，故笑之。於
是齊威王乃益齎黃金千鎰，白璧十雙，車馬百
駟。髡辭而行，至趙，趙王與之精兵十萬，革車千
乘。楚王聞之，夜引兵而去。

　威王大說，置酒後宮，召髡賜之酒。問曰，先
生能飲幾何而醉。對曰，臣飲一斗亦醉，一石亦
醉。威王曰，先生飲一斗而醉，惡能飲一石哉，
其說可得聞乎。髡曰，賜酒大王之前，執法在
傍，御史在後，髡恐懼俯伏而飲，不過一斗徑醉
矣。若親有嚴客，髡帣韝鞠䏶，待酒於前，時賜餘
瀝，奉觴上壽，數起，飲不過二斗徑醉矣。若朋
友交遊，久不相見，卒然相睹，歡然道故，私情
相語，飲可五六斗徑醉矣。若乃州閭之會，男女
雜坐，行酒稽留，六博投壺，相引爲曹，握手無
罰，目眙不禁，前有墮珥，後有遺簪，髡竊樂
此，飲可八斗而醉二參。日暮酒闌，合尊促坐，
男女同席，履舄交錯，杯盤狼藉，堂上燭滅，主
人留髡而送客，羅襦襟解，微聞薌澤，當此之
時，髡心最歡，能飲一石。故曰，酒極則亂，樂
極則悲，萬事盡然，言不可極，極之而衰。以諷
諫焉。齊王曰善，乃罷長夜之飲。以髡爲諸侯主
客，宗室置酒，髡嘗在側。

Vocabulary

*淳于髡   Chúnyú Kūn, a clever Warring States rhetorician, adviser to 齊威王 King Wēi of Qí

六蓺   *liù yì* (n), the "Six Arts" > the "Six Canons"

禮   *Lǐ*, the *Canon of Ritual*

節   *jié* (v), to regulate, restrain

樂   *Yuè*, the *Canon of Music*

發   *fā* (v), to emit, make manifest

和   *hé* (n), accord, harmony

書   *Shū*, the *Canon of Documents*

道   *dào* (v), to speak of, describe

詩   *Shī*, the *Canon of Poetry*

達意   *dá yì* (v+o), "to convey the intention" (from 論語)

易   *Yì*, the *Canon of Change*

春秋   *Chūnqiū*, the *Spring and Autumn Annals*

義   *yì* (n), right, appropriate action, glossed as ≈ 宜

太史公   *Tàishǐ gōng*, the Grand Scribe, refers to either Sīmǎ Qiān, the

author of the 史記, or to his father, 司馬談 Sīmǎ Tán, who started the project.

*恢恢   *huī huī* (v), [descriptive of] being vast

微   *wēi* (v), to be minute, subtle > (adv), subtly

中   *zhòng* (v), to hit the center

解   *jiě* (v), to cut > to resolve

紛   *fēn* (v), to be in profuse disorder > (n) confusion

*贅壻   *zhuì xù* (n), a man who marries into a clan

滑稽   *gǔjī* (v), to be of ready wit and verbally adroit

多辨   *duō biàn* (v), disputatious

數   *shuò* (adv), frequently

屈辱   *qū rù* (v), to submit to humiliation

齊威王   King Wēi of Qí, reigned 356–320 B.C.

隱   *yǐn* (n), a riddle

淫樂   *yín lè* (n), wanton pleasure

*沉湎   *chén miǎn* (v), to be sunk deep (in a drunken binge)

委　*wěi* (v), to delegate, entrust

卿大夫　*qīng dàifū* (n), high officials

荒亂　*huāng luàn* (v), to be dissolute and disorderly

侵　*qīn* (v), to encroach, raid

且　*qiě* (fw), tentative future marker

危亡　*wéi wáng* (v), to be on the brink of destruction

說　*shuì* (v), to [attempt to] persuade

國　*guó* (n), capital of a state

庭　*tíng* (n), courtyard

*蜚　*fēi* (v), to fly (same as 飛)

已　*yǐ* (v), to bring to an end > "that's the end of it."

*沖　*chōng* (v), to rise rapidly, soar

鳴　*míng* (v), to sing, call out

驚　*jīng* (v), to startle, alarm

朝　*cháo* (v), to bring to court

令長　*lìng zhǎng* (n), local officials (a 令 governs a region of 10,000 people or more; a 長 governs smaller districts)

賞　*shǎng* (v), to reward

奮兵　*fèn bīng* (v+o), to rouse an army

*振驚　*zhèn jīng* (v), to alarm and frighten

*威行　*wēi xíng* (v), to prevail through strength

*田完　Tián Wán, i.e., Chén Wán, son of 陳厲公 Duke Lì of Chén, who fled to Qí and whose descendant was appointed marquis of Qí

世家　*Shì jiā*, "Hereditary Houses," a category of biography in the 史記 for lineages of feudal lords and other important clans

發兵　*fā bīng* (v), to send out troops

加　*jiā* (v), to set [troops] facing . . .

之　*zhī* (v), to go to

趙　Zhào, a state in north China during the 戰國 period

請　*qǐng* (v), to request

救　*jiù* (v), to rescue

*齎　*jī* (v), to present

斤　*jīn* (m), 256 grams (in 戰國)

駟　*sì* (m), team of 4 horses

冠　　　*guàn* (n), hat

纓　　　*yīng* (n), hat tassel

索　　　*suǒ* (n), string

絕　　　*jué* (v), to break

先生　　*xiānshēng* (respectful pronoun), Elder

傍　　　*páng* (n), side, border (旁)

*穰田　*ráng tián* (v), to offer a sacrifice in the fields to assure bounty

操　　　*cāo* (v), to grasp in hand

豚蹄　　*tún tí* (n), pig's foot

*盂　　*yú* (n), bowl

祝　　　*zhù* (v), to pray

*甌樓　*ōu lóu* (v), descriptive bi-nome for high ground (according to commentary)

滿　　　*mǎn* (v), to fill

*簍　　*gōu* (n), a basket

*污邪　*wū yé* (v), descriptive bi-nome for damp low ground

車　　　*jū* (n), cart, pronounced *t'i̯å*

五穀　　*wǔ gǔ* (n), the five major grains

蕃　　　*fán* (v), to flourish

熟　　　*shóu* (v), to ripen

穰穰　　*ráng ráng* (v), to be abundant

家　　　*jiā* (n), household, *kå*

狹　　　*xiá* (v), to be narrow > skimpy

奢　　　*shē* (v), to be lavish

*鎰　　*yì* (m), 320 grams

璧　　　*bì* (n), ceremonial jade disk

雙　　　*shuāng* (m), a pair

辭　　　*cí* (v), to take leave

精兵　　*jīng bīng* (n), crack troops

革車　　*gé jū* (n), leather-covered war chariots

乘　　　*shèng* (m), measure for chariots

引兵　　*yǐn bīng* (v), withdraw one's troops

說　　　*yuè* (v), to be delighted (= 悅)

後宮　　*hòu gōng* (n), the "rear palace," the women's quarters in a palace

召　　　*zhào* (v), to summon

賜　　　*cì* (v), to bestow

幾何　　*jǐ hé* (n), how many?

斗　　　*dǒu* (m), measure of volume, 1.94 liters

石　　　*shí* (m), measure of volume, 10 斗, 19.4 liters

惡　　*wū* (fw), "how?"

執法　*zhí fǎ* (v+o), to maintain, uphold the laws

御史　*yù shǐ* (n), the censor, whose job is to impartially make accusations against anyone guilty of crimes

俯伏　*fǔ fú* (v), to prostrate oneself

徑　　*jìng* (adv), right away

親　　*qīn* (n), parents

嚴客　*yán kè* (n), important visitor

*袨韝　*juàn gōu* (v+o), to roll up one's sleeves

*鞠脞　*jú jì* (v), to kneel humbly (脞 = 跽)

餘瀝　*yú lì* (n), leftover drops

奉觴　*fèng shāng* (v+o), to offer up the goblet

上壽　*shàng shòu* (v+o), to wish for [someone's] long life

交遊　*jiāo yóu* (n), companion

久　　*jiǔ*, (adv) for a long time

卒然　*cù rán* (adv), suddenly

睹　　*dǔ* (v), to see, to discern

*道故　*dào gù* (v+o), to speak of former [matters]

州閭　*zhōu lǔ* (n), one's village (in the 周 system, 州 = 2,500 households, 閭 = 25 households)

會　　*huì* (n), meeting

稽留　*jī liú* (v), to tarry, remain

六博　*liù bó* (n), a betting game (using 6 white and 6 black strips of bamboo)

投壺　*tóu hú* (n), "pitch pot," a game of tossing arrows into a pot

曹　　*cáo* (n), companion (one of similar nature) > teammate

握　　*wò* (v), to hold in the hand

罰　　*fá* (v) to penalize, punish

眙　　*chì* (v), to fix one's gaze on

墮　　*duò* (v), to drop

珥　　*ěr* (n), earrings

簪　　*zān* (n), ornamental hatpin or hairpin

竊　　*qiè* (v), to steal > a humble form of speech: "Although I know I shouldn't"

二參　*èr sān*, 20–30 percent, that is, a little (參 = 三). Some scholars take this to mean 2/3.

酒闌　*jiǔ lán*, lit., "the wine is finished" > the drinking has wound down

合尊　*hé zūn* (v+o), to combine in one bottle

促坐　*cù zuò* (v), to sit close together

履舃　*lǚ xì* (n), shoes, footwear

交錯　*jiāo cuò* (v), to mix together

盤　*pán* (n), a platter

狼藉　*láng jí* (v), to be strewn about

滅　*miè* (v), to extinguish

羅襦　*luó rú* (n), a finely woven silk shirt (worn under other clothes)

襟　*jīn* (n), lapels, collar

聞　*wén* (v), to smell

薌澤　*xiāng zé* (n), fragrant vapors (薌 = 香)

極　*jí* (v), to go to [its] extreme

盡　*jìn* (v), to exhaust > (adv), entirely

衰　*shuāi* (v), to decline, decay

諷諫　*fèng jiàn* (v), to criticize through indirection

主客　*zhǔ kè* (n), an official who oversees the treatment of visitors

宗室　*zōng shì* (n), the royal clan

嘗　*cháng* (adv), invariably (= 常)

側　*cè* (n), the side [of the body]

Notes

1.　This passage is the complete biography of Chúnyú Kūn in the 史記 as recorded in the 滑稽列傳 "Biographies of Court Wits" chapter (史記 126).

2.　Note how Sīmǎ Qiān introduces Chúnyú Kūn with a nominal sentence that establishes an identity: "the man named Chúnyú Kūn = a son-in-law adopted into a clan in the state of Qí." During the late Warring States period and into the Hàn, the aristocratic, feudal society looked down on the practice of adopting a bridegroom to continue a clan.

3. 使 is used as a full verb here, "to send on a mission." Thus one who is sent on a mission is a 使, *shǐ*.

4. The statement 齊威王之時喜隱 seems odd: since the *time* is the topic, *who* delights in riddles seems unclear. The later sentences in the series—好爲淫樂長夜之飲，沉湎不治，委政卿大夫—reveal that the king himself is the unspoken topic.

5. In 國且危亡, the 且 is best viewed as a marker of provisional futurity. That is, from the perspective of those looking at the situation, it seemed that surely 齊 would soon meet with disaster. The 且 captures this quality of tentative judgment.

6. The shocked king asks two questions about his proposed gifts to Zhào. The first expects a negative answer, "No, I don't think the presents too few." The second suggests that Chúnyú Kūn's explanation had better be good. This account of Chúnyú Kūn's mission to Zhào has a classic persuasion format: Chúnyú Kūn gets the king's attention through an extravagant action and then explains his intentions through a pointed anecdote.

7. In Chúnyú Kūn's explanation of his drinking, notice the regular four-character style. Sometimes transition words introduce a four-character phrase, as in the scene-shifting expressions 若朋友交遊 and 若乃州閭之會. 若 and 若乃 are frequently used to mark changes in topic in an enumeration of possibilities.

8. The relationship between 言 and 不可極 in 言不可極 seems to be **verb-object** rather than topic-comment.

Questions

1. Explain the relevance of Sīmǎ Qiān's quotation from Confucius as the introduction to biographies of men famous for their way with words. What about the quotation from the Grand Scribe?

2. Explain Chúnyú Kūn's question about the bird? Why did the king then respond as he did?

3. What year is 威王八年?

4. Why did Chúnyú Kūn's hat-tassel string break?

5. Is 與 a coverb in 趙王與之精兵十萬? Explain.

6. What is the analogy that Chúnyú Kūn suggests in the story of the farmer?

7. Chúnyú Kūn's story of his drinking is a long and elaborate set piece. What is its point? The king seems to acknowledge a veiled criticism. What is it?

Review

1. Explain the use of 以 in 禮以節人, 樂以發和, etc.

2. Explain the difference in the placement of time words between 三年不蜚又不鳴 and 威行三十六年.

3. What part of speech is 大 in 楚大發兵加齊?

4. 少 ordinarily is *intransitive*, that is, it has no direct object. Does it take an object in the phrase 少之? What does the phrase mean?

5. To what in the story does 所持者 refer? To what does 所欲者 refer?

6. What part of speech is 執法 in 執法在傍?

Sentence Patterns

1. 且

    國且危亡，在於旦暮。

    吳王從臺上觀，見且斬愛姬，大驚。

    事成功立，然後德且見也。

Bibliographic Exercises

1. Find out more about the 六藝. Fung Yu-lan's *A History of Chinese Philosophy* (Princeton: Princeton University Press, 1952), volume 1, is a good place to begin. With what emperor do we usually associate the establishment of the 六藝 as official canon?

2. Look up 恢恢. Give another early example of its usage.

3. Look up the phrase 令長 in Charles O. Hucker, *A Dictionary of Official Titles in Imperial China* (Stanford: Stanford University Press, 1985). Do these titles appear before the 秦?

Part Three

Advanced Texts

Lesson 25

孟子

Mèng Kě 孟軻 (ca. 371 B.C.–289 B.C.), was the great debater of the early Confucian tradition. Like many other "persuaders" 遊說者 of the Warring States period, he traveled from court to court seeking the patronage of a feudal lord willing to accept his approach to governing. In the end, however, he seems to have given up hope of finding a ruler who could break free of the narrow approaches of power politics and see the more fundamental advantages of Confucian benevolent rule 仁政. Like Confucius before him, Mèng Kě finally sought to influence the world and transmit his views through his role as a teacher.

The three selections below are among the most famous passages in the 孟子. In the first, the initial passage in the book, Master Mèng obliquely argues that the king's true advantage lies in not speaking of advantage at all. That is, his person, his wealth, and his realm are most secure when he stresses humaneness and right action and sets aside all explicit concern for profit. The second selection—in which 孟子 proves that the Confucian virtues are innate in all people—is another example of grand rhetorical argument that becomes very important in later 道學 Neo-Confucian philosophy. The final selection, the longest entry in the 孟子, is an extended argument in which 孟子 attempts to persuade King Xuān of Qí to realize his own inner potential: it is tightly organized as a progressive series of answers to the king's question, "Through what do you know that I can [protect the populace and thus become a true king]?" 何由知吾可也?

The 孟子 as a text seems to have changed little since the Hàn dynasty when Zhào Qí 趙岐 (d. A.D. 201) wrote the first surviving commentary. The selections below include Zhào's comments as well as those of Zhū Xī 朱熹 (1130–1200) and Jiāo Xún (1763–1820) 焦循. Zhū Xī made 孟子 one of the so-called Four Books, which were the core of his teaching curriculum.[1] Zhū Xī's Four Books then became basic texts for the imperial examination system in the Míng and Qīng dynasties, assuring 孟子's continuing centrality. Jiāo Xún, coming from the mid-Qīng dynasty, presents a sophisticated perspective from the end of the premodern era.

Suggestions for Further Reading

Graham, Angus C. *Disputers of the Tao: Philosophical Argument in Ancient China*. La Salle, Ill.: Open Court, 1989.

Mencius. Trans. D. C. Lau. Harmondsworth, Eng.: Penguin Classics, 1970.

Xiè Bingyíng 謝冰瑩 et al., eds. 四書讀本. 臺北: 三民, 1966. (This very convenient edition with 注音符號 has commentary and translations into modern Chinese suitable for beginning students.)

梁惠王，上，一

孟子見梁惠王。趙岐曰，梁惠王，魏惠王也。惠，諡也，王，號也。時天下有七王，皆僭號者也。魏惠王居於大梁，故號曰梁王。王曰，叟不遠千里而來，亦將有以利吾國乎。孟子對曰，王何必曰利。亦有仁義而已矣。王曰何以利吾國。大夫曰何以利吾家。士庶人曰何以利吾身。上下交征利而國危矣。征，取也。史記魏世家曰，上下爭利，國則危矣。案征利猶爭利也。萬乘之國，弒其君者，必千乘之家。千乘之國，弒其君者，必百乘之家。

---

1. The three others are *The Analects* 論語, *The Greater Learning* 大學, and *The Doctrine of the Mean* 中庸.

萬取千焉，千取百焉，不爲不多矣。苟爲後義而
先利，不奪不饜。未有仁而遺其親者也。未有義
而後其君者也。王亦曰仁義而已矣。何必曰利。朱
熹集注曰，此章言仁義根於人心之固有，天理之公也。利心生於物我之相
形，人欲之私也。循天理，則不求利而自無不利。徇人欲，則求利未得而
害已隨之。

Vocabulary

孟子　Mèng Zǐ (ca. 371–289 B.C.), the Warring States Confucian philosopher

梁惠王　Liáng Huì Wáng, King Huì of Wèi (r. 370–335 B.C.); also, title of the first chapter of 孟子.上，一 "first part [of two], first section"

見　(1) *xiàn* (v), to appear, (2) *jiàn* (v), to see

趙岐　Zhào Qí (d. A.D. 201), late Hàn dynasty editor of the only extant version of *Mèng Zǐ*.

謚　*shì* (n), funerary name

號　*hào* (n), public designation

僭　*jiàn* (v), to overstep one's position

大梁　Dà Liáng, the capital of 魏, the present city of 開封 Kāifēng

叟　*sǒu* (n), old person; here, a polite form of address

遠　*yuàn* (v), to consider distant

士　*shì* (n), the nobility and officials

庶人　*shù rén* (n), the commoners

交　*jiāo* (adv), mutually

*征利　*zhēng lì* (v-o), to compete for profit = 爭利

危　*wéi* (v), to be endangered

魏世家　"Wèi shì jiā," "The History of the Wèi Ruling Clan" in the 史記

案　*àn* (n), "in the editor's opinion . . ."

乘　*shèng* (m), counter for carts

弑　*shì* (v), to assassinate

苟　　*gǒu* (fw), "if . . . ,"

奪　　*duó* (v), to take by force

厭　　*yàn* (v), to be satisfied

遺　　*yí* (v), to leave aside, neglect

朱熹　Zhū Xī (1130–1200), 道學 thinker who added 孟子 to the 四書

章　　*zhāng* (n), section [of text]

天理　*tiān lǐ* (n), Heavenly Principle, an important 道學 concept

公　　*gōng* (v), to be open to public agreement

循　　*xún* (v), to follow, to be obedient to

徇　　*xún* (v), to follow, to sacrifice oneself for

公孫丑，上，六

孟子曰，人皆有不忍人之心。趙岐曰，言人人皆有不忍加惡於人之心也。先王有不忍人之心，斯有不忍人之政矣。以不忍人之心行不忍人之政，治天下可運之掌上。所以謂人皆有不忍人之心者，今乍見孺子將入於井，皆有怵惕惻隱之心。非所以內交於孺子之父母也。非所以要譽於鄉黨朋友也。非惡其聲而然也。趙岐曰，孺子，未有知小子也。所以言人皆有是心，凡人暫見小小孺子將入井，賢愚皆有驚駭之情。情發於中，非為人也。非惡有不仁之聲名，故怵惕也。由是觀之，無惻隱之心非人也。無羞惡之心非人也。無辭讓之心非人也。無是非之心非人也。惻隱之心，仁之端也。羞惡之心，義之端也。辭讓之心禮之端也。是非之心，智之端也。趙岐曰，端者首也。朱熹曰，惻隱、羞惡、辭讓、是非，情也。仁、義、禮、智，性也。心，統性情者也。端，緒也。因其情之發，而性之本然可得而見，猶物在中而緒見於外也。焦循曰，自人道溯之天道，自人之德性溯之天德，則氣化流行，生生不息，仁也。由其生生有自然之條理，觀其條理之秩然有序，可以知禮矣。觀於條理之截然不可

亂，可以知義矣。在天爲氣化之生生，在人爲生生之心。是乃仁之爲德也。在天爲氣化推行之條理，在人爲其心知之通乎條理而不紊。是乃智之爲德也。惟條理是以生生。條理苟失，則生生之道絕。人之有是四端也，猶其有四體也。有是四端而自謂不能者，自賊者也。趙岐曰，自謂不能爲善，自賊害其性，使不爲善也。謂其君不能者，賊其君者也。趙岐曰，謂君不能爲善而不匡正者，賊其君，使陷惡也。凡有四端於我者，知皆擴而充之矣，若火之始然，泉之始達。苟能充之，足以保四海。苟不充之，不足以事父母。

Vocabulary

上六 *shàng liù*, the sixth section in the first part of the 公孫丑 Gōngsūn Chǒu chapter of 孟子

忍 *rěn* (v), to endure > to be unmoved by evil done to others

惡 *è* (v), to be bad > (n), bad [things], badness

斯 *sī* (n), this > (fw), in this case . . . > thus

行 *xíng* (v), to carry out, perform

運 *yùn* (v), to revolve

掌 *zhǎng* (n), palm of the hand

乍 *zhà* (adv), suddenly

孺子 *rú zǐ* (n), small child

井 *jǐng* (n), well

*怵惕 *chù tì* (v), alarmed with fear

*惻隱 *cè yǐn* (v), pained with concern

內 *nà* (v), to receive, accept = 納

交 *jiāo* (n), [social] intercourse

譽 *yù* (n), praise

*鄉黨 *xiāng dǎng* (n), village; in 周, 黨 = 50 households, 鄉 = 250 households

惡 *wù* (v), to detest

凡 *fán* (fw), in the general case of . . .

暫 *zhàn* (adv), for a brief time

賢愚   *xián yú* (n), the worthy and the doltish (complementary pair)

驚駭   *jīng hài* (v), to be startled

聲名   *shēng míng* (n), reputation

羞惡   *xiū wù* (v), to feel shame and revulsion

是非   *shì fēi* (n), judgment [of the truth of a proposition]

辭讓   *cí ràng* (v), to give way, yield

端   *duān* (n), tip, beginning

統   *tǒng* (v), to regulate, bind together

緒   *xù* (n), thread tip

*本然   *běn rán* (n), basic nature

焦循   Jiāo Xún (1763–1820), one of the great Qing dynasty philologists, wrote 孟子正義

溯   *sù* (v), to go upstream

*氣化   *qì huà* (n), transformations of *qì*, (the "stuff" of the universe)

流行   *liú xíng* (v), to move in a flow

*生生   *shēng shēng* (v-o), to bring forth, bringing forth [life]

息   *xí* (v), to rest

*條理   *tiáo lǐ* (n), articulated order

*秩然   *zhì rán* (v), to be very orderly

序   *xù* (n), ranked order

*截然   *jié rán* (v), to be clearly separated

推行   *tuī xíng* (v), to proceed by substitution

通   *tōng* (v), to penetrate, comprehend

乎   *hū* (fw), locative marker ≅ 于

*紊   *wèn* (v), to be disordered

四體   *sì tǐ* (n), the four limbs

賊   *zéi* (v), to steal

匡正   *kuāng zhèng* (v), to correct

陷   *xiàn* (v), to trap, ensnare

擴   *kuò* (v), to broaden

充   *chōng* (v), to fill up

然   *rán* (v), to set afire = 燃

泉   *quán* (n), a spring of water

達   *dá* (v), to reach, to arrive

保   *bǎo* (v), to protect, secure

四海   *sì hǎi* (n), [the land within] the four seas

事   *shì* (v), to serve

梁惠王，上，七

齊宣王問曰，齊桓晉文之事可得聞乎。孟子對曰，仲尼之徒無道桓文之事者，是以後世無傳焉。臣未之聞也。無以，則王乎。朱熹曰，以已通用。無以，必欲言之而不止也。曰，德何如則可以王矣。曰，保民而王，莫之能禦也。曰，若寡人者可以保民乎哉。曰，可。曰，何由知吾可也。曰，臣聞之胡齕曰王坐於堂上，有牽牛而過堂下者。王見之，曰牛何之。對曰將以釁鐘。王曰舍之，吾不忍其觳觫若無罪而就死地。對曰然則廢釁鐘與。曰何可廢也，以羊易之。不識有諸。曰，有之。曰，是心足以王矣。百姓皆以王為愛也。臣固知王之不忍也。王曰，然誠有百姓者。齊國雖褊小，吾何愛一牛。即不忍其觳觫若無罪而就死地，故以羊易之。曰，王無異於百姓之以王為愛也。以小易大，彼惡知之。王若隱其無罪而就死地，則牛羊何擇焉。王笑曰，是誠何心哉。我非愛其財而易之以羊也。宜乎百姓之謂我愛也。曰，無傷也，是乃仁術也。見牛未見羊也。君子之於禽獸也，見其生，不忍見其死。聞其聲，不忍食其肉。是以君子遠庖廚也。王說曰，詩云，他人有心，予忖度之，夫子之謂也。夫我乃行之，反而求之，不得吾心。夫子言之，於我心有戚戚焉。此心之所以合於王者，何也。曰，有復於王者曰吾力足以舉百鈞而不足以舉一羽，明足以察秋毫

之末而不足以見輿薪，則王許之乎。曰，否。今
恩足以及禽獸而功不至於百姓者，獨何與。然則
一羽之不舉爲不用力焉，輿薪之不見爲不用明
焉。百姓之不見保爲不用恩焉。故王之不王，不
爲也，非不能也。曰，不爲者與不能者之形，何以
異。曰，挾泰山以超北海，語人曰我不能，是誠
不能也。爲長者折枝，語人曰我不能，是不爲
也，非不能也。故王之不王非挾泰山以超北海之
類也。王之不王是折枝之類也。老吾老以及人之
老，幼吾幼以及人之幼，天下可運於掌。詩云，
刑于寡妻，至于兄弟，以御于家邦。言舉斯心，
加諸彼而已。故推恩足以保四海，不推恩無以保
妻子。古之人所以大過人者無他焉，善推其所爲
而已矣。今恩足以及禽獸而功不至於百姓者，獨
何與。權然後知輕重，度然後知長短。物皆然，
心爲甚。王請度之。抑王興甲兵，危士臣，構怨
於諸侯，然後快于心與。王曰，否，吾何快於是。
將以求吾所大欲也。曰，王之所大欲，可得聞
與。王笑而不言。曰，爲肥甘不足於口與，輕煖
不足於體與，抑爲采色不足視於目與，聲音不足
聽於耳與，便嬖不足使令於前與。王之諸臣皆足
以供之而王豈爲是哉。曰，否，吾不爲是也。
曰，然則王之所大欲可知已。欲辟土地，朝秦
楚，莅中國，而撫四夷也。以若所爲求若所欲，猶
緣木而求魚也。朱注，若，如此也。王曰，若是其甚

乎。曰，殆有甚焉。緣木求魚，雖不得魚，無後
災。以若所爲求若所欲，盡心力而爲之，後必有
災。曰，可得聞與。曰，鄒人與楚人戰，則王以爲
孰勝。曰，楚人勝。曰，然則小固不可以敵大，
寡固不可以敵衆，弱固不可以敵彊。海內之地，
方千里者九，齊集有其一。趙岐曰，集會齊地可方千里。以
一服八，何以異於鄒敵楚哉。蓋亦反其本矣。今
王發政施仁，使天下仕者皆欲立於王之朝，耕者
皆欲耕於王之野，商賈皆欲藏於王之市，行旅皆
欲出於王之塗。天下之欲疾其君者，皆欲赴愬於
王，孰能禦之。王曰，吾惛，不能進於是矣。願
夫子輔吾志，明以教我，我雖不敏，請嘗試之。
曰，無恆產而有恆心者，惟士爲能。若民則無恆
產，因無恆心。苟無恆心，放辟邪侈，無不爲已。
及陷於罪，然後從而刑之，是罔民也。焉有仁人
在位，罔民而可爲也。是故明君制民之產，必使
仰足以事父母，俯足以畜妻子。樂歲終身飽，凶
年免於死亡，然後驅而之善，故民之從之也輕。
今也，制民之產，仰不足以事父母，俯不足以畜
妻子。樂歲終身苦，凶年不免於死亡。此惟救死
而恐不贍，奚暇治禮義哉。王欲行之，則盍反其
本矣。五畝之田，樹之以桑，五十者可以衣帛
矣，雞豚狗彘之畜，無失其時，七十者可以食肉
矣。百畝之田，勿奪其時，八口之家可以無肌
矣。謹庠序之教，申之以孝悌之義，頒白者不負

戴於道路矣。老者衣帛食肉，黎民不肌不寒，然
而不王者，未之有也。

Vocabulary

齊宣王　King Xuān of Qí (r. 319– 301 B.C.)

齊桓公　Duke Huán of Qí (r. 685– 634 B.C.)

晉文公　Duke Wén of Jìn (r. 636– 628 B.C.)

仲尼　Zhòngní, i.e., 孔子

徒　*tú* (n), follower

王　*wàng* (v), to rule as king

禦　*yù* (v), to guard against, block

胡齕　Hú Hè, a retainer of King Xuān

堂上　*táng shàng* (n), the upper end of the audience hall

牽　*qiān* (v), to pull

釁　*xìn* (v), to consecrate [with blood]

鐘　*zhōng* (n), bell [cast in bronze]

舍　*shě* (v), to set aside, reject = 捨

*觳觫　*hú sù* (v), to tremble with fear

就　*jiù* (v), to arrive at

死地　*sǐ dì* (n), "place of death," here, execution ground

廢　*fèi* (v), to abandon

與　*yú* [fw: question final] = 歟

諸　*zhū*, fusion of 之乎

愛　*ài* (v), to be stingy about

固　*gù* (v), to be solid, secure > (adv), certainly

誠　*chéng* (adv), truly, indeed

*褊　*biǎn* (v), to be narrow, thus 褊小 = small

即　*jí* [fw: "since it is the case ..."]

異　*yì* (v), to be strange > to treat as strange

彼　*bǐ* (n), that, those

惡　*wū* [fw: question initial]

若　*ruò* (fw), "if ...,"

隱　*yǐn* (v), to feel sorrow for

擇　*zé* (v), to select

*仁術　*rén shù* (n), humane technique

遠　*yuàn* (v), to keep distant

*庖厨 *páo chú* (n), kitchen

說 *yuè* (v), to be delighted = 悅

他人 *tuō rén* (n), other people

予 *yú* (n), I

*忖 *cǔn* (v), to reckon

*忖度 *cǔn duò* (v), to measure

夫子 *fū zǐ* (n), honorific pronoun, here, "you, sir"

*戚戚 *qī qī* (v), to be moved within

復 *fù* (v), to report

鈞 *jūn* (m), 30 斤, (1 斤 ≈ 256 g)

羽 *yǔ* (n), feather

明 *míng* (n), clearness of vision

毫 *háo* (n), fur, fine hair

末 *mò* (n), tip, end

否 *fǒu* (v), "It is not."

輿 *yú* (n), a cart

薪 *xīn* (n), firewood

許 *xǔ* (v), to grant, agree to

恩 *ēn* (n), benevolence

獨 *dú* (adv), in particular, "precisely"

挾 *jiā* (v), to hold under the arm

泰山 Mt. Tài, a sacred mountain in 山東 Shāndōng province

語 *yù* (v), to inform

長者 *zhǎng zhě* (n), old person

*折枝 *zhé zhī* (v-o), lit., "to break a limb," perhaps means "massage"

幼 *yòu* (v), to be young

*刑 *xíng* (v), to provide a model = 型

*寡妻 = 寡人之妻

*御 *yù* (v), to advance, set forward

家邦 *jiā bāng* (n), clan and state

諸 = 之乎, equivalent to 之 於

妻子 *qī zǐ* (n), wife and children

權 *quán* (n), measuring weight > (v), to measure weight

度 *duò* (v), to measure length

抑 *yì* (fw), "or perhaps"

甲兵 *jiǎ bīng* (n), armor and weapons

*構怨 *gòu yuàn* (v-o), create resentment

快 　　 *kuài* (v), to delight, satisfy

肥甘 　 *féi gān* (n), fatty and sweet [foods] = delicious food

輕煖 　 *qīng nuǎn* (n), light [clothes in summer] and warm [in winter]

采色 　 *cǎi sè* (n), brilliant colors

*便嬖 　 *piān bì* (n), [king's] favorites

已 　　 *yǐ* (fw), here, equivalent to 矣

辟 　　 *pì* (v), to open up [land]

*蒞 　　 *lì* (v), to oversee, govern

中國 　 *zhōng guó* (n), the central states

撫 　　 *fǔ* (v), to pacify

四夷 　 *sì yí* (n), barbarians of the four directions

緣 　　 *yuán* (cv), to rely on

災 　　 *zāi* (n), disaster

殆 　　 *dài* (adv), almost [with a negative implication]

*鄒 　　 Zōu, a small state near 齊

孰 　　 *shú* (fw), "which?" (often of 2 choices)

敵 　　 *dí* (v), to be a match for

彊 　　 *qiáng* (v), to be strong = 強

方 　　 *fāng* (n?), a square of . . .

服 　　 *fú* (v), to submit to > to cause to submit

盍 　　 *hé* = 盇, a fusion of 何不

施 　　 *shī* (v), to apply, bring to bear

仕 　　 *shì* (v), to serve [in office]

野 　　 *yě* (n), undeveloped land

賈 　　 *gǔ* (n), merchant

藏 　　 *cáng* (v), to store [goods]

行旅 　 *xíng lǚ* (n), traveler

塗 　　 *tú* (n), road = 途

疾 　　 *jí* (v), to criticize

赴 　　 *fù* (v), to go to

愬 　　 *sù* (v), to inform, lodge a complaint

惛 　　 *hūn* (v), to be dense, stupid

輔 　　 *fǔ* (v), to help

敏 　　 *mǐn* (v), to be quick in apprehension, clever, sensitive

恆 　　 *héng* (v), to be constant

產 　　 *chǎn* (n), livelihood

*放辟 　 *fàng pì* (v), to be abandoned and dissolute

*邪侈 　 *xié chǐ* (v), to be depraved and extravagant

陷 　　 *xiàn* (v), to trap

罔　　*wǎng* (n), net > (v), to catch in a net = 網

仰　　*yǎng* (v), to look up [to the older]

俯　　*fǔ* (v), to look down [to the younger]

畜　　*xù* (v), to care for, tend

*樂歲　*lè suì* (n), a good harvest

終身　*zhōng shēn* (v), to live out one's life

飽　　*bǎo* (v), to have a full stomach

凶　　*xiōng* (n), famine

驅　　*qū* (v), to gallop, hasten

之　　*zhī* (v), to go to

贍　　*shàn* (v), to be sufficient

奚　　*xī* (fw), equivalent to 何以

暇　　*xiá* (n), leisure time

盍　　*hé* (fw), fusion of 何不, "why not"

桑　　*sāng* (n), mulberry

帛　　*bó* (n), silk cloth

雞　　*jī* (n), chicken

豚　　*tún* (n), pig

彘　　*zhì* (n), boar, pig

畜　　*chù* (n), animals

時　　*shí* (n), season > breeding time

飢　　*jī* (v), to be hungry

謹　　*jǐn* (v), to be careful, reverent

庠序　*xiáng xù* (n), local school in 周 dynasty

申　　*shēn* (v), to extend

悌　　*tì* (n), brotherly affection

頒白　*bān bái* (v), to have hair turning white

負　　*fù* (v), to carry on the back

戴　　*dài* (v), to carry on the head

黎民　*lí mín* (n), the dark-haired populace, i.e., the people

寒　　*hán* (v), to be cold

Lesson 26

莊子

Zhuāng Zhōu 莊周 is a central figure in both Chinese thought and literature. His wildly imaginative parables give unforgettable life and color to a skeptical yet enthusiastic philosophy that was a major precursor to later Daoism. His ingenious attacks on human habits of category making provide stories and images that became part of the Chinese cultural universe and deeply influence later Chinese thinking on language and the limits of knowledge.

The four selections below are found in the "Inner Chapters" 內篇 *Nèi Piān*, which are believed to best represent the writings of Zhuāng Zhōu himself. The first text is the well-known story of the *peng* bird from the opening section of 逍遙遊 *Xiāoyáo Yóu* "Free and Easy Wandering," the first chapter of *Zhuāng Zǐ*. Through disorienting shifts of scale, Zhuāng Zǐ here explores what truly untrammeled wandering might be like. The second selection reflects Zhuāng Zǐ's role as a radically skeptical logician: using a word, for Zhuāng Zǐ, commits one to the existence of the corresponding object, but Zhuāng Zǐ here demonstrates that most of our word-based commitments are highly suspect and—in the end—incoherent. The third selection is perhaps the best known of Zhuāng Zǐ's parables, the dream of the butterfly. The final selection is the story of Butcher Dīng's discussion with Lord Wénhùi about carving up an ox, in which Zhuāng Zǐ explores the relationship between knowledge, learning, action, and the Way.

The selections include substantial annotation because *Zhuāng Zǐ* is very difficult. Zhuāng Zǐ does not hesitate to make up expressions whose meanings are still debated. His parables often remain open to many, sometimes contradictory, readings. The commentary tradition provides a sense of the range of possibilities to help one navigate through the more difficult passages. The selections rely primarily on Qián Mù's 錢穆 judicious citation of commentary in his 莊子纂箋 and on Guó Qìngfán's 郭慶藩 very useful 莊子集釋.

Introduction to the Commentators
Cited in This Lesson

Major Commentaries

向秀   Xiàng Xiù (221–300): writer of the first major commentary, which disappeared in the Jìn dynasty.

郭象   Guō Xiàng (d. ca. 312): writer of the first major extant commentary on 莊子. He was part of the resurgence of philosophical Daoism after the collapse of the Hàn.

司馬彪   Sīmǎ Biāo (d. 306): Jìn dynasty crown prince, who established a reputation both as a degenerate (in order to disqualify himself for the throne) and as a scholar.

崔譔   Cūi Zhuàn (Jìn dynasty): little is known of this writer, whose notes are recorded in Lù Démíng's 經典釋文.

陸德明   Lù Démíng (558–627): wrote the great compendium of Southern Dynasties commentary, 經典釋文, which is the only source for much of the earlier commentary tradition.

成玄英   Chéng Xuányīng (fl. 632): Tang dynasty scholar who wrote a subcommentary on the authoritative Guō Xiàng commentary.

王念孫   Wáng Niànsūn (1744–1831): one of the most important Qīng dynasty philologists.

俞樾   Yú Yuè (1821–1907): prolific writer, scholar, and editor during the late Qīng dynasty.

郭慶藩   Guō Qìngfán (1844–96): a late Qing writer and philologist.

王先謙   Wáng Xiānqiān (1842–1917): student of 郭慶藩; compiler
         of the last great compendium of Qīng dynasty philology.

馬其昶   Mǎ Qíchǎng (d. 1930): late Qīng scholar with Tóngchéng
         桐城 affiliations.

Lesser Commentaries

葉秉敬   Yè Bǐngjìng (fl. 1615): late Míng eclectic scholar.

林雲銘   Lín Yúnmíng (fl. 1673): early Qīng scholar and eccentric
         literatus.

陳壽昌   Chén Shòuchāng, a mid-Qīng scholar.

奚侗   Xī Tóng, a Qīng scholar.

吳汝綸   Wú Rǔlún (1840–1903): an activist, follower of Zēng
         Guófān, Lǐ Hóngzhāng, and other late Qīng reformers.

Other Annotators Whose Comments Appear in This Lesson

洪頤煊   Hóng Yíxuān (b. 1765): a mid-Qing scholar, philologist
         and bibliophile.

李頤   Lǐ Yí: a Jin 晉 dynasty scholar whose comments are pre-
         served in the 經典釋文.

林希逸   Lín Xīyì (fl. 1252): a late Southern Sòng scholar, poet, and
         official whose discussion of 莊子 survives in the 道藏.

羅勉道   Luó Miǎndào: a late Southern Sòng writer whose com-
         ments also are preserved in the 道藏.

陸長庚   Lù Chánggēng, a Ming dynasty scholar.

王闓運   Wáng Kǎiyùn (1832–1916), a late Qing educator, scholar,
         and poet.

蕭鋼   Xiāo Gāng (503–51), better known as the Jiǎnwén Emperor
         of the Liáng 梁簡文帝, an accomplished poet and writer.

宣穎   Xuān Yǐng, an early Qing scholar.

嚴復 Yán Fù (1853–1921), a polymathic scholar, translator and cultural figure. He served as the president of what became 北京大學.

楊慎 Yáng Shèn (1488–1559), a Ming dynasty official and a prolific writer.

支遁 Zhīdùn (314–366), an important Jìn 晉 dynasty Buddhist monk who opposed Neo-Daoist nihilism.

Suggestions for Further Reading

Graham, Angus C. *Chuang-tzu: The Seven Inner Chapters and Other Writings from the Book of Chuang-tzu.* London: George Allen & Unwin, 1981.

———. *Disputers of the Tao: Philosophical Argument in Ancient China.* La Salle, Ill.: Open Court, 1989.

Guó Qìngfán 郭慶藩. 莊子集釋. 北京: 中華, 1985.

Mair, Victor, ed. *Experimental Essays on Chuang Tzu.* Honolulu: University of Hawaii Press, 1983.

Qián Mù 錢穆. 莊子纂箋. 4th ed. 香港: 東南, 1962.

Watson, Burton. *The Complete Works of Chuang Tzu.* New York: Columbia University Press, 1968

逍遙遊 Selection

北冥有魚，其名爲鯤。陸德明曰，北冥，北海也。東方朔十洲記云水黑色謂之冥海，無風洪波百丈。李頤曰，鯤，大魚名。崔譔曰鯤當爲鯨。羅勉道曰，爾雅，鯤，魚子。楊慎曰，莊子乃以至小爲至大，便是滑稽之開端。鯤之大，不知其幾千里也。化而爲鳥，其名爲鵬。崔譔曰，鵬古鳳字。鵬之背，不知其幾千里也。怒而飛，其翼若垂天之雲。是鳥也，海運，則將徙於南冥。司馬彪曰，運轉也。林希逸曰，海動必有大風。今諺有六月海動之語。南冥者，天池也。郭象曰，非冥海不足以運其身，非九萬里不足以負其翼。齊諧者，志怪者也。簡文曰，齊

諧，書也。羅勉道曰，齊諧者，齊人諧虐之言。諧之言曰，鵬之
徙於南冥也，水擊三千里，崔譔曰，將飛舉翼，擊水踉蹡。
摶扶搖而上者九萬里，司馬彪曰，圜飛而上也。上行謂之扶
搖。爾雅，扶搖謂之飆。去以六月息者也。成玄英曰，六月半
歲。至天池而息。陸長庚曰，息，氣也。宣穎曰，大塊噫氣爲風，六月氣
盛，故多風。野馬也，塵埃也，生物之以息相吹也。郭
象曰，野馬者，遊氣也。成玄英曰，天地之間，生物氣息，更相吹動。穆
按，此言野馬塵埃雖至微，亦有所憑而移動也。天之蒼蒼，其正
色耶，其遠而無所至極耶。其視下也，亦若是則
已矣。王先謙曰其謂鵬。借人視天，喻鵬視下，極言其摶上之高。且
夫水之積也無厚，則負大舟也無力。覆杯水於坳
堂之上，則芥李頤曰，芥，小草。爲之舟。置杯焉，則
膠。崔譔曰，膠，著地也。水淺而舟大也。風之積也不
厚，則其負大翼也無力。故九萬里，則風斯在下
矣，而後乃今培風。王念孫曰，培之爲言馮也。馮，乘也。背
負青天而莫之夭閼者，司馬彪曰，夭，折也。李頤曰，閼，塞
也。而後乃今將圖南。馬其昶曰，此言乘氣以遊天地間者，必待
厚積，乃可遠舉。蜩與學鳩笑之曰，洪頤煊曰文選注引司馬彪
云，學鳩，小鳥。我決起而飛，李頤曰，決疾貌。馬敘論曰，決借
爲趹。槍或作搶。榆枋，音方。支遁曰，槍，突也。時則不
至，王念孫曰，則，猶或也。而控於地而已矣。司馬彪曰，
控，投也。奚以之九萬里而南爲。適莽蒼者，三飡而
反，司馬彪曰，莽蒼，近郊之色也。崔譔曰，三飱，猶言竟日。腹猶
果然。陸德明曰，果然，飽貌。適百里者，宿舂糧。適千
里者，三月聚糧。之二蟲又何知。馬其昶曰，之，是也。

斥鷃鳩。小知不及大知。小年不及大年。奚以知其然
也。朝菌不知晦朔，<small>司馬彪曰，陰濕則生，見日便死，亦謂之大</small>
<small>芝，生於朝而死於暮，故曰朝菌。</small>蟪蛄不知春秋，此小年
也。楚之南有冥靈者，以五百歲爲春，五百歲爲
秋。<small>羅勉道曰，麟、鳳、龜、龍，謂之四靈。冥靈者，冥海之龜也。</small>
上古有大椿者，以八千歲爲春，八千歲爲秋。<small>司</small>
<small>馬彪曰，冥靈大椿，並木名也。以葉生爲春，以葉落爲秋。冥靈生於楚之</small>
<small>南，以二千歲爲一年。</small>而彭祖乃今以久特聞。衆人匹之，
不亦悲乎。湯之問棘也是已。窮髮之北，<small>成玄英曰，</small>
<small>以草爲毛髮。北方寒冱之地，草木不生，故名窮髮。所謂不毛之地。</small>有
冥海者，天池也。有魚焉，其廣數千里，未有知其
修者。其名爲鯤。有鳥焉，其名爲鵬。背若泰
山，翼若垂天之雲。摶扶搖羊角而上者九萬里。
絕雲氣，負青天，然後圖南，且適南冥也。斥鷃笑
之曰，彼且奚適也。我騰躍而上，不過數仞而
下，翱翔蓬蒿之間，此亦飛之至也。而彼且奚適
也。此小大之辯也。故夫知<small>音智。</small>效一官，行<small>下孟反。</small>
比一鄉，德合一君，而徵一國者，其自視也，亦若
此矣。<small>郭慶藩曰，而讀爲能。司馬彪曰，徵信也。</small>而宋榮子猶
然笑之。且舉世而譽之而不加勸，舉世而非之而
不加沮。定乎內外之分，辯乎榮辱之竟。斯已
矣。彼於世，未數數然也。雖然，猶有未樹也。
夫列子御風而行，泠然善也。旬有五日而後反。
彼於致福者，未數數然也。此雖免乎行，猶有所
待者也。若乎乘天地之正，而御六氣之辯，以遊

無窮者，彼且惡乎待哉。故曰，至人無己，神人無
功，聖人無名。

Vocabulary

逍遙　　*xiāo yáo* (v), to be "free and easy"

遊　　　*yóu* (v), to wander

北冥　　*běi míng* (n), the "Northern Darkness"

鯤　　　*kūn* (n), the "leviathan" (lit., "fingerling")

東方朔　Dōngfāng Shuò, a Hàn dynasty man of letters

*十洲記　*Shí zhōu jì, An Account of the Ten Isles*, attributed to 東方朔, about the Taoist Isles of the Immortals

洪波　　*hóng bō* (n), turbulent waves

鯨　　　*jīng* (n), "leviathan," whale

爾雅　*Ěr Yǎ*, a late Warring States compendium of glosses on early texts

至小　　*zhì xiǎo* (v), to be the smallest

便　　　*biàn* (fw), then, directly then

滑稽　　*gǔ jī* (v), to be comical

開端　　*kāi duān* (n), starting point

鵬　　　*péng* (n), "roc"

鳳　　　*fèng* (n), "phoenix" [male]

背　　　*bèi* (n), the back

怒　　　*nù* (v), to exert oneself (努)

翼　　　*yì* (n), wings

垂　　　*chuí* (v), to hang, drape

徙　　　*xǐ* (v), to move

諺　　　*yàn* (n), a proverb

池　　　*chí* (n), pool, pond

負　　　*fù* (v), to bear on the back

翼　　　*yì* (n), wings

齊諧　　*Qí Xié* (n), a book (?)

志怪　　*zhì guài* (v), to record the strange

諧虐　　*xié nüè* (n), joke, jest

擊　　　*jí* (v), to strike

*踉蹌　*liàng qiàng* (v), to wobble, move uneasily

搏　　　*tuán* (v), to twist

扶搖 *fú yáo* (n), the whirlwind

圜 *huán* (v), to move in a circle

*飆 *biāo* (n), a violent wind

息 *xí* (v), to rest, (n), breath

大塊 *dà kuài*, the "Great Clod," i.e., the Earth

*噫 *ài* (v), to belch

盛 *shèng* (v), to be abundant

野馬 *yě mǎ* (*di̯ǎ må*), descriptive of haze

塵埃 *chén āi* (n), dirt, dust

微 *wēi* (v), to be minute, subtle

憑 *píng* (v), to rely on

移動 *yí dòng* (v), to move

蒼蒼 *cāng cāng* (v), deep [blue]

色 *sè* (n), appearance, color

耶 *yé* (fw), final interrogative marker for nominal sentences

極 *jí* (n), extreme, limit

喻 *yù* (v), to use as a comparison

極言 *jí yán* (v), to say as much as possible about

且夫 *qiě fú* (fw), "now . . ."

積 *jī* (v), to accumulate

覆 *fù* (v), to overturn

*坳 *ào* (n), a depression

*芥 *jiè* (n), chaff

膠 *jiāo* (n), glue > (v), to stick

著 *zhuó* (v), to stick to

斯 *sī* (fw), [under] these [circumstances]

培 *péi* (v), to bank up, pile up

馮 *píng* (v), to rely on 憑

乘 *chéng* (v), to ride

*夭閼 *yāo è* (v), to impede

折 *zhé* (v), to fold or break

塞 *sè* (v), to block up

圖 *tú* (v), to plan

遠舉 *yuǎn jǔ* (v), to rise and go far away

*蜩 *tiáo* (n), cicada

*學鳩 *xué jiū* (n), a type of pigeon (鷽鳩)

文選 *Wén xuǎn*, the 昭明文選, the most important literary anthology in early imperial China

決 *jué* (v), in a rushing manner

疾 *jí* (v), to be quick, swift

*趹 *jué* (v), to travel quickly

槍	*qiāng* (n), a spear	*芝	*zhī* (n), a type of fungus
搶	*qiāng* (v), to hit, to strike	*蟪蛄	*huì gū* (n), a type of cicada
突	*tú* (v), to be sudden, abrupt	冥靈	*míng líng* (v), to be obscure and divine
*榆枋	*yú fāng* (n), two types of elm	麟	*lín* (n), "unicorn"
控	*kòng* (v), to throw, hit	龜	*guī* (n), tortoise
投	*tóu* (v), to throw	龍	*lóng* (n), dragon
奚	*xī* (n), "how," 何[以]	椿	*chūn* (n), a type of tree
爲	*wéi* [interrogative final particle]	並	*bìng* (fw), both
適	*shì* (v), to go to	葉	*yè* (n), leaf
*莽蒼	*mǎng cāng* (v), descriptive of bushes	彭祖	*Péng Zǔ* (n), the "Chinese Methuselah," lived 800 years
*三湌	*sān cān* (n), three meals	匹	*pī* (v), to match
腹	*fù* (n), belly	湯	Tāng, sage emperor, founded 商 dynasty
猶	*yóu* (adv), still		
果然	*guǒ rán* (v), to be full	*棘	Jí, an official
宿	*sù* (n), the previous night	窮髮	*qióng fǎ* (v), to be without hair
舂糧	*chōng liáng* (v), to pound grain in a mortar	毛髮	*máo fǎ* (n), hair, fur
聚	*jù* (v), to gather	*寒沍	*hán hù* (v), to be freezing cold
*菌	*jùn* (n), a type of mushroom	修	*xiū* (v), to be long
晦朔	*huì shuò* (n), dusk/dawn, end of month/beginning of month	泰山	*Tài Shān*, Mt. Tai, one of the five sacred mountains
陰濕	*yīn shī* (v), dark and damp	羊	*yáng* (n), goat
		角	*jué* (n), horn [on an animal]

且　qiě (fw), "provisionally," "about to"

斥鴳　chì yàn (n), a marsh quail

騰躍　téng yuè (v), to leap

仞　rèn (m), 7 尺

翱翔　áo xiáng (v), to soar

蓬蒿　péng hāo (n), scrub plants

辯　biàn (v), to distinguish, differentiate (辨)

效　xiào (v), [here] to contribute

比　bì (v), to shelter (庇)

*而　ér, perhaps equivalent to 能

徵　zhēng (v), to be verifiably true

*猶然　yóu rán (v), perhaps 猶 = 迶, self-satisfied

舉　jǔ (adj), the entire, all

舉世　jǔ shi (n), all the world

譽　yù (v), to praise

勸　quàn (v), to encourage, urge on

沮　jǔ (v), to block

榮辱　róng rù (n), glory and disgrace

竟　jìng (n), border, boundary

*數數然　shuò shuò rán (v), avidly anxious

御　yù (v), to [ride in a] chariot

泠然　líng rán (v), descriptive of cool

免　miǎn (v), to avoid

六氣　liù qì (n), six "vapors," for example: 陰陽風雨晦明

窮　qióng (v), to go to the end of

惡　wū (adv), "how . . ?"

齊物論 *Selection One*

今且有言於此，不知其與是類乎，其與是不類乎。類與不類，相與為類，則與彼無以異矣。雖然，請嘗言之。有始也者。有未始有始也者。有未始有夫未始有始也者。有有也者。有無也者。有未始有無也者。有未始有夫未始有無也者。俄而有無矣，而未知有無之果孰有孰無也。今我則

已有謂矣，而未知吾所謂之其果有謂乎，其果無
謂乎。天下莫大於秋毫之末，而太山爲小。莫壽
乎殤子，而彭祖爲夭。天地與我並存，而萬物與
我爲一。既已爲一，且得有言乎。既已謂之一
矣，且得無言乎。一與言爲二，二與一爲三。自此
以往，巧歷不能得，況其凡乎。故自無適有，以至
於三，而況自有適有乎。無適焉，因是已。

Vocabulary

齊	*qí* (v), to make equal, make even	壽	*shòu* (v), to live a long life
論	*lùn* (n), a discourse	殤子	*shāng zǐ* (n), a child who dies young
且	*qiě* (fw), "in a provisional way"	夭	*yāo* (v), to die young
類	*lèi* (v), to be of the category	並	*bìng* (v), to combine > (adv), at the same time
嘗	*cháng* (v), to try to . . .	存	*cún* (v), to exist, remain
始	*shǐ* (v), to begin to	既	*jì* + v (cv), since v has happened, . . .
夫	*fú* (adj), that (demonstrative pronoun)	*巧歷	*qiǎo lì* (v), to be skilled at reckoning, 歷 = 曆
俄	*é* (adv), suddenly		
孰	*shú* (fw), which? (often, as here, of two possibilities)	況	*kuàng* (fw), the more so . . .
		凡	*fán* (adj), in the general case
謂	*wèi* (n), a technical term, "reference"	適	*shì* (v), to go toward
毫	*háo* (n), fur		

齊物論 *Selection Two*

昔者莊周夢爲胡蝶，栩栩然胡蝶也。 陸德明曰，栩栩，喜貌。或曰，歡暢貌。自喻適志與。 李頤曰，喻，快也。奚侗曰，字當作愉。錢穆注，自喻，猶云自謂。不知周也。俄然覺，則蘧蘧然周也。 李頤曰，蘧蘧，有形貌。王闓運曰，蘧蘧，重貌。嚴復曰，大宗師蘧然覺，則蘧然自是覺貌。不知周之夢爲胡蝶與。胡蝶之夢爲周與。周與胡蝶，則必有分矣。此之謂物化。

Vocabulary

胡蝶　*hú dié* (n), butterfly

*栩栩然　*xū xū rán* (v), in a delighted manner

x 貌　x *mào*, "descriptive of x"

歡暢　*huān chàng* (v), to be exuberant

喻　*yù* (v), (1) to inform; (2) to be pleased, 喻 = 愉

適志　*shì zhì* (v), to accord with one's resolve

與　*yú* (fw), "?" = 歟

*蘧蘧然　*qú qú rán* (v), descriptive either of having a substantial shape or of waking up

大宗師　*Dàzōngshī*, chapter title in 莊子

*物化　*wù hùa* (n), "transformation of things"

養生主 *Selection*

庖丁爲文惠君解牛。手之所觸，肩之所倚，足之所履，膝之所踦，砉然嚮然，奏刀騞然。莫不中音，合於桑林之舞，乃中經首之會。文惠君曰，譆，善哉，技蓋至此乎。庖丁釋刀對曰，臣之所好者，道也。進乎技矣。始臣之解牛之時，所見

無非牛也。三年之後，未嘗見全牛也。方今之
時，臣以神遇而不以目視。官知止而神欲行。向秀
曰，專所司察而後動，謂之官智。縱手放意，無心而得，謂之神欲。依
乎天理。韓非曰，理者，成物之文也。批大卻，導大窾，因
其固然。技經肯綮之未嘗，俞樾曰，技，疑枝之誤。枝經，
猶經絡也。陸德明曰，肯，著骨肉也。司馬彪曰，綮，猶結處也。王闓運
曰，嘗，試也。而況大軱乎。良庖歲更刀，割也。族庖
月更刀，折也。今臣之刀，十九年矣。所解，數
千牛矣。而刀刃若新發於硎。彼節者有閒而刀刃
者無厚。以無厚入有閒，恢恢乎，其於遊刃，必有
餘地矣。是以十九年而刀刃若新發於硎。雖然，
每至於族，吾見其難為。怵然為戒，視為止，行
為遲。動刀甚微，謋然已解，如土委地。提刀而
立，為之四顧，為之躊躇滿志。善刀而藏之。文
惠君曰，善哉，吾聞庖丁之言，得養生焉。

Vocabulary

主　*zhǔ* (n), "host," the one who presides in . . .

庖　*páo* (n), kitchen

丁　*dīng* (n), (1) "man" [of lower class]; (2) a name

*文惠　Wénhuì, i.e. 梁惠王

解　*jiě* (v), to cut

觸　*chù* (v), to touch, make contact with

肩　*jiān* (n), shoulder

倚　*yǐ* (v), to lean on

履　*lǚ* (v), to tread on

膝　*xī* (n), knees

踦　*jǐ* (v), to lean into

*砉然　*huò rán* (v), the sound of flesh and bone separating

*嚮然　*xiàng rán* (v), reverberating

奏　*zòu* (v), to wield, move

*騞然 *huò rán* (v), the sound of flesh and bone rending

中 *zhòng* (v), to hit the center

*桑林 *sāng lín* (n), mulberry grove

*經首 *jīng shǒu* (n), name of a dance(?)

*譆 *xī*, "Ah"

技 *jì* (n), technique

蓋 *gài* (fw), "I conclude does perhaps"

進 *jìn* (v), to advance

未嘗 *wèi cháng* (adv), "not yet once"

方今 *fāng jīn* (n), just now

遇 *yù* (v), to encounter

*官知 *guān zhì* (n), knowledge from the five senses (五官)

專 *zhuān* (v), to use exclusively

*司察 *sì chá* (v), to investigate (司＝伺)

縱手 *zòng shǒu* (v), to release one's grip

放 *fàng* (v), to let loose

意 *yì* (n), intentions

欲 *yù* (n), desires

依 *yī* (v), to rely on

理 *lǐ* (n), inherent patterns

文 *wén* (n), manifest patterns

批 *pī* (v), to hit (with the hand)

*卻 *què* (n), a hole

導 *dǎo* (v), to lead

*窾 *kuǎn* (n), a rift

*固然 *gù rán* (v), following Graham, that which it has innately

*技經 *jì jīng* (n), cartilage(?)

*肯綮 *kěn qǐ* (n), tendons(?)

誤 *wù* (n), a mistake

*經絡 *jīng luò* (n), veins and arteries

結 *jié* (v), to tie, join

試 *shì* (v), to try out, investigate

*軱 *gū* (n), large bone

更 *gēng* (v), to exchange

割 *gē* (v), to rip, hack

族 *zú* (adj), ordinary

刃 *rèn* (n), knife blade

*硎 *xíng* (n), whetting stone

節 *jié* (n), joint

*恢恢然 *huī huī rán* (v), spacious

*怵然 *chù rán* (v), fearful

戒   *jiè* (v), to caution, guard against

遲   *chí* (v), to delay, go slow

*謋然   *huò rán* (v), describes sound of separating

委地   *wěi dì* (v+o), fall to the ground

躊躇   *chóu chú* (v), pace back and forth

*善   *shàn* (v), to wipe (繕)

藏   *cáng* (v), to store away

Lesson 27

史記

Sīmǎ Qiān 司馬遷 (ca. 145–86 B.C.) endured the pain and disgrace of castration in order to complete his father's project of writing a new history of their civilization. This history is the great 史記, the *Records of the Grand Historian*, a multilayered account of Chinese history from the mythic emperors through the reign of Hàn Wǔdì 漢武帝, the "Martial Emperor" (r. 140–87 B.C.). The 史記 proved enormously influential, and its structure became the model for dynastic histories to follow. The 史記 has five sections:

1. 本紀 *Běn jì* "Basic Annals," the accounts of the reigns of emperors and kings

2. 表 *Biǎo* "Tables," a concise tabular chronology of the rulers of the various states before the Hàn and a genealogy of the families ennobled during the Hàn

3. 書 *Shū* "Treatises," historical essays on various topics: ritual, music, the calendar, etc.

4. 世家 *Shì jiā* "Hereditary Families," accounts of the rulers of the major feudal states of the pre-Qín period (plus Confucius and a few important men from the early Hàn)

5. 列傳 *Liè zhuàn* "Biographies," biographies of historically important people as well as accounts of various types of significant though lesser figures, arranged by category

(obedient officials, jesters, assassins, virtuous women, barbarians, and the like)

More than a simple chronicle of the events at the centers of power, the 史記 presents the act of writing, of transmitting the records of the past, as driven by complex motives that elevate the 史—an office heretofore better translated simply as "scribe"—to the new status of "historian." What then does history mean to Sīmǎ Qiān? First, it provides object lessons in the patterns of human events. Historical narrative, with its breadth of scale, clarifies the consequences of actions: this is the metaphor of history as "mirror" shared by both ancient China and early Western cultures. A second, related function is the preservation of useful information on the development and prior structure of current institutions. Historical writing also performs acts of compensation, of recording for all time good deeds unrewarded and evil unpunished in its own day. This third role points to a fourth basic duty of the historian. The earlier historical chronicle, the *Zuǒ zhuàn* 左 傳, records the idea of the "three undiminishing" types of actions 三不 朽: to establish virtue 立德, to establish meritorious deeds 立功, and to establish [wise] speech 立言. Yet there is no guaranteed immortality, and it is the historian's responsibility to record these actions for future generations.

The selection below is the story of Bó Yí 伯夷 and Shū Qí 叔齊, the first "biography" in the 史記. An undercurrent running throughout the biography is the difficulty of fulfilling the historian's task of recording deeds and words, given the contradictions and uncertainties in the source materials. A second theme—appropriate for the first biography—is precisely the historian's duty to struggle against the manifest injustice of life and seek out the stories of people of worth who, far from the centers of power, would otherwise vanish without a trace.

Suggested Further Reading

Durrant, Stephen W. *The Cloudy Mirror: Tension and Conflict in the Writings of Sima Qian*. Albany: State University of New York Press, 1995.

Sima Qian. *Records of the Grand Historian: Han Dynasty*. Translated by Burton Watson. Hong Kong : Research Centre for Translation,

The Chinese University of Hong Kong; New York: Columbia University Press, 1993.

Sima Qian. *Records of the Grand Historian: Qin dynasty*. Translated by Burton Watson. Hong Kong: Research Centre for Translation, Chinese University of Hong Kong; New York: Renditions–Columbia University Press, 1993.

Watson, Burton. *Records of the Grand Historian of China*. New York: Columbia University Press, 1961.

伯夷列傳

夫學者載籍極博，猶考信於六藝，詩書雖缺，然虞夏之文可知也。孔子刪詩三百五篇，今亡五篇，刪書一百篇，今亡四十二篇。然尚書有堯典，舜典，大禹謨，則虞夏之文，可考而知也。堯將遜位，讓於虞舜，舜禹之閒，岳牧咸薦，岳，四岳，官名。一人而總四岳諸侯之事。牧，九州之牧。乃試之於位，典職數十年，功用既興，然後授政，示天下重器，王者大統，傳天下若斯之難也。而說者曰，說者，謂諸子雜記也。堯讓天下於許由，許由不受，恥之逃隱。及夏之時，有卞隨、務光者，此何以稱焉。堯舜讓位，若斯之難，則許由、隨、光之讓，或說者之妄稱，未必實有其人。太史公曰，余登箕山，其上蓋有許由冢云。孔子序列古之仁聖賢人，如吳太伯、伯夷之倫詳矣。余以所聞由、光義至高，其文辭不少概見，何哉。以由、光義至高，而詩書之文辭不少略見，則其人終屬有無之間，未可據以為實。孔子曰，伯夷叔齊，不念舊惡，怨是用希。求仁得仁，又何怨乎。余悲伯夷之意，睹軼詩可異焉。軼詩，即下采薇之詩也。不入三百篇，故云軼。其詩有涉於怨，與孔子之言不合，故可異。

其傳曰，伯夷叔齊，孤竹君之二子也。父欲立叔齊，及父卒，叔齊讓伯夷，伯夷曰，父命也，遂逃去。叔齊亦不肯立而逃之。國人立其中子。於是伯夷叔齊聞西伯昌善養老，盍往歸焉。及至，西伯卒，武王載木主，號爲文王，東伐紂。伯夷叔齊叩馬而諫曰，父死不葬，爰及干戈，可謂孝乎。以臣弒君，可謂仁乎。左右欲兵之，太公曰，此義人也，扶而去之。武王已平殷亂，天下宗周，而伯夷叔齊恥之，義不食周粟，隱於首陽山，采薇而食之。及餓且死，作歌。其辭曰，

登彼西山兮，采其薇矣，
以暴易暴兮，不知其非矣，
神農虞夏忽焉沒兮，我安適歸矣，
于嗟徂兮，命之衰矣。

遂餓死于首陽山。由此觀之，怨耶非耶。或曰，天道無親，常與善人，若伯夷叔齊，可謂善人者非耶，積仁絜行，如此而餓死。且七十子之徒，仲尼獨薦顏淵爲好學，然回也屢空糟糠不厭，而卒蚤夭，天之報施善人，其何如哉。盜跖日殺不辜，肝人之肉，暴戾恣睢，聚黨數千人，橫行天下，竟以壽終，是遵何德哉。此其尤大彰明較著者也。若至近世，操行不軌，事犯忌諱，而終身逸樂，富厚累世不絕，或擇地而蹈之，時然後出言，行不由徑，非公正不發憤，而遇禍災者，不可

勝數也。余甚惑焉，儻所謂天道，是耶非耶。子
曰道不同，不相爲謀。亦各從其志也。故曰，富
貴如可求，雖執鞭之士，吾亦爲之，如不可求，從
我所好。歲寒然後知松柏之後凋。舉世混濁，清
士乃見，豈以其重若彼，其輕若此哉。君子疾没
世而名不稱焉。賈子曰，貪夫徇財，烈士徇名，夸
者死權，衆庶馮生。同明相照，同類相求。雲從
龍，風從虎，聖人作而萬物睹。伯夷叔齊雖賢，
得夫子而名益彰，顏淵雖篤學，附驥尾而行益
顯。巖穴之士，趨舍有時，若此類名堙滅而不
稱，悲夫。閭巷之人，欲砥行立名者，非附青雲
之士，青雲上，聖賢立言傳世者。惡能施於後世哉。

Vocabulary

載籍 *zài jí* (n), written documents

極 *jí* (adv), extremely

博 *bó* (v), to be broad, extensive

考信 *kǎo xìn* (v), to examine and verify

六藝 *liù yì*, "The Six Arts": ritual, music, archery, chariot driving, writing, and mathematics > "The Six Classics": 詩 *Poetry*, 書 *Documents*, 禮 *Ritual*, 樂 *Music*, 易 *Change*, and

春秋 Spring and Autumn Annals.

詩 *Shī*, the *Classic of Poetry*

書 *Shū*, the *Classic of Documents*, also called the 尚書 *Shàng Shū*.

缺 *quē* (v), to lack, be incomplete

虞 *Yú*, the name of the period when 舜 ruled.

夏 *Xià*, the first of the three early dynasties (三代), 2205–1766 B.C. (traditional dates)

删 *shān* (v), to cut away > to edit

堯 Yáo, the first great sage-emperor of Confucian "history," traditionally said to have ruled 2356–2255 B.C.

堯典 "Yáo diǎn," the first section of the 尚書

舜 Shùn, the second sage-emperor, ruled 2255–2205 B.C. (traditional dates)

舜典 "Shùn diǎn," the second section of the 尚書

禹 Yǔ, sage-founder of the 夏 dynasty

大禹謨 "Dà Yǔ mó," "The Plan of Great Yǔ," a section of the 尚書

遜位 *xùn wèi* (v), to cede the throne

岳 *yuè* (n), refers to the four leaders of barbarian tribes acknowledged as vassals by Yáo and Shùn

牧 *mù* (n), shepherd > leader

薦 *jiàn* (v), to recommend

試 *shì* (v), to try out

典職 *diǎn zhí* (v), to preside at a post

授 *shòu* (v), to hand to

重器 *zhòng qì* (n), heavy utensils > the ritual symbols of authority

許由 Xǔ Yóu, a legendary hermit

恥 *chǐ* (v), to be ashamed

逃 *táo* (v), to flee

隱 *yǐn* (v), to go into hiding

卞隨 Biàn Suí, a virtuous recluse. When offered the throne by 禹, he threw himself into a river and drowned.

務光 Wù Guāng, another virtuous recluse

稱 *chēng* (v), to state, claim

太史公 Tàishǐ Gōng, "The Grand Historian," i.e., 司馬遷's father, 司馬談

箕山 Jī shān, Mt. Jī, a mountain in modern Hénán 河南 province

冢 *zhǒng* (n), grave mound

序列 *xù liè* (v), to list in ordered sequence

吳太伯 Wú Tàibó, "Grand Earl of Wú," the older brother of 周文王's father, who yielded his title to his more virtuous younger brother, then departed to

Wú, which was considered the far south

伯夷   Bó Yí, a virtuous recluse

倫   *lún* (n), category, type, group

叔齊   Shú Qí, younger brother of Bó Yí

伯...希   See 論語 5.23

怨   *yuàn* (v), to hold a grievance

念   *niàn* (v), to recall, keep in mind

是用   *shì yòng*, an inversion of 用是

希   *xī* (v), to be rare, few, = 稀

求...乎   See 論語 7.15

睹   *dǔ* (v), to look at carefully

軼   *yì* (v), to lose > (adj) remnant

三百篇   *Sān bǎi piān*, another name for the 詩經, which has 305 poem titles

涉   *shè* (v), to ford > to enter into

孤竹   Gūzhú, a state during the Shang dynasty (in modern Hebei)

立   *lì* (v), establish [as heir]

西伯昌   Xī Bó Chāng, "The Western Earl, Chāng," i.e., 周文王, the father of the founder of the Zhōu dynasty. Because of his virtue, he became preeminent among the Shāng aristocracy. His name was 昌.

盍   *hé* (fw), 何不

木主   *mù zhǔ* (n), a wooden funerary placard

伐   *fā* (v), to wage punitive war

紂   Zhòu, the "bad last" king of the Shāng dynasty

叩   *kòu* (v), to pull [to a stop]

爰   *yuán* (n), at this point 於是

干戈   *gān gē* (n), shield and spear > warfare

兵   *bīng* (n), weapon > (v), to hit

太公   Tài Gōng, Lǚ Shàng 呂尚, an important adviser to 武王, also known as "He for whom my father looked," or 太公望

扶   *fú* (v), to shield, protect

平   *píng* (v), to pacify

殷   Yīn, another name for the 商

宗　　*zōng* (v), to honor the ancestor

周　　Zhōu, the dynasty founded by 武王

粟　　*sù* (n), grain

首陽山　Shǒuyáng Shān, Mt. Shouyang, in modern Shanxi 陝西 province

兮　　*xī* (fw), "Hey!" a breathing mark in songs

薇　　*wéi* (n), ferns and moss

暴　　*bào* (v), to be violent, use force

神農　Shén Nóng, a mythical emperor, established agrarian society

没　　*mò* (v), to sink > to vanish, > die

適　　*shì* (v), to go toward

于嗟　*xū jiē*, "Alas" 于 = 吁

徂　　*cú* (v), to go (also, to die 殂)

衰　　*shuāi* (v), to decline

親　　*qīn* (v), close friend > favorite

積　　*jī* (v), to accumulate

絜　　*jié* (v), to purify

行　　*xìng* (n), conduct

七十子　*qī shí zǐ*, Confucius' 70 students

顏淵　Yán Yuān, Confucius' favorite disciple, Yán Huí 顏回, 字 Zǐyuān 子淵

好學　*hào xué*, to delight in learning

屢　　*lǚ* (adv), frequently. See 論語 11.18.

糟糠　*zāo kāng* (n), grain that has been used in brewing (糟) and the husks from grain (糠) > fare eaten by the very poor

厭　　*yàn* (v), to weary of

蚤　　*zǎo* (v), to be early = 早

夭　　*yǎo* (v), to die young

施善　*shī shàn* (v-o), to enact the good

盜跖　*Dào Zhí*, "Robber Zhí," whose evil deeds are described in the chapter "盜跖," in 莊子

不辜　*bù gū* (v), to be innocent

肝　　*gān* (n), liver

戾　　*lì* (v), to be perverse

恣睢　*zì suī* (v), to be unrestrained

橫　　*héng* (v), to go slantwise > go by crooked (evil) ways

遵　　*zūn* (v), to follow

尤　　*yóu* (adv), especially

彰明　*zhāng míng* (v), to be brilliantly clear

較著　*jiào zhù* (v), to be brightly manifest

操行　*cāo xìng* (n), conduct

軌　　*guǐ* (n), carriage rut; (v), to be on track, on the right path

犯　　*fàn* (v), to violate, transgress

忌諱　*jì huì* (n), taboos

逸樂　*yì lè* (n), unimpeded pleasure

累世　*lěi shì* (n), successive generations

蹈　　*dào* (v), to tread, step on

徑　　*jìng* (n), byway, shortcut

發憤　*fā fèn* (v), to express indignant anger

不可勝　*bùkě shēng*, cannot successfully (completely) do . . .

儻　　*tǎng* (fw), if

道 . . . 謀　See 論語 15.40

鞭　　*biān* (n), a whip

富 . . . 好　See 論語 7.12

寒　　*hán* (v) to be cold

松柏　*sōng bó* (n), pine and cypress (evergreens)

凋　　*diāo* (v), to wither

歲 . . . 凋　See 論語 9.28

舉世　*jǔ shì* (n), the entire generation

混濁　*hún zhó* (v), to be turbid, dirty

疾　　*jí* (v), to detest

賈子　Jiǎ Zǐ, "Master Jiǎ," Jiǎ Yì 賈誼 (ca. 201–169 B.C.), important early Hàn writer and official. See the "Owl Fù" 鵩鳥賦 *Fú niǎo fù.*

貪　　*tān* (v), to covet, to desire

烈　　*liè* (v), to be ardently virtuous

夸　　*kuā* (v), to be boastful (of one's abilities)

權　　*quán* (n), authority

馮　　*píng* (v), to rely on = 憑

雲 . . . 睹　See the Hexagram 乾 *Qián* in the 易經

篤　　*dǔ* (v), to be earnest

驥尾　Jì *wěi*, the fabulous horse Jì's tail

巖穴 *yán xuè* (n), cliffs and caves

趨舍 *qū shě* (v), to hurry toward (to select for use) and to reject

堙滅 *yīn miè* (v), to vanish

閭巷 *lǘ xiàng* (n), villages and small alleys

砥   *dǐ* (n), whetstone > (v), to polish

惡   *wū* (fw), how?

Lesson 28

王羲之，蘭亭集序

Wáng Xīzhī 王羲之 (A.D. 321–79) is known today as one of China's greatest calligraphers. Born into the Lángyé Wáng 琅邪王 clan, Wáng rose to prominence in Eastern Jìn elite society and served in both civil and military offices.[1]

Wáng Xīzhī's "Preface to the *Orchid Pavilion Collection*" is a masterpiece of *xíng shū* 行書, "running script."[2] The actual content of the preface, however, has largely been overshadowed by its status as a work of art. Wáng composed the essay (also know as the "Account of Orchid Pavilion") as the introduction to a collection of poetry written by the participants in an elite springtime excursion to the Orchid Pavilion near the city of Kuàijī (modern Shàoxīng). Written in a loosely parallel style with many structurally balanced sentences, the essay describes the occasion and then explains the significance of the poetry composed at the time. Wáng's account of the relationship between writing, personality, and the circumstances of composition shows an important symmetry between reading and writing in the Chinese tradition. That is, Wáng observes that precisely because "men of old" wrote

1. Members of the great aristocratic clans of medieval China were referred to by the place of origin of the clan. Although the Tàiyuán Wáng clan, for example, originated in the northern city of Tàiyuán, most members of the Southern dynasties aristocracy from that clan had no direct connection with the city, which had long been under non-Chinese control.

2. According to one account, the Táng dynasty emperor Tàizōng 唐太宗 (r. 627–649) had the original buried with him.

under similar circumstances with similar feelings, we today can understand them. Equally, if we honestly record our reactions to our circumstances, people of the future will be able to read us as we read writers of the past. This continuity of human sensibility and endurance of language offset the strong, melancholy sense in the essay of the fading of all things and have made it a canonical affirmation—deeply influential in later times—of the power of the written word.

永和九年永和，晉穆帝年號。，歲在癸丑，暮春之初，會於會膾稽山陰之蘭亭時當暮春，王羲之與謝安，孫綽等以上巳日，會於蘭亭。會稽，今紹興府。山陰，縣名。，修禊事也。禊，祓除不祥也。三月上巳日，臨水洗濯，除去宿垢謂之禊。群賢畢至，少長咸集。此地有崇山峻嶺，茂林修竹。又有清流激湍脫平聲映帶左右，引以爲流觴曲水。因曲水以泛觴。列坐其次，雖無絲竹管弦之盛，一觴一詠，亦足以暢敘幽情。是日也，天朗氣清，惠風和暢。仰觀宇宙之大，俯察品類之盛。所以遊目騁懷，足以極視聽之娛，信可樂也。夫人之相與，俯仰一世，或取諸懷抱，晤言一室之內。一種人，是倦於涉獵者。或因寄所託，放浪形骸之外。又一種人，是曠達不拘者。雖取舍萬殊，靜躁不同，此兩種人或取或舍，或靜或躁。當其欣於所遇，暫得於己，快然自足，曾不知老之將至。總是一樣得意。及其所之之，往也。既倦，情逐事遷，感慨係之矣。又一樣興盡。向之所欣，俯仰之間，已爲陳跡，猶不能不以之興懷。況修短隨化，終期於盡。人命長短，總歸於盡。古人云，死生亦大矣，豈不痛哉。莊子德充符，仲尼曰，死生亦大矣。每覽昔人興感之由，若合一契，未嘗不臨文嗟悼，不能喻之於懷。_{我未嘗不臨此興感之文，而爲之嗟悼，亦不能自解其所以然。}固知一生死爲虛誕，齊彭殤爲妄作。_{莊子齊物論，予惡乎知夫死者不悔其始之蘄生乎，此一死生之說也。莫壽乎殤子，而彭祖爲夭，此齊彭殤之說也。}後之視今，亦猶今之視昔，悲夫。故列敘時人，錄其所述，雖世殊事異，所以興懷，其致一也。_{古今同一興感。}後之覽者，亦將有感於斯文。_{後人亦重死生，覽我斯文，亦當同我之感。}

Vocabulary

王羲之 Wáng Xīzhī (321–79), Jìn dynasty literatus

蘭亭 Lán tíng, "Orchid Pavilion"

集 *jí* (n), a [literary] collection

序 *xù* (n), a "preface"

*永和 *Yǒnghé*, reign period, A.D. 345–57

*晉穆帝 Jìn Mùdì (r. 345–61), an emperor during the Eastern Jìn dynasty

年號 *nián hào* (n), reign period

歲 *suì* (n), 太歲, the planet Jupiter

癸丑 *guǐ chǒu*, 50th stem-branch combination for marking years

暮春 *mù chūn* (n), last month of spring, i.e., 3rd Month

會 *huì* (v), to meet

*會稽 Kuàijī, modern Shàoxīng

*膾 *kuài* (n), minced meat

*謝安 Xiè Ān (320–85), aristocratic literatus and savior of the Jìn dynasty

*孫綽 Sūn Chuò (ca. 301–80), a gentleman at leisure

等 *děng* (n), "group of . . ."

*上巳 *shàng sì* (n), first *sì* day of the month

*紹興 Shàoxīng, in Zhéjiāng

修 *xiū* (v), to cultivate, prepare

*禊 *xì* (n), rite of purification

*祓 *fú* (v), to ritually purify

祥 *xiáng* (v), to be auspicious

宿垢 *sù gòu* (n), prior defilement

畢 *bì* (v), to complete > (adv) completely

咸 *xián* (adv), all

崇 *chóng* (v), to be lofty and exalted

峻 *jùn* (v), to be lofty and steep

嶺 *lǐng* (n), mountain range

茂 *mào* (v), to flourish

修 *xiū* (v), to be long

激 *jī* (v), to be violent, rushing

湍 *tuān* (n), rapids

映 *yìng* (v), to reflect a gleam

觴 *shāng* (n), goblet

曲 *qū* (v), to bend

泛 *fàn* (v), to float

列 *liè* (v), to put in a row

次 *cì* (n), place, position

絲竹 *sī zhú* (n), "silk and bamboo," a term for stringed and pipe instruments

管弦 *guǎn xián* (n), "pipes and strings," musical instruments

詠 *yǒng* (v), to chant

暢 *chàng* (v), to expand, stretch

敘 *xù* (v), to put in order, describe (put in descriptive order)

幽 *yōu* (v), to be secluded, withdrawn, hidden

朗 *lǎng* (v), to be bright

和 *huō* (v), to be balmy

仰 *yǎng* (v), to look up

宇宙 *yǔ zhòu* (n), the universe

俯 *fǔ* (v), to look down

品類 *pǐn lèi* (n), categories

*騁 *chěng* (v), to gallop

娛 *yú* (v), to give pleasure to

諸 *zhū*, fusion of 之 + 乎

*晤言 *wù yán* (v), to speak face to face

倦 *juàn* (v), to grow weary

*涉獵 *shè liè* (v), to search here and there

寄 *jì* (v), to lodge

託 *tuō* (v), to entrust to

放浪   *fàng làng* (v), to be un-bridled

骸   *hái* (n), skeleton

拘   *jū* (v), to confine, be confined

殊   *shū* (v), to be different

躁   *zào* (v), to be agitated, easily excited

欣   *xīn* (v), to be delighted

遇   *yù* (v), to encounter

遷   *qiān* (v), to move, change

感慨   *gǎn kǎi* (v), to be deeply moved (usually to sorrow)

向   *xiàng* (n?), [the time] just a while ago

陳跡   *chén jī* (n), "set out traces"

況   *kuàng* (fw), "all the more . . ."

終   *zhōng* (v), to end > (adv) in the end

豈   *qǐ* (fw), how can . . . ?, implies a negative answer

覽   *lǎn* (v), to look at, examine

昔   *xí* (n), former times

契   *qì* (n), a tally (which is broken in half as part of making an agreement, so the two halves should match to be authentic)

嗟   *jiē* (v), to sigh

悼   *dào* (v), to mourn

喻   *yù* (v), to explain through comparison

誕   *dàn* (n), a lie

妄   *wàng* (v), to act foolishly, recklessly

殤   *shāng* (v), to die young

惡   *wū* (fw), "how . . . ?"

*蘄   *qí* (v), to seek [by prayer]

夭   *yǎo* (v), to die young

猶   *yóu* (fw), still

述   *shù* (v), to relate, transmit, describe

致   *zhì* (v), to deliver (cause to arrive) > (n), where [it] arrives, direction

斯   *sī* (n), this

斯文   *sī wén* (n), "this text" > culture in general

Lesson 29

陶潛

In the Chinese tradition, Táo Qián 陶潛 (365–427) is the poet of simplicity and authenticity. For the past thirteen hundred years, his writings have provided a model for "gentlemen in retirement": officials in exile, men who were driven from office or who failed to attain it, or simply literati who chose not to serve the state.

Táo Qián came from a minor aristocratic clan in an age when family status was vitally important to one's success in the world. After serving briefly as a local official, Táo Qián decided to quit, to withdraw from court society and return to his farm. On his estate, he developed a style—both of writing and of living—that was stripped of distracting ornamentation. While he had little influence in his own day, his writings became widely appreciated during the Táng dynasty.

The five selections below are among Táo Qián's most famous writings. The first, the "Biography of Mister Five Willows," is a fictional biography that serves as a self-portrait. The second, "An Account of Peach Blossom Spring," depicts a peaceful rural community beyond the reach of central authority that has been an inspiration to poets, painters and officials who longed to escape the ceaseless demands of their own society. The three poems that complete the selection reveal Táo Qián's style of easy elegance—a simplicity and directness based on the paring down of language, structure, imagery, and imagination—that never falls into crudeness.

Suggestions for Further Reading

Hightower, James Robert. *The Poetry of T'ao Ch'ien*. Oxford: Clarendon Press, 1970.

Kwong, Charles Yim-tze. *Tao Qian and the Chinese Poetic Tradition: The Quest for Cultural Identity*. Michigan Monographs in Chinese Studies, no. 66. Ann Arbor: University of Michigan Press, 1994.

Owen, Stephen. "The Self's Perfect Mirror: Poetry as Autobiography." In Lin Shuen-fu and Stephen Owen, eds., *The Vitality of the Lyric Voice*. Princeton: Princeton University Press, 1986.

Táo Shù 陶澍, ed. 靖節先生集. 香港: 中華, 1973.

五柳先生傳

先生不知何許人也，亦不詳其姓氏。宅邊有五柳樹，因以爲號焉。閑靜少言，不慕榮利。好讀書，不求甚解，每有會意，便欣然忘食。性嗜酒，家貧不能常得。親舊知其如此，或置酒而招之。造飲輒盡，期在必醉，既醉而退，曾不吝情去留。環堵蕭然，不蔽風日。短褐穿結，簞瓢屢空，晏如也。常著文章自娛，頗示己志。 忘懷得失，以此自終。

贊曰黔婁有言，不戚戚於貧賤，不汲汲於富貴。味其言茲若人之儔乎。銜觴賦詩，以樂其志。無懷氏之民歟。葛天氏之民歟。

Vocabulary

陶潛	Táo Qián (365–427), a famous poet known for his 田園 poetry	傳	*zhuàn* (n), biography
		何許	*hé xǔ*, "what place?"

詳　*xiáng* (v), to be detailed

宅　*zhái* (n), home, household

號　*hào* (n), style-name

閑　*xián* (v), to be at leisure

慕　*mù* (v), to admire, yearn for

好　*hào* (v), to like

會　*huì* (v), to meet

意　*yì* (n), intention

欣然　*xīn rán*, delighted

嗜　*shì* (v), to be fond of

貧　*pín* (v), to be poor

親舊　*qīn jiù* (n), family and old friends

置　*zhì* (v), to set out

招　*zhāo* (v), to summon, invite

*造　*zào* (v), [unusual usage] to begin

輒　*zhé* (fw), "invariably then . . ."

期　*qī* (n), period > appointed time > expectation

曾　*zēng* (fw), to the very end

吝　*lìn* (v), to be stingy > be concerned about in a petty way

*環堵　*huán dǔ*, [a house of] small circumference

*蕭然　*xiāo rán* (v), desolate, rundown

蔽　*bì* (v), to cover, shade, block

*褐　*hé* (n), coarse cloth

穿　*chuān* (v), to pierce

*簞瓢　*dān piáo* (n), rice-basket and ladle (this is an allusion to the 論語)

屢　*lǚ* (adv), often

*晏如　*yàn rú* (v), to be at ease

著　*zhù* (v), to write

文章　*wén zhāng*, literary compositions

娛　*yú* (v), to entertain

頗　*pō* (adv), rather

贊　*zàn* (n), evaluation (the author's comments in a biography)

*黔婁　Qián Lóu, a recluse from Qí during the Chūnqiū period.

*戚戚　*qī qī* (v), to be worried and sad (another allusion to the 論語)

*汲汲　*jí jí* (v), to be anxiously striving

味　*wèi* (v), to taste, savor

茲　*zī* (n), this

*若人 *ruò rén*, "this type of per-son"

儔 *chóu* (n), companion

銜 *xián* (v), to hold in mouth (like a horse's bit)

觴 *shāng* (n), a goblet

賦 *fù* (v), to compose [a poem]

*無懷氏 Mr. Wúhuái, an ancient emperor in a time of sim-ple, agrarian plenty.

歟 *yú* (fw), question mark

*葛天氏 Mr. Gétiān, an ancient emperor who ruled with-out speech and without action

桃花源記

晉太元中，武陵人捕魚爲業。緣溪行，忘路之遠
近。忽逢桃花林，夾岸數百步，中無雜樹，芳草鮮
美，落英繽紛。漁人甚異之。復前行，欲窮其
林。林盡水源，便得一山。山有小口，髣　若有
光，便舍船從口入。初極狹，纔通人。復行數十
步，豁然開朗。土地平曠，屋舍儼然，有良田美
池，桑竹之屬。阡陌交通，雞犬相聞。其中往來
種作，男女衣著，悉如外人。黃髮垂髫，並怡然
自樂。見漁人，乃大驚，問所從來，具答之。便
要還家，設酒殺雞作食。村中聞有此人，咸來問
訊。自云先世避秦時亂，率妻子邑人來此絕境，
不復出焉，遂與外人間隔。問今是何世，乃不知
有漢，無論魏、晉。此人一一爲具言所聞，皆嘆
惋。餘人各復延其家，皆出酒食。停數日，辭
去。此中人語云，不足爲外人道也。既出，得其
船，便扶向路，處處誌之。及郡下，詣太守說如
此。太守即遣人隨其往，尋向所誌，遂迷不復得

路。南陽劉子驥，高尚士也，聞之，欣然親往，未
果，尋病終。後遂無問津者。

Vocabulary

源   *yuán* (n), source, head [of a stream]

記   *jì* (n), "account"

晉   Jìn dynasty (265–419)

*太元   *Tàiyuán*, an Eastern Jìn reign period (376–97)

*武陵   Wǔlíng, a town in modern Hunan

捕   *bǔ* (v), to catch, arrest

緣   *yuán* (v), to follow along

溪   *xī* (n), stream, ravine

逢   *féng* (v), to encounter

夾   *jiá* (v), to line both sides

岸   *àn* (n), river bank

芳   *fāng* (v), to be fragrant

鮮   *xiān* (v), to be fresh

*落英   *luò yīng*, fallen petals

*繽紛   *bīn fēn* (v), in tangled profusion

髣髴   *fǎng fú* (v), to appear [with a vague resemblance]

狹   *xiá* (v), to be narrow

纔   *cái* (adv), just [barely]

*豁然   *huō rán* (v), to be expansive

*開朗   *kāi lǎng* (v), bright and open

*曠   *kuàng* (v), to be broad, open

*儼然   *yǎn rán* (v), to be dignified > [here] well-regulated

池   *chí* (n), pond

桑   *sāng* (n), mulberry tree

屬   *shǔ* (v), to belong to > (n), [of the] category . . .

阡陌   *qiān mò* (n), field paths

犬   *quǎn* (n), dog

著   *zhuó* (v), to wear > (n), clothing

悉   *xī* (adv), entirely

黃髮   *huáng fǎ* (n), "yellow-haired," i.e., an old person

髫   *tiáo* (n), bangs (worn by children)

*怡然   *yí rán* (v), pleased, happy

具   *jù* (adv), [in] complete [detail]

咸　*xián* (adv), all

訊　*xùn* (v), to inquire

云　*yún* (v), to say

避　*bì* (v), to flee

秦　Qín dynasty (255–206 B.C.)

率　*shuài* (v), to lead

邑　*yì* (n), city

絕境　*jué jìng* (n), remote region

間　*jiàn* (v), to come between

隔　*gé* (v), to be on opposite sides

漢　Hàn dynasty (206 B.C.–A.D. 220)

魏　Wèi dynasty (A.D. 220–65)

*嘆惋　*tàn wàn* (v), sigh with surprised sorrow

延　*yán* (v), to extend > to invite

辭　*cí* (v), to take leave

語　*yù* (v), to inform, tell

道　*dào* (v), to say, convey

扶　*fú* (v), to stick close to

向　*xiàng* (adj), former

郡　*jùn* (n), commandery, [military] prefecture

詣　*yí* (v), to go to, reach

太守　*tài shòu* (n), [military] prefect

即　*jí* (fw), thereupon, immediately

遣　*qiǎn* (v), to send, dispatch

尋　*xún* (v), to follow, seek out

迷　*mí* (v), to stray, get lost

*南陽　Nányáng, in Hénán

*驥　Jì (name of a great horse)

高尚　*gāo shàng* (v), lofty

親　*qīn* (adv), in person

果　*guǒ* (v), to produce results

尋　*xún* (adv), soon thereafter

問津　*wèn jīn*, "to ask about the crossing," i.e., to seek the way (an allusion to the 論語)

歸田園居五首錄二
第一

少無適俗韻，性本愛邱山。

誤落塵網中，一去三十年。

羈鳥戀舊林，池魚思故淵。

開荒南野際，守拙歸園田。

方宅十餘畝，草屋八九間。

榆柳蔭後簷，桃李羅堂前。

曖曖遠人村，依依墟里煙。

狗吠深巷中，雞鳴桑樹顛。

戶庭無塵雜，虛室有餘閒。

久在樊籠裏，復得返自然。

Vocabulary

少	*shào* (v), to be young	荒	*huāng* (n), waste land
適	*shì* (v), to accord with	際	*jì* (n), border
韻	*yùn* (n), rhyme, tune	拙	*zhuó* (v), to be clumsy
邱	*qiū* (n), hill	畝	*mǔ* (m), area of land
誤	*wù* (v), to err	間	*jiān* (m), area within roof pillars
塵	*chén* (n), dirt, dust		
網	*wǎng* (n), net	*榆	*yú* (n), elm
*羈	*jī* (n), bridle > (v), to rein	簷	*yán* (n), eaves
		羅	*luó* (n), net
戀	*liàn* (v), to have affection for	*曖曖	*ài ài* (v), to be dark with shade
思	*sī* (v), to long for	*依依	*yī yī* (v), to be hazy, indistinct
淵	*yuān* (n), deep pool		

*墟	*xū* (n), small village	閒	*xián* (v), to be at leisure
里	*lǐ* (n), ward, village	*樊	*fán* (n), bird cage
煙	*yān* (n), mist, smoke	籠	*lóng* (n), basket > cage
吠	*fèi* (v), to bark	返	*fǎn* (v), to return, go back
巷	*xiàng* (n), alley		
顛	*diān* (n), top [of tree, etc.]		

第三

種豆南山下，草盛豆苗稀。

晨興理荒穢，帶月荷鋤歸。

道狹草木長，夕露沾我衣。

衣沾不足惜，但使願無違。

Vocabulary

種	*zhǒng* (v), to plant	*荷	*hè* (v), to carry on shoulder
盛	*shèng* (v), to flourish	鋤	*chú* (n), hoe
苗	*miáo* (n), sprouts	狹	*xiá* (v), to be narrow
稀	*xī* (v), to be sparse	夕	*xì* (n), dusk, night
晨	*chén* (n), dawn	惜	*xí* (v), to be concerned about
理	*lǐ* (v), to order, arrange	違	*wéi* (v), to go astray from
*穢	*huì* (n), weeds		
帶	*dài* (v), to encircle		

飲酒二十首錄一
第五
結廬在人境，而無車馬喧。

問君何能爾，心遠地自偏。

採菊東籬下，悠然望南山。

山氣日夕佳，飛鳥相與還。

此中有眞意，欲辨已忘言。

Vocabulary

結　*jié* (v), to tie, plait

盧　*lú* (n), hut

喧　*xuān* (n), clamor

*爾　*ěr* (v), to be like this

偏　*piān* (v), to be off to one side

採　*cǎi* (v), to pick, pluck

菊　*jú* (n), chrysanthemum

籬　*lí* (n), hedge

*悠然　*yōu rán* (v), distanced, detached

辨　*biàn* (v), to discern, judge, decide

Part Four

唐宋文選
Selected Táng and Sòng Dynasty Writings

Lesson 30

陳玄祐，離魂記

天授三年，清河張鎰，因官家於衡州。性簡靜，寡知友。無子，有女二人。其長早亡。幼女倩娘，端妍絕倫。鎰外甥太原王宙，幼聰悟，美容範。鎰常器重，每曰，他時當以倩娘妻之。後各長成。宙與倩娘常私感想於寤寐，家人莫知其狀。後有賓寮之選者求之，鎰許焉。女聞而鬱抑，宙亦深恚恨。託以當調，請赴京，止之不可，遂厚遣之。宙陰恨悲慟，決別上船。日暮，至山郭數里。夜方半，宙不寐，忽聞岸上有一人行聲甚速，須臾至船。問之，乃倩娘徒行跣足而至。宙驚喜發狂，執手問其從來。泣曰，君厚意如此，寢夢相感。今將奪我此志，又知君深情不易，思將殺身奉報，是以亡命來奔。宙非意所望，欣躍特甚。遂匿倩娘于船，連夜遁去。倍道兼行，數月至蜀。凡五年，生兩子，與鎰絕信。其妻常思父母，涕泣言曰，吾曩日不能相負，棄大義而來奔君。向今五年，恩慈間阻。覆載之下，胡顏獨存也。宙哀之曰，將歸，無苦。遂俱歸衡州。既至，宙獨身先至鎰家，首謝其事。鎰曰，倩娘病在閨中數年，何其詭說也。宙曰，見在舟中。鎰大驚，促使人驗之。果見倩娘在船中，顏色怡暢，訊使者曰，大人安否。家人異之，疾走報鎰。室中女聞喜而起，飾粧更衣，笑而不語，出與相迎，翕然而合爲一體，其衣裳皆重。其家以事不正，祕之。惟親戚間有潛知之者。後四十年間，夫妻皆喪。二男並孝廉擢第，至丞尉。玄祐少常聞此說，而多異同，或謂其虛。大曆末，遇萊蕪縣令張仲規，因備述其本末。鎰則仲規堂叔，而說極備悉，故記之。

Lesson 31

杜甫詩選

望嶽

岱宗夫如何，
齊魯青未了。
造化鍾神秀，
陰陽割昏曉。
盪胸生曾雲，
決眥入歸鳥。
會當凌絕頂，
一覽眾山小。

春望

國破山河在，
城春草木深。
感時花濺淚，
恨別鳥驚心。
烽火連三月，

家書抵萬金。
白頭搔更短，
渾欲不勝簪。

客至

舍南舍北皆春水，
但見群鷗日日來。
花徑不曾緣客掃，
蓬門今始爲君開。
盤飧市遠無兼味，
樽酒家貧只舊醅。
肯與鄰翁相對飲，
隔籬呼取盡餘杯。

畫鷹

素練風霜起，
蒼鷹畫作殊。
㧐身思狡兔，
側目似愁胡。
絛鏇光堪摘，
軒楹勢可呼。
何當擊凡鳥，
毛血灑平蕪。

倦夜

竹涼侵臥內，
野月滿庭隅。
重露成涓滴，
稀星乍有無。
暗飛螢自照，
水宿鳥相呼。
萬事干戈裏，
空悲清夜徂。

月夜

今夜鄜州月，
閨中只獨看。
遙憐小兒女，
未解憶長安。
香霧雲鬟濕，
清輝玉臂寒。
何時倚虛幌，
雙照淚痕乾。

客亭

秋窗猶曙色，
落木更高風。
日出寒山外，
江流宿霧中。
聖朝無棄物，
衰病已成翁。
多少殘生事，
飄零任轉蓬。

石壕吏

暮投石壕村，
有吏夜捉人。
老翁踰牆走，
老婦出看門。
吏呼一何怒，
婦啼一何苦。
聽婦前致詞，
三男鄴城戍。
一男附書至，
二男新戰死。
存者且偷生，
死者長已矣。
室中更無人，
惟有乳下孫。

有孫母未去，
出入無完裙。
老嫗力雖衰，
請從吏夜歸。
急應河陽役，
猶得備晨炊。
夜久語聲絕，
如聞泣幽咽。
天明登前途，
獨與老翁別。

彭衙行

憶昔避賊初，
北走經險艱。
夜深彭衙道，
月照白水山。
盡室久徒步，
逢人多厚顏。
參差谷鳥吟，
不見遊子還。
癡女饑咬我，
啼畏虎狼聞。
懷中掩其口，
反側聲愈嗔。
小兒強解事，

故索苦李餐。
一旬半雷雨，
泥濘相攀牽。
既無禦雨備，
徑滑衣又寒。
有時經契闊，
竟日數里間。
野果充餱糧，
卑枝成屋椽。
早行石上水，
暮宿天邊煙。
小留同家窪，
欲出蘆子關。
故人有孫宰，
高義薄曾雲。
延客已曛黑，
張燈啓重門。
煖湯濯我足，
剪紙招我魂。
從此出妻孥，
相視淚闌干。
眾雛爛熳睡，
喚起霑盤飧。
誓將與夫子，
永結爲弟昆。

遂空所坐堂，
安居奉我歡。
誰肯艱難際，
豁達露心肝。
別來歲月周，
胡羯仍構患。
何當有翅翎，
飛去墮爾前。

Lesson 32

韓愈，原道

博愛之謂仁，行而宜之之謂義，由是而之焉之謂道，足乎己無待於外之謂德。仁與義爲定名，道與德爲虛位。<small>道德之實非虛，而道德之位則虛也。</small>故道有君子小人，而德有凶有吉。<small>如易言，恆其德，貞。婦人吉，夫子凶之類。此所以謂之德虛位也。</small>老子之小仁義，<small>老子，大道廢，有仁義非毀之也，其見者小也。</small>坐井而觀天，曰天小者，非天小也。彼以煦煦<small>許、</small>爲仁，孑孑爲義，其小之也則宜。<small>煦煦，小惠貌。孑孑，孤立貌。老子錯認仁義，故以爲小。</small>其所謂道，道其所道，非吾所謂道也。其所謂德，德其所德，非吾所謂德也。<small>老子，道可道，非常道。又，上德不德，是以有德。老子不知有仁義，并錯認道德。</small>凡吾所謂道德云者，合仁與義言之也，天下之公言也。老子所謂道德云者，去仁與義言之也，一人之私言也。周道衰，孔子没，火于秦，<small>秦李斯，請吏官非秦記，皆燒之。</small>黃老于漢，<small>黃老，黃帝、老子也。</small>佛于晉魏梁隋之間。<small>後漢明帝夜夢金人飛行殿庭。以問于朝，而傅毅以佛</small>

238

對。帝遣使往天竺，得佛經及釋迦像。自後佛法ҳ中夏。此特南舉晉梁，北舉魏隋也。其言道德仁義者，不入於楊，則入於墨。不入於老，則入於佛。入于彼，必出于此。入者主之，出者奴之。入者附之，出者污之。入于楊、墨、佛、老者，必出于聖人之學。主異端者，必以聖人爲奴。附異端者，必以聖人爲迂也。噫，後之人其欲聞仁義道德之說，孰從而聽之。老者曰，孔子，吾師之弟子也。佛者曰，孔子，吾師之弟子也。老者、佛者，謂治老佛治道者。如孟子所謂墨者是也。爲孔子者，習聞其說，樂其誕而自小也，亦曰吾師亦嘗師之云爾。爲，治也。言治孔子之道者，喜佛老之怪誕，而自以儒道爲小，而願附之。不惟舉之於其口，而又筆之於其書。筆之于書，如莊子天運篇，孔子見老子而語仁義。老子曰，仁義慘然乃憤吾心，亂莫大焉，孔子歸，三日不談之類也。噫，後之人雖欲聞仁義道德之說，其孰從而求之。甚矣，人之好怪也，不求其端，不訊其末，惟怪之欲聞。端，始也。末，終也。佛老之說甚怪，而人好之。故反足以勝吾道。古之爲民者四，今之爲民者六。古之教者處其一，今之教者處其三。農之家一，而食粟之家六。工之家一，而用器之家六。賈之家一，而資焉之家六。奈之何民不窮且盜也。古之時，人之害多矣。害，指下文蟲、蛇、禽，獸、饑、寒、顛、病等語。有聖人者立，然後教之以相生相養之道。爲之君，爲之師。書，天降下民，作之君，作之師。驅其蟲蛇禽獸而處之中土。寒然後爲之衣，飢然後爲之食。木處而顛，土處而病也，然後爲之宮室。爲之工以贍其器用，爲之賈以通其有無，爲之醫藥以濟其夭死，爲之葬埋祭祀以長其恩愛，爲之禮以次其先後，爲之樂以宣其湮鬱，爲之政以率其怠倦，爲之刑以鋤其強梗。相欺也，爲之符璽斗斛權衡以信之。相奪也，爲之城郭甲兵以守之。害到而爲之備，患生而爲之防。今其言曰，聖人不死，大盜不止。剖斗折衡，而民不爭。其言指老氏之書。嗚呼，其亦不思而已矣。如古之無聖人，人之類滅久矣。何也。無羽毛鱗介以居寒熱也，無爪牙以爭食也。言人不若禽獸之有羽毛鱗介爪牙，必待聖人衣食之。若無聖人，豈能至今有人之類乎。是故君者，出令者也。臣者，行君之令而致之民者也。民者，出粟米麻絲，作器皿，通貨財，以事其上者也。君不出令，則失其所以爲君。臣不行君之令而致之民，則失其所以爲臣。民不出粟米麻絲，作器皿，通貨財，以事其上，則誅。今其法曰，必棄而君臣，去而父子，禁而相生相養之道，其法指佛老之教。而，汝也。以求其所謂清淨寂滅者。嗚呼，其亦幸而出於三代之後，不見黜於禹、湯、文、武、周公、孔子也。其亦不幸而不出於三代之前，不見正於禹、湯、文、武、周公、孔子也。帝之與王，其號雖殊，其所以爲聖一也。夏葛而冬裘，渴飲而饑食，其事雖殊，其所以爲智一也。今其言曰，曷不爲太古之無事。是亦責冬之裘者曰，曷不爲葛之之易也。責饑之食者曰，曷不爲飲之之易也。傳曰，古之欲明明德於天下者，先治其

國。欲治其國者，先齊其家。欲齊其家者，先修
其身。欲修其身者，先正其心。欲正其心者，先
誠其意。然則古之所謂正心而誠意者，將以有爲
也。佛老托于無爲，大學功在有爲。今也欲治其心，而外天
下國家，滅其天常。子焉而不父其父，臣焉而不
君其君，民焉而不事其事。孔子之作春秋也，諸
侯用夷禮，則夷之，進於中國，則中國之。經
曰，夷狄之有君，不如諸夏之亡。詩曰，戎狄是
膺，荊舒是懲。今也，舉夷狄之法，而加之先王
之教之上，幾何其不胥而爲夷也。夫所謂先王之
教者，何也。博愛之謂仁，行而宜之之謂義，由
是而之焉之謂道，足乎己無待於外之謂德。其文
詩書易春秋。其法禮樂刑政。其民士農工賈。其
位君臣父子，師友賓主，昆弟夫婦。其服麻絲。
其居宮室。其食粟米果蔬魚肉。其爲道易明，而
其爲教易行也。是故以之爲己，則順而祥。以之
爲人，則愛而公。以之爲心，則和而平。以之爲
天下國家，無所處而不當。是故生則得其情，死
則盡其常。郊焉而天神假，格、廟焉而人鬼饗。
曰，斯道也，何道也。曰，斯道吾所謂道也，非
向所謂老與佛之道也。堯以是傳之舜，舜以是傳
之禹，禹以是傳之湯，湯以是傳之文武周公，文
武周公傳之孔子，孔子傳之孟軻，軻之死，不得
其傳焉。荀與楊也，擇焉而不精，語焉而不詳。荀
卿，名況。趙人。嘗推儒墨道德之行事興懷。漢，楊雄，字子雲，所撰有

法言十三卷。由周公而上，上而爲君，故其事行。由周公而下，下而爲臣，故其說長。事行，謂得位以行道。說長，謂立言以明道也。然則如之何而可也，曰，不塞不流，不止不行。佛老之道，不塞不止。聖人之道，不流不行。人其人，僧道俱令還俗。火其書，絕其惑人之說。廬其居，寺觀改作民房。明先王之道以道同導之。鰥寡孤獨廢疾者有養也。其亦庶乎其可也。

Lesson 33

歐陽修

縱囚論

信義行於君子，而刑戮施於小人。刑入於死者，乃罪大惡極，此又小人之尤甚者也。寧以義死不苟幸生而視死如歸，此又君子之尤難者也。方唐太宗之六年，錄大辟囚三百餘人。縱使還家，約其自歸以就死。是以君子之難能，期小人之尤者以必能也。其囚及期，而卒自歸無後者，是君子之所難而小人之所易也。此豈近於人情哉。或曰，罪大惡極，誠小人矣。及施恩德以臨之，可使變而爲君子。蓋恩德入人之深，而移人之速，有如是者矣。曰，太宗之爲此，所以求此名也。然安知夫縱之去也，不意其必來以冀免，所以復來乎。夫意其必來而縱之，是上賊下之情也。意其必免而復來，是下賊上之心也。吾見上下交相賊以成此名也。烏有所謂施恩德與夫知信義者哉。不然，太宗施德於天下，於茲六年矣。不能使小人不爲極惡大罪。而一日之恩，能使視死如歸，而存信義，此又不通之論也。然則何爲而可，曰，縱而來歸，殺之無赦。而又縱之，而又來，則可知爲恩德之致爾。然此必無之事也。若夫縱而來歸而赦之，可偶一爲之爾。若屢爲之，則殺人者皆不死。是可爲天下之常法乎。不可爲常者，其聖人之法乎。是以堯舜三王之治，必本於人情。不立異以爲高不逆情以干譽。

醉翁亭記

環滁皆山也。其西南諸峰，林壑尤美。望之蔚然而深秀者，瑯琊也。山行六七里，漸聞水聲潺潺，而瀉出於兩峰之間者，釀泉也。峰回路轉，有亭翼然，臨於泉上者，醉翁亭也。作亭者誰，山之僧智仙也。名之者誰，太守自謂也。太守與客來飲於此，飲少輒醉，而年又高，故自號醉翁也。醉翁之意不在酒，在乎山水之間也。山水之樂，得之心而寓之酒也。若夫日出而林霏開，雲歸而巖穴暝，晦明變化者，山間之朝暮也。野芳發而幽香，佳木秀而繁陰，風霜高潔，水落而石出者，山間之四時也。朝而往，暮而歸。四時之景不同，而樂亦無窮也。至於負者歌於塗，行者休於樹，前者呼，後者應，傴僂提攜，往來而不絕者，滁人遊也。臨溪而漁，溪深而魚肥。釀泉爲酒，泉香而酒洌。山肴野蔌，雜然而前陳者，

太守宴也。宴酣之樂，非絲非竹。射者中，弈者
勝。觥籌交錯，坐起而喧嘩者，眾賓懽也。蒼顏
白髮，頹乎其中者，太守醉也。已而夕陽在山，
人影散亂，太守歸而賓客從也。樹林陰翳，鳴聲
上下，遊人去而禽鳥樂也。然而禽鳥知山林之
樂，而不知人之樂。人知從守之樂，而不知太守
之樂其樂也。醉能同其樂，醒能述以文者，太守
也。太守謂誰，廬陵歐陽修也。

Lesson 34

蘇軾

賈誼論

非才之難，所以自用者實難。惜乎賈生王者之佐，而不能自用其才也。賈誼，雒陽人。年二十餘，文帝召以爲博士，一歲中至大中大夫。天子議以爲賈生任公卿之位，絳灌之屬盡害之，乃短賈生。帝於是疏之。出爲長沙王太傅。後召對宣室，拜爲梁王太傅。帝雖納其言，而終不見用。卒以自傷哭泣而死，年三十三。夫君子之所取者遠，則必有所待。所就者大，則必有所忍。古之賢人，皆負可致之才，而卒不能行其萬一者，未必皆其時君之罪，或者其自取也。愚觀賈生之論，如其所言，雖三代何以遠過。得君如漢文，猶且以不用死。然則是天下無堯舜，終不可有所爲耶。仲尼聖人，歷試於天下。苟非大無道之國，皆欲勉強扶持，庶幾一日得行其道。將之荊，先之以冉有，申之以子夏。荊，楚本號。將適楚，而先使二子繼往者，蓋欲觀楚之可任與否，而謀其可處之位與。君子之欲得其君，如此其勤也。孟子去齊，三宿而後出晝，猶曰王其庶幾召我。君子之不忍棄其君，如此其厚也。公孫丑問曰，夫子何爲不豫。孟子曰，方今天下，舍我其誰哉，而吾何

246

爲不豫。君子之愛其身，如此其至也。夫如此而不用，然後知天下果不足與有爲，而可以無憾矣。若賈生者，非漢文之不能用生，生之不能用漢文也。夫絳侯親握天子璽而授之文帝，灌嬰連兵數十萬，以決劉呂之雌雄，_{高后時，諸呂欲危劉氏。大將軍灌嬰，與齊王襄連合，以待呂氏之變，共誅之。}又皆高帝之舊將。此其君臣相得之分，豈特父子骨肉手足哉。賈生洛陽之少年，欲使其一朝之間，盡棄其舊而謀其新，亦已難矣。爲賈生者，上得其君，下得其大臣，如絳灌之屬，優游浸漬，而深交之，使天子不疑，大臣不忌，然後舉天下而唯吾之所欲爲，不過十年，可以得志。安有立談之間，而遽爲人痛哭哉。觀其過湘，爲賦以弔屈原，縈紆鬱悶，趯然有遠舉之志。其後以自傷哭泣，至於夭絕。是亦不善處窮者也。夫謀之一不見用，則安知終不復用也。不知默默以待其變，而自殘至此。嗚呼，賈生志大而量小，才有餘而識不足也。古之人，有高世之才，必有遺俗之累。是故非聰明睿智之主，則不能全其用。古今稱苻堅得王猛於草茅之中，一朝盡斥去其舊臣，而與之謀。彼其匹夫略有天下之半，其以此哉。愚深悲生之志，故備論之。亦使人君得如賈生之臣，則知其有狷介之操，一不見用，則憂傷病沮，不能復振。而爲賈生者，亦謹其所發哉。

前赤壁賦

壬戌之秋，七月既望，蘇子與客泛舟，遊於赤壁之下。建安十三年，曹操自江陵追劉備。備求救于孫權。權將周瑜請兵三萬拒之。瑜部將黃蓋，建議以 艦載荻柴，先以書詐降。時東南風急，蓋以十艦著前，餘船繼進，去二里許，同時火發。火烈風猛，燒盡北船，操軍大敗。石壁皆赤。清風徐來，水波不興。舉酒屬客，誦明月之詩，歌窈窕之章。少焉，月出於東山之上，徘徊於斗牛之間。白露橫江，水光接天。縱一葦之所如，凌萬頃之茫然。浩浩乎如馮平虛御風，而不知其所止。飄飄乎如遺世獨立，羽化而登仙。於是飲酒樂甚，扣舷而歌之。歌曰，桂棹兮蘭槳，擊空明兮泝流光。渺渺兮予懷，望美人兮天一方。客有吹洞簫者，依歌而和之，其聲嗚嗚然，如怨如慕，如泣如訴，餘聲嫋嫋，不絕如縷。舞幽壑之潛蛟，泣孤舟之嫠離婦。嫠婦，寡婦也。蘇子愀然，正襟危坐，而問客曰，何為其然也。客曰，月明星稀，烏鵲南飛，此非曹孟德之詩乎。文選，魏武帝短歌曰，月明星稀，烏鵲南飛，遶樹三匝，無枝可依。孟德，曹操字也。是為魏武帝。西望夏口，東望武昌，山川相繆，同繚。鬱乎蒼蒼，此非孟德之困於周郎者乎。周瑜，字公瑾，曹操呼為周郎。方其破荊州，劉琮降。下江陵，自江陵至赤壁。順流而東也，舳艫千里，旌旗蔽空，釃酒臨江，橫槊賦詩，釃，酌酒也。槊，矛屬。曹氏父子，鞍馬間為文，往往橫槊賦詩。固一世之雄也，而今安在哉。況吾與子漁樵於江渚之上，侶魚蝦而友麋鹿，駕一葉之扁舟，舉匏樽以相屬。
寄蜉蝣於天地，渺滄海之一粟。哀吾生之須臾，
羨長江之無窮。挾飛仙以遨遊，抱明月而長終。
知不可乎驟得，託遺響於悲風。蘇子曰，客亦知
夫水與月乎。逝者如斯，而未嘗往也。此句說水。盈
虛者如彼，而卒莫消長也。此句說月。蓋將自其變者
而觀之，則天地曾不能以一瞬。自其不變者而觀
之，則物與我皆無盡也，而又何羨乎。且夫天地
之間，物各有主。苟非吾之所有，雖一毫而莫
取。惟江上之清風，與山間之明月，耳得之而為
聲，目遇之而成色，取之無禁，用之不竭，是造
物者之無盡藏也，而吾與子之所共適。客喜而
笑。洗盞更酌。肴核既盡，盃盤狼藉。相與枕藉
乎舟中，不知東方之既白。

後赤壁賦

是歲十月之望，步自雪堂，將歸於臨皋。蘇軾年四十
七，在黃州寓居臨皋亭。就東坡築雪堂，自號東坡居士。二客從
予，過黃泥之坂。霜露既降，木葉盡脫。人影在
地，仰見明月。顧而樂之，行歌相答。已而歎
曰，有客無酒，有酒無肴，月白風清，如此良夜
何。客曰，今者薄暮，舉網得魚，巨口細鱗，狀
如松江之鱸，顧安所得酒乎。歸而謀諸婦，婦
曰，我有斗酒，藏之久矣。以待子不時之需。於
是攜酒與魚，復遊於赤壁之下。江流有聲，斷岸

千尺，山高月小，水落石出。曾日月之幾何，而
江山不可復識矣。予乃攝衣而上，履巉巖，披蒙
茸_{披，開也。蒙茸，草卉叢生也。}踞虎豹，登虯龍，攀栖鶻
之危巢，俯馮_{平。}夷之幽宮_{馮夷，水神。息于深淵之幽宮。}
蓋二客不能從焉。劃然長嘯，草木震動，山鳴谷
應，風起水湧。吾亦悄然而悲，肅然而恐，凜乎
其不可留也。反而登舟，放乎中流，聽其所止而
休焉。時夜將半，四顧寂寥，適有孤鶴，橫江東
來。翅如車輪，玄裳縞衣，戛然長鳴，掠予舟而
西也。須臾客去，予亦就睡。夢一道士，羽衣蹁
躚，過臨皋之下，揖予而言曰，赤壁之遊樂乎。
問其姓名，俛_{同俯}而不答。嗚呼噫嘻，我知之矣。
疇昔之夜，飛鳴而過我者，非子也耶。道士顧
笑，予亦驚寤，開戶視之，不見其處。

念奴嬌　赤壁懷古

大江東去，浪淘盡，千古風流人物。故壘西邊，人道是，三國周郎赤壁。亂石崩雲，驚濤裂岸，捲起千堆雪。江山如畫，一時多少豪傑。

遙想公瑾當年，小喬初嫁了，雄姿英發。羽扇綸巾，談笑間，強虜灰飛煙滅。故國神遊，多情應笑我，早生華髮。人間如夢，一樽還酹江月。

Lesson 35

朱熹，中庸章句序

中庸何爲而作也。子思子憂道學之失其傳而作也。蓋自上古聖神，繼天立極，而道統之傳有自來矣。其見於經，則「允執厥中」者，堯之所以授舜也。「人心惟危，道心惟微，惟精惟一，允執厥中」者，舜之所以授禹也。堯之一言，至矣盡矣，而舜復益之以三言者，則所以明夫堯之一言，必如是而後可庶幾也。

蓋嘗論之，心之虛靈知覺，一而已矣。而以爲有人心道心之異者，則以其或生於形氣之私，或原於性命之正，而所以爲知覺者不同，是以或危殆而不安，或微妙而難見耳。然人莫不有是形，故雖上智不能無人心，亦莫不有是性，故雖下愚不能無道心。二者雜於方寸之間，而不知所以治之，則危者愈危，微者愈微，而天理之公，卒無以勝夫人欲之私矣。精則察夫二者之間而不雜也，一則守其本心之正而不離也。從事於斯，無

少間斷，必使道心常爲一身之主，而人心每聽命
焉，則危者安，微者著，而動靜云爲，自無過不
及之差矣。

夫堯舜禹，天下之大聖也。以天下相傳，天下
之大事也。以天下之大聖行天下之大事，而其授
受之際丁寧告戒，不過如此，則天下之理，豈有
以加於此哉。自是以來，聖聖相承，若成湯文武
之爲君，皋陶伊傅周召之爲臣，既皆以此而接夫
道統之傳。若吾夫子，則雖不得其位，而所以繼
往聖，開來學，其功反有賢於堯舜者。然當是
時，見而知之者，惟顏氏曾氏之傳得其宗。及曾
氏之再傳，而復得夫子之孫子思，則去聖遠而異
端起矣。子思懼夫愈久而愈失其眞也。於是推本
堯舜以來相傳之意，質以平日所聞父師之言，更
互演繹，作爲此書，以詔後之學者。蓋其憂之也
深，故其言之也切。其慮之也遠，故其說之也
詳。其曰天命、率性則道心之謂也。其曰擇善固
執，則精一之謂也。其曰君子時中，則執中之謂
也。世之相後千有餘年，而其言之不異如合符
節。歷選前聖之書，所以提挈綱維，開示蘊奧，
未有若是其明且盡者也。

自是而又再傳以得孟氏，爲能推明是書，以承
先聖之統。及其沒而遂失其傳焉。則吾道之所
寄，不越乎言語文字之間，而異端之說日新月
盛，以至於老佛之徒出，則彌近理而大亂眞矣。

然而尚幸此書之不泯，故程夫子兄弟者出，得有所考，以續夫千載不傳之緒，得有所據，以斥夫二家似是之非。蓋子思之功於是為大，而微程夫子，則亦莫能因其語而得其心也。惜乎其所以為說者不傳，而凡石氏之所輯錄，僅出於其門人之所記，是以大義雖明，而微言未析。至其門人所自為說，則雖頗詳盡而多所發明，然倍其師說而淫於老佛者，亦有之矣。熹自蚤歲，即嘗受讀而竊疑之，沉潛反復，蓋亦有年，一旦恍然似有以得其要領者，然後乃敢會眾說而折其中。既為定著章句一篇，以俟後之君子，而一二同志，復取石氏書，刪其繁亂，名以輯略，且記所嘗論辯取舍之意，別為或問，以附其後。然後此書之旨，支分節解，脈絡貫通，詳略相因，巨細畢舉，而凡諸說之同異得失，亦得以曲暢旁通而各極其趣。雖於道統之傳不敢妄議，然初學之士或有取焉，則亦庶乎行遠升高之一助云爾。

　　　　　　淳熙己酉春三月戊申新安朱熹序

Appendixes

Appendix A

Issues in the Linguistic Aspects of Literary Chinese

Topic and Subject in Classical Chinese

Dingxu Shi

When we study a language, we usually classify the data into different groups and establish a field of inquiry for each group. In the field of *syntax*, we study the structures of phrases and sentences, constituent order, and structural changes. *Semantics* is the study of meaning at various levels. *Discourse analysis* investigates patterns of conversation and the overall organization of thoughts above the sentence level. Other fields are phonetics, phonology, and morphology.

The grammatical notion of subject-predicate discussed in this section describes the *semantic* relation among constituents in *wén yán* sentences and is similar to the corresponding English concept, with some definable differences.

> When the subject represents the *agent* of an action, the predicate represents the *action*.

> If the predicate is a *noun phrase*, the subject is usually an entity that is the *equivalent* of the predicate.

> When the predicate is an *adjective* (stative verb) phrase, the subject is the entity *described* by the predicate.

In the case of a *passive* sentence, the subject is the *patient* of
the passive verb; that is, it is the entity being affected by the
action.

The notion of subject-predicate applies to the *underlying* form of sentences in syntax. The underlying forms tell us how each *wén yán* sentence should be interpreted in terms of what happened to what or
which element is related to which. They may not appear in actual *wén
yán* texts. Indeed, the initial task in reading a *wén yán* text is to find
the underlying form for each sentence.

In some cases, the underlying subject-predicate form surfaces in
the normal form. The subject then occupies the sentence-initial position as the topic. This happens when the subject is what the writer
wants to talk about. In many cases, however, the abstract process of
topicalization moves part of the underlying sentence to the topic position—the initial position in the sentence—because that part is what the
writer wants to talk about. The rest of the sentence becomes the comment, namely, what the writer wants to say about the topic. For example, in English we can say the following sentence when certain contextual conditions are met:

John, I know.

The underlying form of the sentence can be represented as:

I know John.

and that is how we understand the sentence, with some subtle difference in meaning. The same can be said about many *wén yán* sentences.
In

汝之女吾已代嫁 (袁枚:《祭妹文》)

the topic 汝之女 is the object of the verb in the underlying sentence:

吾已代嫁汝之女

The underlying object is then moved to the topic position because it is
the entity the writer wants to talk about.

Sometimes, the writer inserts a *resumptive pronoun* 之 or 焉 into
the comment to mark the underlying position of the topic. In the topic-
comment construction

服領以南王自治之 《漢書, 西南夷兩粵朝鮮傳》

the topic 服領以南 is the object of the verb 治 in the underlying form, and its position is now occupied by the resumptive pronoun 之.

The issue of topicalization can be examined from a slightly different angle. When the *wén yán* writer constructs a sentence, he often starts with an entity that he picks up from the previous discourse and wants to discuss further. This entity will be written down as the first item in the sentence, that is, as the topic, and the further discussion will be the comment. The topic therefore represents old information, and the comment new information. The comment has the overall shape of a (subject-predicate) sentence, but the position that the topic would occupy in the underlying form is now empty or marked by a resumptive pronoun 之 or 焉.

Sometimes, a *wén yán* author talks about a particular entity in a consecutive sequence of sentences. Since this entity is the topic of all the sentences, it would be redundant and repetitive to write the topic in every sentence. Usually the author uses the topic only at the beginning of the sequence and simply adds more and more comments to the topic. In other words, the author creates a chain of comments that share the same topic. For example, in the following sequence of sentences, the topic 馬 is shared by four comments. 馬 is the possessor of 蹄 in the first comment and the possessor of 毛 in the second, but is the subject in the third and fourth comments:

馬，[ ]蹄可以踐霜雪，[ ]毛可以御風寒，[ ]齕草飲水，[ ]翹足而陸 《莊子, 馬蹄》

In the example below, the topic is the direct object of both comments, and its position is marked by the resumptive pronoun 之.

若是者，古謂之民賊，今謂之良臣 · (韓愈:《原毀》)

Generally speaking, topic-comment is the order in which ideas are presented in *wén yán* texts or the way in which the writer's thoughts flow in *wén yán* discourse. Subject-predicate is the framework for establishing the relationship among various constituents in a sentence and the format for coding the semantic content of each sentence in *wén yán* syntax. Each relation has its own domain of function, and the two are different facets of *wén yán* grammar.

Syntax and Phonology in Old Chinese

Most languages have a system of building words by affixation, that is, sounds attached to the beginnings, middles, or ends of words that add information to the root word.

> In English, the suffix "-s" is a standard way of indicating plural nouns: "one book"/ "many books."

> The suffix "-ed" signals the past tense: "Yesterday I talked with Jim."

> The prefix "re-" denotes repeated action: "She reshot the scene."

In most cases, the affixes are inflections that have regular grammatical functions (as in forming plurals or the past tense in English), and for many languages, "grammar" traditionally has been a matter of learning the right affix to add. Thus, when European scholars began to study Old Chinese, some believed the language lacked a grammar precisely because it had no obvious system of syntactically significant affixes.[1]

The modern study of Old Chinese, however, has uncovered patterns of sounds in the early language that offer tantalizing suggestions of a long-lost system of affixes. Many scholars who work in the field of historical phonology—the study of those early sound systems—have sought to systematize these hints. Even though a regular structure of case markings and verbal inflections has not been found—and few hold out hope for such a system—scholars have sought to identify word families and smaller, more local patterns of correlation between sound and meaning.

WORD FAMILIES

Word families are the other half of the story of affixation: they are the groups of words related to one another through affixes added to root words. In English, we have, for example:

> move   movement   removal   movie   . . .

---

1. Jerry Norman, *Chinese*, p. 84.

Two sets of patterns in Old Chinese suggest that a similar logic of word building through root + affix may have been at work. The first is the addition of a prefix *ɦ.[2] In some cases, it seems to turn transitive verbs into intransitives or passives:

見 *jiàn* < *kens "to see"　見 *xiàn* < *ɦkens "to appear"

敗 *bài* < *prats "to defeat"　敗 *bài* < *ɦprats "to be defeated"

In other cases, the role of the prefix is unclear:

朝 *zhāo* < *trjaw "morning"　朝 *cháo* < *ɦtrjaw "(morning ceremony:) audience, court, attend court"

間 *jiān* < *kren "interval, space between"　閑 *xián* < *ɦkren "(empty interval in time:) leisure"

夾 *jiā* < *krep "be on both sides, press between"　狹 *xiá* < *ɦkrep "narrow"

倉 *cāng* < *tshang "storeroom, granary"　藏 *cáng* < *ɦtshang "to hide"

The second pattern of word formation is the use of an *-s suffix, which seems to create nouns from verbs or verbs from nouns:[3]

傳 *chuán* < *dron "to transmit"　傳 *zhuàn* < *drons "a record"

研 *yán* < *ngen "to grind"　硯 *yàn* < *ngens "inkstone"

磨 *mó* < *maj "to grind"　磨 *mò* < *majs "grindstone"

納 *nà* < *nup "to bring in"　內 *nèi* < *nups "inside"

---

2. This discussion, including examples, translations, and reconstruction of Old Chinese, comes from William H. Baxter, *Handbook of Old Chinese Phonology*, Trends in Linguistics Studies and Monographs 64 (Berlin and New York: Mouton de Gruyter, 1992), pp. 218–20. In earlier discussions of this pattern, the distinction was between voiced and unvoiced initials in Middle Chinese.

3. These examples also come from Baxter, *Handbook of Old Chinese Phonology*, pp. 315–19. Earlier discussions of this pattern by and large pointed to the distinction between different tones in Middle Chinese, since the second member of each pair is a departing tone in modern Mandarin. In fact, Baxter uses the *-s suffix examples as part of his discussion of the historical development of the departing tone.

責 *zé* < *tsrek "to exact, demand payment"   債 *zhài* < *tsreks "debt"

塞 *sè* < *sɨk "to block"   塞 *sài* < *sɨks "border, frontier"

衣 *yī* < *ʔjɨj "clothing"   衣 *yì* < *ʔjɨjs "to wear, to clothe"

王 *wáng* < *wjang "king"   王 *wàng* < *wjangs "to be king"

These patterns of relationship have encouraged scholars to pay attention to other possible semantic or syntactic groupings encoded in the sound system of Old Chinese. In the study of late Old Chinese, Edwin Pulleyblank in particular has sought to tease out the connection between morphology, semantics, and syntax. The remainder of this essay discusses some aspects of the links Pulleyblank has proposed in his *Outline of Classical Chinese Grammar*.[4]

MORPHOLOGY, SEMANTICS, AND SYNTAX: SOME EXAMPLES

Pronouns

First-person pronouns can be divided into two groups: those beginning with a j- in Middle Chinese (the Archaic initial remains uncertain), and those beginning with ŋ-:[5]

1. 余 jɨ̌ã   予 jɨ̌ã'   台 jɨ   朕 drim[6]
2. 吾 ŋɔ   我 ŋa'   卬 ŋaŋ

Pulleyblank suggests that in Shang times group (1) represented singular and group (2) plural forms. However, if this pattern worked at all, it had already been blurred by early Zhou times.

The two pairs—余/予 and 吾/我—in the later Zhou perhaps marked a difference in *case*. That is, both 予 and 我 tend to appear only as the objects of verbs rather than as subjects. The data are not entirely conclusive, and a dispute about the exact nature of the distinc-

4. I treat the *Outline* as a summary of the sorts of patterns about which Pulleyblank feels reasonably certain.

5. The discussion of pronouns comes from Pulleyblank, *Outline*, pp. 76–78.

6. Pulleyblank speculates that 朕 *zhèn* had the same initial in Old Chinese. See Pulleyblank, *Outline*, n. 22, p. 164.

tion has simmered ever since Bernard Karlgren made the argument for case in 1920.

All second-person pronouns had the initial *n-, which corresponds to second-person pronouns in Tibeto-Burman. The readings, in Pulleyblank's reconstruction of Early Middle Chinese are:

爾 ɲiă'   汝 ɲiă'   而 ɲi   若 ɲiak   乃 ɲəj'   戎 ɲuwŋ

Again, the exact distinctions being made remain elusive. 而, for example, seems to have been used only as the object of verbs, whereas 爾 and 汝 appear in both subject and object positions.

Negatives

Consider the two sets of characters:

  1a. 不 puw   verb negation

   b. 弗 put   verb negation + aspect (?) > fusion of 不 + 之

   c. 非 puj   negation of noun (identity)

   d. 否 puw'   "no"

  2a. 無 muă   "there is no . . ." or "do not . . .";
     毋 mum   "do not . . ."

   b. 勿 mut   "do not . . ." + aspect (?) > fusion of 毋 + 之;
     蔑 mɛt   "there is no . . ." + aspect (?)

   c. 微 muj   contrafactual function word, "were it not that . . ."

   d. 未 muj^h aspectual negative, "not yet"

   e. 亡 muaŋ   "there is no/none"

   f. 罔 muaŋ' "there is no . . ."

   g. 莫 mak   negative distributive, "in no case . . ."

Negatives in Old Chinese had either *p- or *m- initials. Pulleyblank suggests two correspondences between the groups. First, 勿 is related to 毋 as 弗 is to 不. Initially, the distinction may have been one of aspect, but by the Warring States period, the final *-t in 勿 and 弗 seems to have been taken as the trace of 之 (tɕiǎ/ tɕi) in a fusion.[7] Second, Pulleyblank proposes that 非 (puj) comes from 不 (puw) + 唯 (惟, 維, jwi), the most common copular word, and 微 (muj) comes from *m- + 唯; this correspondence helps to explain the occasional use of 微 as a phrase-initial contrafactual negative function word.

Quantifiers

Many scholars have noted that all the "distributive" quantifiers—adverbs indicating how many of the participants took part in the action of the verb—share a final *-k:

孰 dʐuwk   "which"

各 kak   "each"

或 ɣwək   "in some cases"

莫 mak   "in no case"

The consistency of the *-k final is surely not a coincidence, but given our knowledge of Old Chinese, it is difficult to make further connections between this group and other phonological/syntactic regularities in the language. Nonetheless, it is extremely useful to realize that the first entry, 孰 "which," belongs to this group: its semantic role at times seems to border on the interrogative pronoun 誰 "who," but its syntax as a preverbal modifier follows the same pattern as 各 and 莫.

Complements

WHAT ARE COMPLEMENTS?

Modern Chinese has complements. English has complements. And, in fact, literary Chinese does have the usual sorts of structure we tend to call complements. To understand why this textbook avoids the term, however, we need to clarify the terminology and look in somewhat greater detail at the structures in question.

---

7. This proposal has a long history, with scholars arguing both for and against. For an overview, see Pulleyblank's "Some Notes on Morphology and Syntax in Classical Chinese," in Henry Rosemont, Jr., ed., *Chinese Texts and Philosophical Contexts: Essays Dedicated to Angus C. Graham* (La Salle, Ill.: Open Court, 1991), pp. 34–41.

Complements, as the name suggests, are phrases or words that *complete* a syntactic structure. For example, prepositional phrases in English and other Indo-European languages consist of a preposition and its complement (1). And the entire prepositional phrase in turn can be the complement of a verb (2):

1. "under" + "the bed"

2. "swept under the bed"

Notice that "swept" *can* take an object:

3. "swept the floor"

In (2), however, the prepositional phrase fills the slot in the phrase required by the verb "swept." That is, "He swept" is a dubious sentence in English, and *something*—either a complement or a direct object—must come after the verb for the sentence to sound right.

To give a more formal definition of complements, we can turn to x-bar theory in modern generative grammar.[8] The basic structure of phrases in x-bar theory looks like:

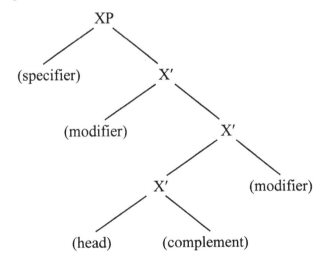

8. Keith Brown and Jim Miller, *Syntax: A Linguistic Introduction to Sentence Structure* (Hammersmith, Eng.: Harper Collins, 1991) provides a good, brief overview of x-bar theory.

The "X" can be either a noun, verb, adjective, or preposition. What the diagram seeks to explain is the hierarchical structure that results when more and more elements are added to a phrase and the ways in which these additions behave and are constrained. For example, we have "that big black dog that ate Billy's homework last night:"

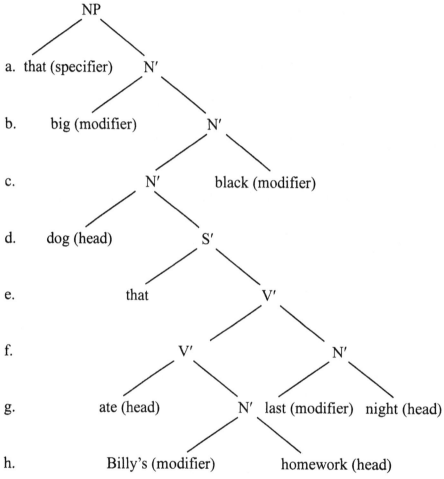

In this framework, the complement of "ate" (level g)—the item "closest" to it and most strongly controlled by it—is the noun phrase "Billy's homework." That is, in this particular case, the complement happens to be the direct object. Verbs in English, as it turns out, have a broader range of complements than nouns, adjectives, or prepositions. Noun complements tend to be limited to such expressions as the "thought *that he might lose*," "the argument *about locatives*," and so on. Adjectives have a similar range: "suspicious *of locatives*," "regretful *about losing*," etc. Prepositions can have nouns, sentences, or other prepositional phrases as their complement: "after *dinner*," "after *John had eaten*," or "out *into the garden*."

NOUN AND ADJECTIVE COMPLEMENTS

In literary Chinese, most questions about complements—particularly for nouns and adjectives—are largely matters of terminology. In English, most complements for nouns and adjectives are simply transformations of similar structures for verbs. That is, "the thought that he might lose" comes from "think that he might lose," "regretful about losing" from "regret losing," and so on. In literary Chinese, the verb phrase itself can be used in either a nominal or a modifier position, and predicate adjectives (he *is doubtful* . . .) are verbs.

> 4. 何由知吾可也   By what do [you] know I can?

The sentence 吾可 is the complement of 知.[9] Since objects are nouns directly governed by verbs, only nouns can be objects; everything else must be a complement. However, if the point of teaching grammar is to heighten awareness of the larger structuring processes in the language, this distinction does not seem strong enough to merit the introduction of new terminology. Consider the verb phrases:

> 5. 知之   know it
>
> 6. 知其可   know his being able
>
> 7. 知吾可   know I can

In (5) and (6), 知 takes an object, a single noun: this textbook calls 吾可 in (7) an object as well.

PREPOSITIONAL COMPLEMENTS

Literary Chinese has no prepositions. Instead, the functions fulfilled by prepositions in other languages are realized by coverbs and locative objects. As with the sentential complements of verbs like 知, this text-

---

9. Neither 孟子 nor 莊子 seems to use sentences as the object of the verbs 信, "to believe," or 疑 "to suspect."

book treats all phrases that are complements of coverbs as their objects. The reasons remain the same: first, to stress the underlying commonalities in the structures of ever more complex sentences, and second, to keep terminology as simple as possible.

VERBAL COMPLEMENTS

This textbook follows a simple rule: if a phrase "behaves" like an object, then it *is* an object. In English, we can say:

> I know this.

> I know where your brother works.

For the purposes of this textbook, "where your brother works" occupies the position of the object of "know" and therefore is its object.

Although this principle reduces the number of issues to be confronted, there still remain two major categories of complements that must be considered: the locative and the resultative.

Locative Complements

In English we can say

> My daughter leaned against me.

but not

> *My daughter leaned.

That is, in English certain verbs require a locative phrase. It so happens that in English, this locative element is expressed as a prepositional phrase, and thus the phrase is termed the "locative complement." In literary Chinese, no preposition is needed before the noun in similar cases. One can say either

> 居堯之宮   reside in Yáo's palace

> 居於王所   reside at the king's residence

The difference is that 於王所 has an explicit locative marking, and 堯之宮 does not.

In literary Chinese, locatives are optionally marked by either 於, 于, or 乎. Wei Peiquan, Alain Peyraube, and Edwin Pulleyblank treat these three characters as coverbs or prepositions more or less on par with such characters as 以, 與, 自, which can also appear either before or after the verb. I suggest that in fact even by the time of late Old Chinese, the locative markers had become fully grammaticalized in a way that the coverbs had not and that the locative markers are a syntactically separate group. First, no coverb has the optional quality of locative markers. When one considers the frequency of use of markers with such verbs as 入, 出, 至, 居 , it becomes clear that in cases in which the thematic role of the object is unambiguous (that is, it is a locative rather than direct object), the marker is indeed optional. Second, coverbs regularly appear in the structure 所 + coverb + main verb, but there are only a few examples of 所于 in the early texts.[10] That is, the locative markers had ceased to be viewed as verbal in nature and had instead become fully grammaticalized function words.

Is a "locative object" then truly an object? Given the principle that "if it behaves like an object, then it is an object," locative phrases are in fact best treated as objects. Two types of behavior are worth particular mention as demonstrating why it is more useful to treat direct and locative objects as subsets of a larger category than to make an unwarranted distinction. First, both direct and locative objects can be represented through 所 constructions:

所欲 　what one desires

所之 　where it goes

Second, both direct and locative objects can be represented through 相 constructions:

相及 　reach one another (locative)

相助 　help one another (direct)

Moreover, one occasionally discovers—even after many years of reading—that what one thought was a transitive verb in fact takes a locative object instead. That is, in a reliable text by a literate author one

---

10. 莊子, for example, has 无所於忤, 无所於逆, 生有所乎萌, and 死有所乎歸.

discovers a locative marker before the verb's object. Given these ways in which direct objects and locative constructions blend together, there is more to be gained than lost in considering both as types of a larger category of object.[11]

As a final note, however, there may still be an important place for "locative complement" as a category. Consider the difference between the following pairs of sentences:

He leaned on the banister.

*On the banister he leaned.

and

I ate a late dinner at the hotel.

At the hotel I ate a late dinner.

"On the banister he leaned" is not allowed because the locative phrase is closely bound to the verb and cannot be moved. "At the hotel" is not part of the core of the sentence (the nuclear sentence) and therefore can be shifted. For understanding the syntax of literary Chinese, the question is whether all verbs have an optional slot available for a locative object (in which case, the locative object is always part of the nuclear sentence), or whether the locative element is determined at the level of the sentence. Perhaps the best test of this distinction is the limits of 所 constructions. Zhuang Zi replied to his friend Hui Zi,

我知之濠上也　I know it on the Hao [River].

Would such a sentence as

我所知之者濠上也　Where I know it is on the Hao River.

be considered acceptable? If not, then 濠上 should be deemed a locative complement. My own sense, no better than an intuition and therefore easily subject to persuasion by examples, is that in fact the sentence is at least marginally acceptable.

<hr />

11. Yáng Bójùn 楊伯峻 and Hé Lèshì 何樂士 in 古漢語語法及其發展 (北京: 語文, 1992) treat unmarked locative complements as locative objects; see p. 534.

Resultative, Purposive, and Descriptive Complements

Modern Chinese has an important construction called the resultative:

我吃飽了   I have eaten [to the extent that I'm] full.

The second verb (飽) is a resultative complement. In this particular instance, the verbs look as if they simply were in coordinate relation: "I eat (with the result that) I am full." But consider the sentence

你嚇死我   You scared me [so that] I [almost] died.

The relation between "scare" 嚇 and "die" 死 cannot be simple coordination because "die" is intransitive, whereas the compound clearly takes an object, "me" 我.[12] The question, then, is whether literary Chinese has similar features that compel one to distinguish between coordinate verbs and resultative complements. The results of this particular line of research seem to suggest not.[13]

One candidate for status as a verb complement is a serial verb construction in which the second verb is introduced by 以:

列子入以告壺子   Liè Zǐ entered to announce it to Hú Zǐ.

This would be analogous to such English sentences as "I went to the store to buy some milk," in which "to buy some milk"—with the verb as an infinitive—is the purposive complement. However, the structure in literary Chinese probably arose as a fusion of 以之 "by means of this," in which the "this" points back to the first verb. The result is a coordinate structure, "V_1 *and, by means of this,* V_2."

---

12. Mei Zulin has looked in detail at the period in which this aspect of resultative constructions begins to appear. See Méi Zǔlín 梅祖麟, 〈從漢代的「動、殺」「動、死」來看動補結構的發展—論中古時期的起詞的施受關係的中立化〉. 語言學論叢 16 (1991), pp. 112–36. His work, in turn, is based on the earlier studies by Ōta Tatsuo 太田辰夫 and Shimura Ryōji 志村良治.

13. Both Mei's work and Cao Guangshun's more recent research suggest that true resultatives began to appear in the spoken language in the late Six Dynasties or more probably in the Táng. See Cáo Guǎngshùn 曹廣順, 近代漢語助詞. 北京: 語文, 1995.

One final possible form of verb complement is what Pulleyblank calls a descriptive complement introduced by either 如 or 猶 (sometimes written as 由):

民歸之由水之就下　　(1) The people will turn to him like water going downward [Pulleyblank]. (2) The people's turning to him will be like water's going downward.

Pulleyblank argues that the absense of a final 也 suggests that 由水之就下 is not an independent predicate.[14] Yet 孟子 also has the sentence:

仁之勝不仁也猶水之勝火　The benevolent's defeating the not-benevolent is like water's defeating fire.

in which the phrase introduced by the 猶 clearly is the predicate. That is, such sentences strongly resemble an ordinary topic-comment structure, and what Pulleyblank takes to be the nuclear sentence becomes a nominalized topic. Pulleyblank may be correct, but the equivocal nature of the evidence does not at present justify the addition of a new category to this textbook's account of syntax.

14. Pulleyblank, *Outline*, p. 57.

Appendix B

Dynastic Timeline, Maps, and Measures

The Dynastic Timeline

The Legendary Emperors

伏羲	Fú Xi
神農	Shén Nóng
黃帝	Huáng Dì
唐帝堯	Táng Dì Yáo
虞帝舜	Yú Dì Shùn

The Sandai 三代

夏 Xià (before 2400 B.C.)[1]
   禹　　Yǔ, the sage founder
   桀　　Jié, the bad last emperor
商 Shāng (before 1700–1045 B.C.) also known as 殷 Yīn
   成湯　Chéng Tāng (before 1700 B.C.), the sage founder
   紂　　Zhòu (1087–1045 B.C.) the bad last emperor
周 Zhōu (1045–255 B.C.)
   西周　Western Zhōu (1045–771 B.C.)
   武王　Wǔ Wáng (1045–1043 B.C.)

---

1. The rough dates for the founding of the Xià and Shāng dynasties come from Kwang-chih Chang, *Shang Civilization* (New Haven: Yale University Press, 1980). The nature of the Xià and early Shāng "states" is still much debated.

成王　Chéng Wáng (1042–1006 B.C.)
　　周公　Regency of Duke of Zhou and
　　召公　Duke of Shào (Wǔ Wáng's brothers)
東周　Eastern Zhōu (770–255 B.C.)
　　春秋　Spring and Autumn Period (770–403 B.C.)
　　戰國　Warring States Period (403–255 B.C.)

Early Imperial China

秦　Qín (255–206 B.C.)

漢　Hàn (206 B.C.–A.D. 220)
　　西漢　Western Hàn (206 B.C.–A.D. 25)
　　王莽　Wáng Mǎng, the usurper (A.D. 8–23)
　　東漢　Eastern Hàn (25–220)

魏　Wèi (220–65)
　　三國　The Three Kingdoms Period (魏 Wèi, 蜀漢 Shǔ Hàn,
　　　　吳 Wú)

晉　Jìn (265–420)
　　西晉　Western Jìn (265–317)
　　東晉　Eastern Jìn (317–420): more accurately, the Jìn was re-
　　　　established south of the Yangtze

The Northern and Southern Dynasties: 南北朝

宋　Sòng (420–79), also called the 劉宋 Liú Sòng

齊　Qí (479–502), also called the 南齊 Southern Qí

梁　Liáng (502–57)

陳　Chén (557–89)

Imperial China

隋　　Suí (589–618)

唐　　Táng (618–907)

五代　The Five Dynasties (907–960)

宋　　Sòng (960–1280)

　　北宋　Northern Song (960–1127)

In the south
南宋　Southern Sòng
(1127–1280)

元　Yuán (1280–1368)

明　Míng (1368–1644)

清　Qīng (1644–1912)

In the north
金　Jīn (1115–1260)

元　Yuán (1260–1368)

The Calendrical Cycle

天干 STEMS	地支 BRANCHES
甲 *jiǎ*	子 *zǐ*
乙 *yǐ*	丑 *chǒu*
丙 *bǐng*	寅 *yín*
丁 *dīng*	卯 *mǎo*
戊 *wù*	辰 *chén*
己 *jǐ*	巳 *sì*
庚 *gēng*	午 *wǔ*
辛 *xīn*	未 *wèi*
壬 *rēn*	申 *shēn*
癸 *guǐ*	酉 *yǒu*
	戌 *xū*
	亥 *hài*

The Sixty-Year Cycle

	0–	1–	2–	3–	4–	5–
-1	甲子	甲戌	甲申	甲午	甲辰	甲寅
-2	乙丑	乙亥	乙酉	乙未	乙巳	乙卯
-3	丙寅	丙子	丙戌	丙申	丙午	丙辰
-4	丁卯	丁丑	丁亥	丁酉	丁未	丁巳
-5	戊辰	戊寅	戊子	戊戌	戊申	戊午
-6	己巳	己卯	己丑	己亥	己酉	己未
-7	庚午	庚辰	庚寅	庚子	庚戌	庚申
-8	辛未	辛巳	辛卯	辛丑	辛亥	辛酉
-9	壬申	壬午	壬辰	壬寅	壬子	壬戌
-0	癸酉	癸未	癸巳	癸卯	癸丑	癸亥

Measurements[2]

Measure	Equivalence	周，春秋，戰國
Length		
寸		2.25 cm
咫	8 寸	18.0 cm
尺	10 咫	22.5 cm
步	6 尺	1.125 m
仞	7 尺	1.575 m
尋	8 尺	1.80 m
丈	10 尺	2.25 m
里	300 步	405.0 m
Area		
畝	100 方步	182.0 m^2
頃	100 畝	4.5 acres
Weight		
銖		0.67 g
兩	24 銖	16.0 g
斤	16 兩	256.0 g
鈞	30 斤	7.68 kg
Volume		
合		19.4 ml
升	10 合	194 ml
豆	4 升	776 ml
斗	10 升	1.94 l
斛	10 斗	19.4 l
鍾	256 升	49.66 l

2. This chart is adapted from Ogawa Tamaki 小川環樹 et al., *Shinjigen* 新字源 (Tokyo: Kakugawa 角川, 1969), p. 1225.

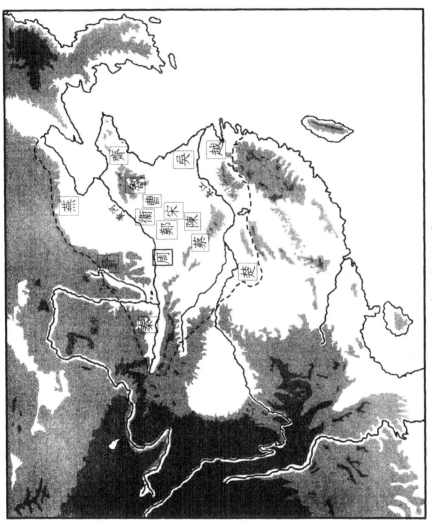

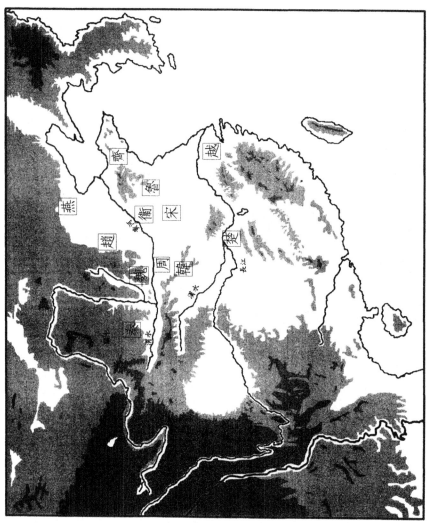

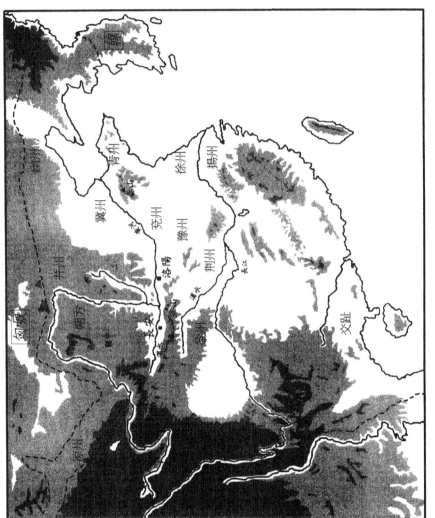

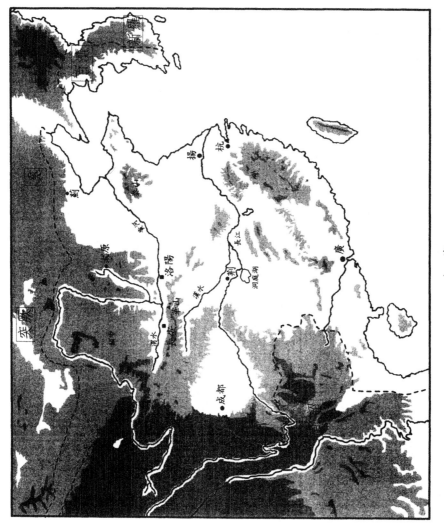

Appendix C

Romanizations and Radicals

Initials

Pinyin	Wade-Giles	注音符號	Pronunciation
b-	p-	ㄅ -	the *b* in "bee"
c-	ts'-	ㄘ -	*ca* is like the *tsa* in "It's a . . ."
ci	tz'u	ㄘ	the *ts* in "its"
ch-	ch'-	ㄔ -	the *ch* in "chuck"
chi	ch'ih	ㄔ	the *chur* in "church"
d-	t-	ㄉ -	the *d* in "dim"
f-	f-	ㄈ -	
g-	k-	ㄍ -	the *g* in "go"
h-	h-	ㄏ -	
ji-	chi-	ㄐ -	the *jea* in "jeans"
ju-	chü-	ㄐ ㄩ -	the *dju* in "adjudicate"
k-	k'-	ㄎ -	the *c* in "cog"
l-	l-	ㄌ -	
m-	m-	ㄇ -	
n	n-	ㄋ -	
p-	p'-	ㄆ -	the *p* in "pump"
qi-	ch'i-	ㄑ -	the *chee* in cheese

Pinyin	Wade-Giles	注音符號	Pronunciation
qu-	ch'ü-	ㄑㄩ-	the *tchyou* in "match you"
r-	j-	ㄖ-	the *r* in "run"
s-	s-	ㄙ-	
si	ssu	ㄙ	the *ss* in "hiss"
sh-	sh-	ㄕ-	
shi	shih	ㄕ	the *shir* in "shirt"
t-	t'	ㄊ-	the *t* in "tea"
w-	w-	ㄨ-	
x-	hs-	ㄒ-	halfway between the *s* in "sea" and *sh* in "she"
z-	ts-	ㄗ-	*ze* is like the *ddsu* in "adds up"
zi	tzu	ㄗ	the *dds* in "adds"
zh-	ch-	ㄓ-	the *j* in "judge"
zhi	chih	ㄓ	the *jer* in "jerk"

Vowels

Pinyin	Wade-Giles	注音符號	Pronunciation
-a	-a	ㄚ	the *a* in "father"
-ai	-ai	ㄞ	
-an	-an	ㄢ	
-ang	-ang	ㄤ	
-ao	-ao	ㄠ	
-e	-e,-o	ㄜ	as in "uh"
-ei	-ei	ㄟ	
-en	-en	ㄣ	
-eng	-eng	ㄥ	

Pinyin	Wade-Giles	注音符號	Pronunciation
er	erh	ㄦ	the *ar* in "far"
-i	-i, -ih	ㄧ	the *ea* in "seat," except in the cases below
	-ih	[ ]	in *zhi, chi, shi, ri*
	-u	[ ]	in *zi, ci, si*
-ia	-ia	ㄧㄚ	
-ian	-ien	ㄧㄢ	
-iang	-iang	ㄧㄤ	
-iao	-iao	ㄧㄠ	
-ie	-ieh	ㄧㄝ	
-in	-in	ㄧㄣ	
-ing	-ing	ㄧㄥ	
-iu	-iu	ㄧㄡ	
-o	-o, -uo	ㄛ	as in "woe"
-ong	-ung	ㄨㄥ	
-ou	-ou	ㄡ	
-u	-u,	ㄨ	the *oo* in "loon" except for the cases below
	-ü	ㄩ	in *ju, qu,* and *xu*
-ua	-ua	ㄨㄚ	
-uai	-uai	ㄨㄞ	
-uan	-uan	ㄨㄢ	
-uang	-uang	ㄨㄤ	
-ui	-ui	ㄨㄟ	

Pinyin	Wade-Giles	注音符號	Pronunciation
-un	-un	ㄨㄣ	
-uo	-uo	ㄨㄛ	
-ü	-ü	ㄩ	
-üan	-üan	ㄩㄢ	
-üe	-üeh	ㄩㄝ	
-un	-un	ㄨㄣ	
-un	-un	ㄨㄣ	

Radicals for Chinese Characters

Below is a list of the 214 traditional radicals. In most cases, the radical indicates some broad category of meaning. This meaning may differ from that of the word itself. 方 is a good example: the word itself means a region or category, but many words with it as a radical mean "a flag" or "a pennant" of one sort or another. In some cases, however, the evolution of a character—and particularly its conventionalization into 楷書 form—has obscured its original signifying elements. In these cases, the early lexicographers identified the character with a radical primarily as a convenience. Some radicals in fact are formal elements that have no particular meaning, or the relationship of their early meaning to the meanings of the characters grouped under them is very loose. I use parentheses ( ) to indicate such merely formal roles or looseness of meaning.

一畫

1	一	*yī*	one > numbers
2	丨	*gǔn*	(down-stroke)
3	丶	*zhǔ*	(dot)
4	丿	*piě*	(slanting stroke)
5	乙 乚	*yǐ*	(bent pattern)
6	亅	*jué*	(hooked stroke)

二畫

7	二	*èr*	(paired strokes)
8	亠	*tóu*	(top stroke)
9	人 亻	*rén*	person
10	儿	*rén*	person (kneeling)
11	入	*rù*	entrance
12	八	*bā*	to split; table
13	冂	*jiōng*	(3-sided stroke)
14	冖	*mì*	covering
15	冫	*bīng*	ice
16	几	*jǐ*	low table > set on
17	凵	*jū*	(open container)
18	刀 刂	*dāo*	knife
19	力	*lì*	strength
20	勹	*bāo*	to wrap, cover
21	匕	*bǐ*	spoon, ladle
22	匚	*fāng*	box
23	匸	*xì*	to partition, hide
24	十	*shí*	(crossed strokes)
25	卜	*bǔ*	divination
26	卩	*jié*	(kneeling; a tally)
27	厂	*hǎn*	cliff
28	厶	*sī*	(private self = 私)
29	又	*yòu*	to take with hand

三畫

30	口	*kǒu*	mouth
31	囗	*wéi*	enclosure
32	土	*tǔ*	earth, dirt
33	士	*shì*	(man)
34	夂	*zhǐ*	to descend
35	夊	*suī*	(a foot)
36	夕	*xī*	dusk > night
37	大	*dà*	big
38	女	*nǚ*	female
39	子	*zǐ*	child
40	宀	*mián*	roof > dwelling
41	寸	*cùn*	(the palm, hand)
42	小	*xiǎo*	small

43	尢兀	*wāng*	lame
44	尸	*shī*	corpse, body
45	屮	*chè*	a sprout
46	山	*shān*	mountain
47	巛川	*chuān*	river
48	工	*gōng*	work, labor
49	己	*jǐ*	(thread tip; self)
50	巾	*jīn*	strip of cloth
51	干	*gān*	(encroach; stem)
52	幺	*yāo*	very small
53	广	*yǎn*	building
54	廴	*yǐn*	road ≈ 彳
55	廾	*gǒng*	to lift up, present
56	弋	*yì*	a stake
57	弓	*gōng*	bow
58	彐	*jì*	beak, bill, snout
59	彡	*shān*	brilliant pattern
60	彳	*chì*	road, travel

四畫

61	心忄小	*xīn*	heart
62	戈	*gē*	halberd
63	戶	*hù*	door
64	手扌	*shǒu*	hand
65	支	*zhī*	to hold; to separate
66	攴攵	*pū*	to beat with a club
67	文	*wén*	pattern
68	斗	*dǒu*	measuring
69	斤	*jīn*	axe
70	方	*fāng*	banners
71	无旡	*wú*	(stuffed, stifled)
72	日	*rì*	sun
73	曰	*yuē*	(mouth + tongue)
74	月	*yuè*	moon
75	木	*mù*	tree
76	欠	*qiàn*	yawn
77	止	*zhǐ*	footstep
78	歹	*è (dǎi)*	wound, death
79	殳	*shū*	staff, stave

80	毋	*wú*	(mother)
81	比	*bǐ*	(lined up)
82	毛	*máo*	fur
83	氏	*shì*	clan
84	气	*qì*	air, vapor
85	水 氵	*shuǐ*	water
86	火 灬	*huǒ*	fire
87	爪	*zhǎo*	claw
88	父	*fù*	father
89	爻	*yáo*	(cross-hatch)
90	爿	*qiáng*	platform > bed
91	片	*piàn*	plank
92	牙	*yǎ*	tooth
93	牛	*niú*	ox
94	犬 犭	*quǎn*	dog

五畫

95	玄	*xuán*	dark, obscure
96	玉 王	*yù*	jade, precious stone
97	瓜	*guā*	melon, gourd
98	瓦	*wǎ*	pottery
99	甘	*gān*	sweetness
100	生	*shēng*	life
101	用	*yòng*	(to use)
102	田	*tián*	farm field
103	疋	*yǎ*	bolt of cloth
104	疒	*chuáng*	sickness
105	癶	*bō*	(to step)
106	白	*bái*	white
107	皮	*pí*	skin
108	皿	*mǐn*	platter
109	目	*mù*	eye
110	矛	*máo*	spear
111	矢	*shǐ*	arrow
112	石	*shí*	stone
113	示 礻	*shì*	altar > ceremony
114	内	*róu*	(paws and tail)
115	禾	*hé*	grain
116	穴	*xuè*	cave, hole
117	立	*lì*	to set up

六畫

118	竹	*zhú*	bamboo
119	米	*mǐ*	rice
120	糸	*mì (sī)*	silk
121	缶	*fǒu*	bottle
122	网 ⺲⺳	*wǎng*	net
123	羊	*yáng*	goat, sheep
124	羽	*yǔ*	feather
125	老	*lǎo*	old person
126	而	*ér*	(beard)
127	耒	*lěi*	plough
128	耳	*ěr*	ear
129	聿	*yù*	brush, pen
130	肉 月 ⺼	*ròu, rù*	meat, flesh
131	臣	*chén*	(eyes open)
132	自	*zì*	nose > self
133	至	*zhì*	arrive
134	臼	*jiù (jú)*	mortar (2 hand lift)
135	舌	*shé*	tongue
136	舛	*chuǎn*	(two hands)
137	舟	*zhōu*	boat
138	艮	*gèn*	(distressed)
139	色	*sè*	appearance
140	艸 ⺾	*cǎo*	grass
141	虎 ⻁	*hǔ*	tiger
142	虫	*huǐ*	bugs
143	血	*xuè*	blood
144	行	*xíng*	travel, road
145	衣 ⻂	*yī*	clothing
146	西 ⻃	*yà (xǐ)*	drape over

七畫

147	見	*jiàn*	to see
148	角	*jué*	horn
149	言	*yán*	to speak
150	谷	*gǔ*	valley
151	豆	*dòu*	bean
152	豕	*shǐ*	pig

153	豸	*zhì*	nimble animals
154	貝	*bèi*	cowry > wealth
155	赤	*chì*	red
156	走	*zǒu*	to run
157	足	*zú*	foot
158	身	*shēn*	body
159	車	*jū*	cart
160	辛	*xīn*	crime, verdict
161	辰	*chén*	farming
162	辵辶	*chuò*	movement
163	邑右阝	*yì*	settlement, town
164	酉	*yǒu*	brewing
165	釆	*biàn*	to pull apart
166	里	*lǐ*	(village)

八畫

167	金	*jīn*	metal
168	長	*cháng*	long (hair)
169	門	*mén*	gate
170	阜左阝	*fù*	mound
171	隶	*dài*	to seize
172	隹	*zhuī*	short-tailed bird
173	雨	*yǔ*	rain > weather
174	青	*qīng*	blue, green
175	非	*fēi*	(denial)

九畫

176	面	*miàn*	face
177	革	*gé*	hides, leather
178	韋	*wéi*	tanned leather
179	韭	*jiǔ*	scallion
180	音	*yīn*	sound
181	頁	*yè*	head (and neck)
182	風	*fēng*	wind
183	飛	*fēi*	to fly
184	食	*shí*	to eat
185	首	*shǒu*	head
186	香	*xiāng*	fragrance

十 畫

187	馬	*mǎ*	horse
188	骨	*gǔ*	bone
189	高	*gāo*	(high place)
190	髟	*biāo*	hair
191	鬥	*dòu*	struggle
192	鬯	*chàng*	fragrant (wine)
193	鬲	*lì*	caldron
194	鬼	*guǐ*	ghost, spirit

十一畫

195	魚	*yú*	fish
196	鳥	*niǎo*	bird
197	鹵	*lǔ*	salt
198	鹿	*lù*	deer
199	麥	*mò*	barley
200	麻	*má*	hemp

十二畫

201	黃	*huáng*	yellow
202	黍	*shǔ*	millet
203	黑	*hēi*	black
204	黹	*zhǐ*	embroidery

十三畫

205	黽	*mǐn*	turtle
206	鼎	*dǐng*	tripod caldron
207	鼓	*gǔ*	drum
208	鼠	*shǔ*	rat

十四畫

209	鼻	*bí*	nose
210	齊	*qí*	evenly arrayed

十五畫

211	齒	*chǐ*	teeth

十六畫

| 212 | 龍 | *lóng* | dragon |
| 213 | 龜 | *guī* | tortoise |

十七畫

| 214 | 龠 | *yuè* | flute |

Appendix D

Glossary of Function Words

"Function words" are characters that have been grammaticalized; that is, they are nouns and verbs that have lost their full semantic weight and have come to serve specialized syntactic functions in literary Chinese. These include coverbs and auxiliaries, which are only partly grammaticalized (that is, we still see them as verbs with meanings closely related to their full verbal usage). The category also contains fully grammaticalized characters like 也. In keeping with the conventional understanding of *xū cí* 虛詞, "empty" (i.e., function) words, I also list characters that have acquired complex functions based more on rhetorical rather than syntactic conventions. The first entry, 一, is an example of this sort of function word.

This glossary is by no means a complete list of function words.[1] Nor does it fully exhaust the range of possibilities for the entries that

---

1. This glossary is built on the list of function words in Zhū Zìqīng 朱自清, Yè Shèngtáo 葉聖陶, and Lǚ Shúxiāng 呂叔湘, *Wényán dúběn* 文言讀本 (Shanghai: Shanghai Jiaoyu, 1980). For convenience and because I found their account judicious, I began with their explanations and examples. I then confirmed the usage by consulting Gāo Shùfán 高樹藩, ed., *Wényánwén xūcí dàcídiǎn* 文言文虛詞大詞典 (Wuhan: Hubei Jiaoyu, 1991); and Liú Qí 劉淇, *Zhùzì biànluè* 助字辨略 (reprinted—Kyoto: Chūbun, 1983). I also consulted the list of function words in Ogawa Tamaki 小川環樹 et al., *Shin jigen* 新字源; and the entries in Morohashi Tetsuji 諸橋轍次, ed., *Dai Kanwa jiten* 大漢和辭典 and the *Hànyǔ dà cídiǎn* 漢語大詞典 (Hong Kong: Sanlian, 1987–95). I also thank Ms. Wu Yushan—for her help in getting me started on this project by translating (and entering) the first half of

are included. I have tried to prevent proliferation of the subcategories of meaning. In particular, I have tried to distinguish between semantic and syntactical differences. Since many important subcategories of semantic distinctions can be grouped under a single syntactic function, I have chosen not to make the syntactic roles for the function words unreasonably complex and multivalent.[2] The entries are arranged by number of strokes, but an index by pronunciation is also provided.

Pronunciation Index Of Function Words

ān	安	306	*ěr*	爾	328	*huì*	會	326
bèi	輩	328	*fán*	凡	297	*huò*	或	311
bǐ	彼	309	*fāng*	方	298	*jī*	幾	322
	俾	317	*fēi*	非	310	*jí*	及	298
bì	比	298	*fěi*	匪	317		即	314
bìng	並	312	*fǒu*	否	309	*jǐ*	幾	323
	并	312	*fú*	夫	298	*jì*	既	321
céng	曾	325		弗	301		幾	323
chā	差	318	*fù*	復	325	*jiàn*	見	308
cháng	嘗	327	*gài*	蓋	327	*jiāng*	將	319
chéng	誠	327	*gēng*	更	307	*jiǎ*	假	321
chū	初	310	*gèng*	更	307	*jiē*	皆	316
chúi	垂	316	*gǒu*	苟	314	*jiè*	藉	330
cǐ	此	303	*gù*	固	310		借	330
cóng	從	321		故	301	*jìn*	浸	325
dài	殆	315		顧	330		浸	325
dàn	但	308	*guǒ*	果	311	*jù*	詎	323
dì	第	322	*hé*	何	306		巨	323
dìng	定	310		曷	317		渠	323
dú	獨	329		盍	317	*jué*	厥	325
ér	而	303	*hū*	乎	299	*kě*	可	301
ěr	耳	305	*hú*	胡	317	*kuàng*	況	311

the *Wényán dúběn* list—and the Chiang Ching-kuo Foundation for providing the funds for hiring Ms. Wu.

2. The 文言文大詞典, for example, gives 之 the syntactic functions of 則, 而, 以, 於, 與, and 且. In many cases, the authors attempt to catch shades of meaning without worrying about the anarchy they impute to literary Chinese as a language.

lìng	令	301	*tǎng*	倘	318	*yì*	益	318
měi	每	307		儻	318	*yīn*	因	305
mí	彌	330	*tè*	特	318	*yōng*	庸	319
mǐ	靡	330	*tú*	徒	318	*yòng*	用	301
miè	蔑	328	*tuō*	他	302	*yóu*	由	301
mò	莫	322		脫	319		猶	324
mǒu	某	315	*wēi*	微	325	*yǒu*	有	305
nǎi	乃	295	*wéi*	唯	320	*yòu*	有	305
	迺	295		惟	320	*yú*	於	309
nài hé	奈何	312		爲	324		于	309
níng	寧	327	*wèi*	未	301		與	327
qí	其	309		爲	324		歟	330
qǐ	豈	317	*wū*	烏	317	*yǔ*	與	326
	幾	323		惡	323	*yuán*	爰	316
qiě	且	300	*wú*	亡	297	*yún*	云	298
rán	然	323		無	324	*zāi*	哉	313
róng	容	318	*wù*	勿	297	*zé*	則	312
rú	如	303	*xī*	兮	299	*zēng*	曾	325
ruò	若	314		奚	317	*zhé*	輒	328
shàng	尚	311	*xiāng*	相	315	*zhě*	者	312
shè	設	321	*xìn*	信	315	*zhèng*	正	302
shěn	矧	316	*xíng*	行	305	*zhī*	之	297
	審	328	*xǔ*	許	320	*zhǐ*	止	298
shèn	甚	316	*xuán*	旋	319		只	298
shǐ	使	311	*yān*	焉	322		祇	316
shì	是	313	*yé*	耶	313		秖	316
	適	328		邪	313	*zhì*	至	304
shū	殊	318	*yě*	也	295	*zhū*	諸	329
shú	孰	322	*yī*	一	295	*zhú*	逐	322
shǔ	屬	331		壹	295	*zhǔ*	屬	331
shù	庶	319		伊	302	*zì*	自	304
shuò	率	319	*yǐ*	已	296	*zòng*	從	321
sī	斯	324		以	300		縱	330
suí	雖	329		矣	307	*zǔ*	足	308
suì	遂	326	*yì*	亦	305			
suǒ	所	309		抑	308			

一畫

一，壹 *yī*

  1. "altogether":「曹參爲相，凡事一遵蕭何約束」

  2. "in fact," "indeed"

    a. contrary to expectation:「不意其怯懦一至於此」

    b. definitely:「今楚王之善寡人一甚也」

    c. 一似:「子之哭也，壹似重有優者」

    d. 一何:「上有絃歌聲，音響一何悲」

  3. "once [this happens, then . . .]":「君正莫不正。一正君而
    國定矣。」

二畫

乃，迺 *nǎi*

  1. pronoun, "you":「豎儒，幾敗乃公事」

  2. rhetorically important word that strongly emphasizes the phrase
    following it

    a. strong assertion of identity:「此書乃後人僞作」;「我
      非知君者，知君者乃蘇君也」;「至拜大將乃韓信
      也」

    b. assertion of causal logic: "then, thereupon":「中原大亂，
      乃南渡江」; "thereafter":「有此父乃有此子」

    c. pointing to disjunction (the unexpected failure of [b]-type
      causality):「名父乃有此不肖之子」

  3. 乃至 "until," "all the way until":「琴棋書畫，騎射拳棒，
    乃至醫卜星相，無所不學」

三畫

也 *yě*

  marker of nominal clauses, most frequently as the final of a nominal sentence. It indicates a "thing," "a state of affairs," the "fact
  that . . . ."

1. statements of identity

   a. categorical identity—"A is a type of B": 「相籍者，下相人也」;「孺子可教也」

   b. circumstantial identity—"All the above, then, is what we mean by . . . .": 「山肴蔌，雜然而前陳者，太守宴也」

2. statements of explanation—"About A, B is the fact of the matter": 「剖竹以代瓦，以其价廉而工省也」;「飲少輒醉，而年又最高，故自號曰醉翁也」

3. statements about a constant situation, a state of affairs[3]

   a. 「環滁皆山也」

   b. with a negative: 「未之聞也」

   c. with an interrogative, asking what *is* the situation: 「何也」

   d. with an exclamatory: 「以一錢之微而死三人，吁，可悲也」

   e. with an imperative: 「君如知此，則無異於民之多怨望也」

4. in a phrase-final rather than sentence-final position, 也 serves the same nominalizing functions: 「向也不怒而今也怒，何也」

已 *yǐ*

1. as an adverb, "already": 「老父已去，高祖適從旁舍來」

2. as a verb, "bring to an end" > "[when this] was done, then . . . ." often used with 而: 「廢以爲侯，已又殺之」,「已忽不見」,「已而釋之」

3. a sentence-final function word often used with 而—"and that's all there is to it": 「吾知其無能爲已」,「言之所盡，知之所至，極物而已」

4. a sentence-final function word, equivalent to 矣: 「王之所大欲可知已」

---

3. Pulleyblank (*Outline*, p. 118) suggests that 也 may have been an aspect marker in contrast with 矣.

凡 *fán*

a modifer of noun phrases, "taken in sum," "in the general case"[4]

1. "every": 「凡今之人，莫如兄弟」

2. "altogether": 「在途凡三十五日」

亡 *wú*[5]

1. a verb, similar to 無: 「一人耕，十人聚而食之，欲天下亡飢，不可得也」

2. a modifier similar to 不: 「常苦枯乾，亡有平歲，穀價翔貴」

3. a statement of denial, "no"; similar to 否: 「請問踏水有道乎。曰，亡，吾無道」

四畫

之 *zhī*

1. "this": 「之子于歸，遠送于野」

2. anaphoric pronoun, used as the object (direct, indirect, or locative) of verbs but not in the topic position: 「吾愛之重之，願汝曹效之」,「姑妄言之妄聽之」,「無之」,「總之」,「均之」

3. marker of modification of nouns: 「是誰之過歟」「虎狼之國」

4. marker of subordination in embedded sentences: 「余之識君二十年」

勿 *wù*

1. a fusion of 毋之: 「無有不如己者，過則勿憚改」,「救趙熟與勿救」

2. a negative imperative: 「己所不欲，勿施於人」

---

4. See Harbsmeier, pp. 153–65.

5. Pulleyblank (*Outline*, p. 109) observes that there is no phonological justification for this reading, especially for early texts. I am simply following the conventional reading.

夫 *fú*

1. an anaphoric pronoun, "that," "that [one] . . . ": 「夫人不言，言必有中」,「君獨不見夫朝趨市者乎」,「子木曰，夫獨無族姻」

2. a function word used at the beginning of a statement, "Now, . . .": 「夫人必自侮，然後人侮之」

3. the fusion of 否乎: 「逝者如斯夫」

方 *fāng*

1. a time marker

    a. "right now": 「今方出之使作雨也」,「國家方危」

    b. "just at the time when . . .": 「方出城門，即逢驟雨」

2. "in unison," "together": 「小民方興，相爲敵讎」

及 *jí*

1. marker of noun coordination: 「陰以兵法部勒賓客及子弟」

2. a coverb, "at the time when, when it happens that . . .": 「吾所以有大患者，爲吾有身，及吾無身，吾有何患」;「彼眾我寡，及其未濟擊之」

比 *bì*

1. a coverb, "by the time that . . .": 「比其反也，則凍餒其妻子」

2. a modifier, "in succession": 「比年傷水災」,「閑者數年比不登」

3. "recently": 「比來不審尊體動止何似」

4. 比比 "always": 「君國比比地動，比比然也」

止, 只 *zhǐ*

"only [this]," "just [this, not that]": 「止可遠觀，不可近翫」

云 *yún*

1. a verb + object, "to say this," that came to be used as a sentence-final function word

    a. "It was thus [said]": 「聞其言不見其人云」

    b. used to weaken the truth claim of the previous sentence, meaning "It was thus [reported]": 「數日無所見，見大人跡云」

2. 云云 a noun phrase: "such as this," "and so on": 「何子之言云云也」

3. 云何 "for what?", "in what manner?": 「不有舟車，云何得達。」

4. 云爾

    a. phrase-final function words, "like this [and that's all]": 「安樂令欒弘…賦詩見贈，答之云爾」

    b. combination of 云 "to say" + 爾 "like this"

兮 *xī*

a metrical pause particle: 「歸去來兮，田園將蕪胡不歸」

五畫

乎 *hū*

1. a sentence-final interrogative used either by itself or with other interrogative function words

    a. by itself: 「許子必種粟而後食乎。可以人而不如鳥乎」

    b. with other question words: 「且乎發七國之難者誰乎」

2. a phrase-final intensive word (which puts rhetorical stress on the preceding phrase), often used in conjunction with phrase-initial modal words such as 寧, 豈, 其, or 果

    a. sentence-final: 「哲人其萎乎」

    b. embedded: 「天乎，吾無罪」,「于是乎有黜者出」

3. same as 於: 「是所重者在乎珠玉而所輕者在乎人民也」

以 *yǐ*

1. coverb (with 以 in particular, the coverb–main verb order can be inverted to stress the object of the coverb as the new information to be conveyed)

    a. "use":「以理喻之」,「喻之以理」,「眾客以次就坐」

    b. "take [at the physical level of having in hand]":「乃以所乘馬贈之」

    c. "take [as an explanation]":「其地多雲霧,以四界逼於高山也」

    d. "take [as a goal]":「余以八月十九日返,而君以中秋後一日行,終不得一晤」

2. a marker of verb coordination (although verb coordination itself can suggest a relationship of antecedent condition, 以 clearly marks this meaning)

    a. to indicate purpose:「繼續努力,以求貫徹」

    b. to indicate result:「發奮忘食,樂以忘憂」

    c. to indicate manner:「呱呱以啼,啞啞以笑」,「談笑以死,白衣冠以送之」

    d. a weak coordination marker:「其責己也重以周,其待人也輕以約」

3. 以上, etc. "from [here] upwards," etc.:「六十分以上為及格,五嶺以南,古稱百粵」

4. 以至 "until":「自王公卿相以至工藝雜流,凡有名者皆留相于館」

且 *qiě*

1. a modifier

    a. "about to," "close to":「驢一鳴,虎大駭,遠遁,以為且噬己也,甚恐」,「積資且千萬」

    b. "for now," "for the moment":「我醉欲眠卿且去」

    c. a modal, used in comparing two actions—"if for the moment we grant . . . ":「明日且未可知,況明年乎」

2. a marker of verbal coordination

    a. simple coordination:「邦無道，富且貴焉，恥也」

    b. to mark simultaneous or alternating actions:「且歌且飲，旁若無人」

    c. to link alternative questions:「敵之不進爲畏我耶。且有所待也」

弗 *fú*

    1. a fusion of 不之:「得之則生，弗得則死」

    2. in later usage, same as 不:「後家居長安，長安諸公莫弗稱之」

未 *wèi*

    1. "not yet":「未之聞也」

    2. "not":「人故不易知，知人亦未易也」; also as in [未可] and [未必]

    3. 未幾 "not for long":「初習法語，未幾又改習英語」

由 *yóu*

a coverb, "through," "via," "by way of," "from":「由此觀之，愛之適以害之也」,「設理士五人，由會員共推之」,「由此楊氏與郭氏爲仇」

用 *yòng*

a coverb, "take ... (as)," "using ...."; almost identical in usage to 以:「衛青霍去病亦以外戚貴，然頗用材能自進」,「用此，其將兵數困辱」

令 *lìng*

    1. a pivot verb, "to cause," "to order":「令人望其氣」

    2. "if [it were made the case that ...]":「令冬月益展一月，足吾事矣」

可 *kě*

    1. a modal auxiliary, usually makes the verb that is its object passive, in contradistinction to 可以, but the distinction is not always observed

       a. "can [be][now]":「蔓草猶不可除，況君之寵弟乎」

b. "may [now]":「可去矣」

c. "should [now]":「但可遣人問迅，不足自往」

d. as an interrogative, "can it be":「我曲楚直，其衆莫不氣，可謂老」

2. (an extended, idiomatic usage) "[can be] approximately":「年可十六七」

正 *zhèng*

1. a modifier of clauses

a. "precisely":「是必羸師以誘我，若往，正墜其計中」

b. "precisely at the time":「曉星正寥落」

c. "precisely [and no other]" > "only":「本所以疑，正爲此耳」

2. "were it just the case that . . . [still]":「正使死，何所懼。況不必死耶。」

他 *tuō*

1. a modifier, "other":「子不我思，豈無他人」,「于是沛公乃夜引兵從他道還」

2. a pronoun

a. "other [things]":「他無所取」

b. "other [matters]":「王顧左右而言他」

c. "other [causes]":「無他，專心而已」

六畫

伊 *yī*

1. a modifier, "that":「所謂伊人，在水一方」(later, 伊人 often refers to a woman)

2. pronoun, "he," "this one":「我就伊無所求，我實亦無可與君者」

3. a phrase-initial particle of uncertain meaning:「伊嘏文王，既右饗之」

此 *cǐ*

pronoun, "this":「此壯士也」,「閑者亦樂此乎」,「予居于此，多可喜，亦多可悲」,「蓋風習移人，賢者不免百有余年於此矣」,「此所謂婦人之仁也」。

如 *rú*

1. a verb, "to be of the type"
   a. "to resemble":「文如其人」
   b. "to be such as":「常樹如松，杉，落葉樹如槐，柳」
   c. "to be as if":「丞相如有驕主色」
2. suffix in descriptive binomes, same as [然]:「三月無君，則皇皇如也」
3. clause-initial modal auxiliary, "if":「如恥之，莫若不爲」
4. a verb, "to go" (archaic usage):「鄭伯如周，始朝桓王也」
5. pronoun, "you," similar to 汝:「各任如曹命，那知吾輩心」
6. with [何]
   a. [如何] "how":「究應如何辦理，寧侯明教」
   b. [如之何] "how about", "what must it be like . . .":「竭力以事大國，則不得免焉，如之何則可」
   c. [如. . .何] "how about," "what can be done about":「君如彼何哉」
7. 不如 "not resemble" > "to be not so good as":「不如決策東鄉」

而 *ér*

1. marker of verbal coordination
   a. to link two verbs, "and":「覺而起，起而歸」
   b. to link two verbs, "but":「知其不可爲而爲之」
   c. to link two sentences, "and":「價廉而物美」
   d. to link two sentences, "but":「價廉而物不美」
2. marker of verbal coordination in which the first verb is strongly linked as the antecedent condition for the second

   a. first verb presents the manner of action:「侃侃而談」,「默爾而笑」,「攀援而登」,「不勞而獲」

   b. to link time verbs with actions:「已而復如初」,「既而悔之」,「俄而客至」,「始而喜」

   c. to link nouns that function as verbs to verbs:「朝而往，幕而歸」,「一日而行千里」,「一言而決」,「匹夫而爲百世師」,「人而無志，終身無成」

   d. to link coverbs and verbs:「由小而知大」,「自古而然」,「爲利而來」,「人材以培養而出」

3. 而已 a sentence-final phrase, "and that is all":「江山之外，第見風帆沙鳥，煙雲竹樹而已矣」。

4. a pronoun, "you," "your":「若歸，試從容問而父」。

自 *zì*

1. reflexive adverb

   a. pointing to oneself as the object of the verb (the true reflexive):「夫人必自侮，然後人侮之」

   b. "of its own accord":「桃李不言，下自成蹊」

   c. "of one's own accord," "by oneself":「不自爲政，卒勞百姓」

2. a coverb, "from":「有朋友自遠方來，自古至今」

3. "if even," "although":「自京師不曉，況於遠方」

4. [自非] "unless":「自非聖人，外寧必有內優」

5. [自餘] "other than":「自餘文人莫有逮者」

至 *zhì*

1. an adverb, "utmost":「其理至淺，何以不達」

2. a verb, "to go as far as," sometimes used with 於

   a. "to include, encompass":「至於犬馬，皆能有養」

   b. "to reach [the time when . . .]":「至人中，所期不賴，至死不悟」

   c. "to reach [the extent of . . .]":「後之亡者多至數十百人」

3. "as for," "as to":「至於日常事務，一以付之屬吏」

因 *yīn*

1. a coverb, "to rely on," "through the agency of": 「因山構屋，因勢利導」，「魏使人因平原君請從於趙」，「因前使絕國功，封騫望侯」

2. an extended anaphoric usage in which the object has been dropped and the implicit object refers to a previous noun, sometimes used with [而]: 「及至頹當城，生子，因名曰頹當」，「避仇至沛，因家焉」，「草木爲之含杯，風雲爲之變色」

有 *yǒu, yòu*

1. read *yǒu*, a verb, "there exists." The verb has varying degrees of grammaticalization and/or rhetorical force. Some variations are listed below:

   a. reduced almost to [於]:「疾學在有尊師」

   b. particularly when the object of 有 is a verb, 有 tends to mean "there is [one who] . . . ":「一男不耕，有受其飢，一女不桑，有受其寒」

2. 有以 equivalent to [有所以], "there is that by means of which . . . ":「刹人以梃與刃，有以異乎」

3. read *yòu*, the same as 又

4. read *yòu*, in numerical expressions:「是後六十有五年，而山戎越燕而伐齊」

亦 *yì*

1. "also," "as well":「施諸己而不願，亦勿施於人」

2. "it's only":「王亦不好士耳。何患無士。」，「竊焉知天道，是亦多言矣」

3. "still, . . . ":「雖不聽子韋之言，亦無損也」

耳 *ěr*

a fusion of 而已, "and that is all":「前言戲之耳」

行 *xíng*

adverb

   a. "about to":「法不信，則君行危矣」

　　b. "thereupon":「漢王怒，行欲斬嬰」

安 *ān*

　interrogative pronoun

　　a. "where":「方此時也，堯安在」

　　b. "why," "how," often before 得, 能, 可, and 敢:「君安得高枕而臥乎」,「吾亦欲東耳，安能鬱鬱久居乎」

七畫

何 *hé*

1. the most widely used interrogative pronoun. In many compounds, it serves as an *inverted object* (何如, 何以, 何由, 何爲, 何自, etc.).

　　a. "what":「內省不疚，夫何憂何懼」,「以此攻城，何城不克」

　　b. "why":「彼丈夫也，我丈夫也，吾何畏彼哉」

　　c. "how":「子在，回何敢死」

　　d. "how . . . !" expressing an exclamation:「何子之不答也」

　　e. "where":「軫不之楚，何歸乎」

2. [何如], [何若]

　　a. used as a predicate, equivalent to 如何, "how," "what is [it] like . . . ?":「讀書之樂樂何如」,「我視君何若」

　　b. used between two objects of comparison, "how can it be as good as . . . ?":「與秦地何如勿與」

3. 何以 equivalent to 以何, "by means of what," "how?":「不爲者與不能者之形何以異」

4. 何嘗 "when has there ever been . . . ?":「何嘗有此言」

5. 何有

　　a. "how can there be . . . ?":「將軍何有當爾」

　　b. "how can there be [difficulties]?":「能以禮讓爲國乎，何有」

6. 何 . . . . 之有 "how can there be...?": 「何難之有」,「何不利之有」

矣 *yǐ*

The range of meanings of [矣] are surprisingly similar to that of modern 了.

1. an aspect marker indicating something completed:
   a. normal perfective: 「晉侯在外，十九年矣」,「險阻艱難，備嘗之矣」,「民之情偽，盡知之矣」
   b. in the future perfect, there are a few other shades of meaning:
      i. to indicate something that will be completed as declared by the speaker: 「夜半，客曰，吾去矣」
      ii. a prediction based on the current situation: 「天下從此多事矣」
      iii. or an imagined consequence, often combined with [則]: 「民爲邦本，民困則國危矣」
2. marker of a change of state: 「孺子可教矣」
3. a sentence-final emphatic marker
   a. an exclamation: 「交友之道難矣」
   b. an imperative: 「先生且休矣，吾將念之」

每 *měi*

1. adverb, "every time": 「每一念至，何時可忘」
2. 每每 "often": 「值歡無復，每每多憂慮」

更 *gèng, gēng*

1. read *gèng*, adverb
   a. "again": 「即日行事，不更計議」,「欲窮千里目，更上一層樓」
   b. "in addition": 「孟長君有一狐白裘入秦獻之昭王，更無他裘」
   c. "increasingly," "yet more": 「洗脂除粉，轉更嫵媚」

    d. "[how can . . .] again . . . ?":「啼鴉衰柳自無聊，更管得離人斷腸」

  2. read *gēng*

    a. verb, "to change," "to exchange":「良庖歲更刀，割也」

    b. adverb, "in alternation":「九卿更進用事」

    c. "in succession":「孝文在代時，前後有三男。及竇太后得幸，前后死，及三子更死，故孝景得立。」

抑 *yì*

  1. a conjunction with modal implications: "or perhaps," used in alternative questions:「敢問天道乎，抑人故也」

  2. "yet alternatively" (in contrastive propositions):「若聖與仁，則吾豈敢，抑爲之不厭，悔人不倦，則可謂云爾已矣」

但 *dàn*

  1. modifier, "only":「不聞耶孃喚女聲，但聞黃河流水鳴濺濺」

  2. "just" (to the exclusion of all else):「汝但出外留客，吾自爲計」

足 *zǔ*

  1. a passive auxiliary (i.e., the topic is usually the *object* of the main verb that follows, in contrast to 足以), "is worthy of . . . ":「是四國者，專足畏也」

  2. 足以 "suffices to," "is adequate to":「適足以結怨深仇，不足以賞天下之費」

  3. 不足 "not worthy of":「豎子不足與謀」,「不足爲外人道也」

見 *jiàn*

  1. a passive marker:「蘇武使匈奴，見留二十年」

  2. sometimes it represents the object of the verb it precedes (i.e., the topic is the *agent* rather than the patient):「家叔以余貧苦，遂見用於小邑」

否 *fǒu*

a negative verb + implicit object: "it is not [so]": 「二三子用我，今日否」

    a. nominalized:「晉人侵鄭以觀其可攻與否」

    b. in tag questions:「如此則動心否乎」

    c. "no" as opposed to 然, "yes:"「許子必織布而後衣乎。曰否」

八畫

其 *qí*

    1. an anaphoric adjective, "its," "that," "their," etc.

        a. before nouns:「工欲善其事，必先利其器」

        b. before verbs (with nominalizing effect):「見其生，不忍見其死」

    2. a modal modifier, "surely" (suggesting either possibility or persuasion):「子其有以語我來」,「爾其無忘乃父之志」

彼 *bǐ*

    1. modifier, "that":「我欲易之，彼四人輔之，羽翼已成，難動矣」

    2. pronoun, "that one":「由是觀之，在彼不在此」

所 *suǒ*

    1. a nominalizing modifier of verbs and coverbs that makes the phrase refer to the object (either direct or locative) of the bound verb:「一日之行，所欲必成」,「所遊必有常」

    2. 所以 "that by means of which":「人類尚智而不尚力，此其所以為萬物之靈也」

於,于 *yú*

    1. marker of locative object:「遇之於塗」

    2. marker of the agent in passive constructions:「善戰者致人，不致於人」

3. in comparative constructions, marks the reference against which the object is being compared, "more than": 「苛政猛於虎」

4. marks a slightly more abstract sort of locative object, "vis-à-vis": 「其民勇於私斗而怯於公戰」

5. 之於 a construction used primarily in the topicalization of locative object (with 焉 usually left as the explicit placeholder in the locative object position), "as related to . . .": 「口之於味也，有同嗜者焉」

6. 於是 "at this point" ("this having happened . . ."): 「於是飲酒樂甚」

初 *chū*

1. "at first when . . .": 「初至一地，必問民俗」

2. "at the beginning" (a word used in the shaping of narrative time): 「初，吏捕條侯，條侯欲自殺，夫人止之」

3. "originally" (typically used in negative contrasts): 「初不中風，但失愛於叔父，故見罔耳」

非 *fēi*

1. the negating word for nominal sentences, "not to be [of the class]": 「子非魚，安知魚之樂」

2. in conditional clauses, "were it not that . . .": 「吾非至予子之門則殆矣」

定 *dìng*

"really," "indeed": 「聞陳王定死，因立楚懷王孫心為楚王」

固 *gù*

1. adverb

   a. "firmly," "insistently": 「朱公欲遣少子，長男固請欲行」

   b. "originally": 「臣固知王之不忍也」

   c. "certainly": 「州縣之設，固不可革也」

2. used in concessive clauses, "while it certainly is true that . . . , [still]": 「今日之事，臣固伏誅，然願請君之衣而擊之焉，以致報仇之意」

3. 固也 "yes, certainly," a positive answer: 「固也，吾欲言之久矣」

果 *guǒ*

1. adverb

   a. "as anticipated": 「趨而視之，果其子也」

   b. "in the end, as a result": 「佞之見佞，果喪其田」

   c. "in fact": 「若然者，人果有如木之質，而又有異木之知矣」

2. clause-initial, "if in fact . . . ": 「果能此道矣，雖愚必明，雖柔必強」

尚 *shàng*

1. adverb, "still": 「視吾舌尚在不」

2. as a rhetorical marker, "if even . . . " (used in conjunction with 何況, 又, etc.): 「禽尚知合群，而況人乎」

3. as a modal, "may [it] still": 「平公之靈，尚輔相余」

況 *kuàng*

a rhetorical marker to intensify contrast: "let alone . . . ," "even more so . . . " (often as 而況 or 何況): 「此不足以欺童子，況吾輩乎」

使 *shǐ*

1. verb, "to send on a mission" > pivot verb, "to cause," "to allow": 「不宜偏私，使內外異法」

2. used to state counterfactual propositions, "if": 「使天下無農夫，舉世皆餓死矣」。

或 *huò*

1. a distributive

   a. "some [things]": 「凡六出奇計，或頗秘，世莫能聞也」

  b. "some[times]":「爲醫或在齊，或在趙」

  c. "some[one]":「或謂孔子曰，子奚不爲政」

 2. "perhaps":「天或啓之，必將爲君，其後必蕃」

 3. "if perhaps . . .":「或又是男，則亦教其以父志爲志」

並 (并) *bìng*

 1. verb, "to line up" > "to combine," "to unify":「魏并山中」

 2. adverb, "together":「諸侯並起」

奈 [. . .] 何 *nài . . . hé*

 1. "what avails it to . . . ," "why?":「男兒死耳，奈何效新亭對泣耶」

 2. "what to do about . . . ?":「食盡援絕，奈何」

九畫

者 *zhě*

an abstract noun, used only in bound forms. Its usual effect is to nominalize verbs bound to it or, in the case of nouns, to indicate the general case or "such a thing as . . . ."

 1. nominalization:「愛人者人恆愛之，敬人者人恆敬之」,「君子務知大者遠者，小人務知小者近者」

 2. the general case:「師者，所以傳道，授業，解惑也」

 3. "such a [person] as":「屈原者，名平，楚之同姓也」

則 *zé*

explicit marker of the comment in topic-comment constructions (this includes other sorts of constructions like contrastive focus, but in this textbook I treat these constructions alike)

 1. topic-comment

  a. "since . . . ," "when . . . ," etc.:「諸兒見家人泣，則隨之泣」

  b. "if . . . , then . . .":「凡物熱則漲，冷則縮」

 2. sentence-initial marker of a "meta-comment:"「予子冠履而斷子手足，子爲之乎。必不爲。何故。則冠履不若手足之貴也」

3. contrastive focus:「衣則不足以蔽體，食則不足以充腹」

是 *shì*

1. pronoun, "this":「誠哉，是言也」

2. verb, "to be":「余是所嫁婦人之父也」(although one should first try to interpret 是 as the pronoun "this," 是 does indeed seem to function as a verb quite early.)

3. used between verb and object when the object is fronted, often combined with 惟:「皇天非人實親，惟德是依」

4. 是以 inversion of 以是, "because of this":「見其生不忍見其死，聞其聲不忍食其肉，是以君子遠庖廚也」

5. 是故 "for this reason":「其言不讓，是故哂之」

哉 *zāi*

an exclamation marker

a. in the middle of the sentence:「異哉，此人之教子也」

b. at the end of the sentence:「小人不忍而亂大謀，惜哉」

c. in a question (often expecting a negative answer, often combined with 豈):「豈可人而不如鳥哉」,「秦以不聞其過亡天下，又何足法哉」

耶，邪 *yé*

The interrogative version of 也, perhaps a fusion of「也乎」

a. sentence-final:「將軍怯耶」

b. in paired phrases:「儻所謂天道，是耶，非耶」

故 *gù*

1. noun, "matter" > "reason":「亂故，是以緩」

2. "[for this] reason":「吾少也賤，故多能鄙事」

3. "if in fact . . .":「故無禮，則手足無所措」

4. "previous," "old," "former":「遂如故知」

5. "previously":「燕太子丹故嘗質於趙」

6. "as previously," "still":「祭以牛羊，故不得福」

7. "intentionally":「我今故與林公來相看」

8. "with particular intention," "especially":「不足以故出兵」

若 *ruò*

1. pronoun, "you":「若歸，試從容問其父，然毋言吾告若也」

2. pronoun, "this"
    a. "this [person's]":「孔子生，不知其父，若母匿之」
    b. "this":「曷爲久居若城而不去也」
    c. "like this," "in this manner":「以若所爲，求若所欲，猶緣木而求魚也」

3. verb, "to be like." Most of its uses closely resemble those of [如]:
    a. "to seem as if":「山有小口，仿佛有光，其人視端容寂，若聽茶聲」
    b. a bound form in making descriptive binomes, same as [然]:「桑之未落，其葉沃若」
    c. clause-initial for making hypothetical conditions, "if":「王若隱其無罪而就死地，則牛羊何則焉」
    d. [不若], [若何], [若之何], [若....何]: see the entries under [如]

4. conjunction, "or":「以萬人若一郡降者，封萬戶」

5. "as to/for [such as]," often combined with 夫:「若僕，則形格勢禁，言之無益也」,「若夫爲不善，非才之罪也」。

苟 *gǒu*

1. "improperly";「臨財毋苟得，鄰難毋苟免」

2. "for the time being":「大適小則爲壇，小適大，苟舍而已，爲用壇」

3. "if":「苟得其養無物不長」

即 *jí*

1. verb, "to arrive at":「來即我某」
    a. coverb, "to be at" (+ place word):「吳王即山鑄錢」

  b. coverb, "to be just at" (+ time word): 「夷賊素聞其名，即時降服」

  c. coverb, "to rely on [having come upon]": 「故世之言道者，或即其所見而名之，或莫之見而意之」

  d. marker of hypothetical clauses, "if it turns out": 「子即反國，何以報寡人」

2. an abstract verb of identity derived from the base meaning: 「梁父即楚將項燕」

3. marker of predicates, "if/once this (the topic) is so, then"

  a. "at that point": 「歲餘，高后崩，即罷兵」

  b. "[only] if [the topic], then . . . ": 「先即制人，後則爲人所制」,「徐行即免死，疾行則及禍」

  c. "even if [the topic], still . . . ": 「今燕雖弱小，即秦王之少婿也」

信 *xìn*

1. adverb, "really": 「卜人皆曰吉，發書視之，信吉」

2. clause-initial, "if really": 「信能行此五者，則鄰國之民仰之若父母矣」

殆 *dài*

adverb, "probably," "almost" (usually used with negative constructions): 「張儀天下賢士，吾殆不如也」

相 *xiāng*

1. adverb, "mutually": 「諸侯相送不出境」

2. adverb that replaces the object—especially personal pronouns—of the modified verb: 「生子無以相活，率皆不舉」

3. 相與 "together" (lit., "mutually give"): 「遂至承天寺尋張懷民，懷民亦未寢，相與步於中庭」

某 *mǒu*

a place-holding pronoun

  a. in place of unknown or lost names, or as a general pronoun: 「於是使勇士某者往殺之」,「其式，某率子某頓首」

    b. to replace real names to avoid error or for the sake of simplicity: 「師冕見…皆坐，告之曰，某在斯，某在斯」

    c. a humble replacement for 我:「諸君賴遭某，故得有今日耳」

    d. as an indefinite adjective:「某時使公主某事，不能辦，以此不任用公」,「具爲區處，某所大木可以爲棺，某亭豬子可以祭」

祇，秖 *zhǐ*

    1. "merely":「雖殺之，無益，祇益禍耳」

    2. later often replacing 止 to mean 只, "only":「所部祇二百人」

爰 *yuán*

    1. locative pronoun, "there" (early usage):「爰有寒泉，在浚之下」

    2. by extension, "at this point":「爰伸筆濡墨而記之」

垂 *chúi*

    adverb, "soon":「吾年垂七十」

皆 *jiē*

    distributive, "all":「國老皆賀子文」

甚 *shèn*

    1. modifier, "extreme/extremely":「生者甚少」,「秦人視之亦不甚惜」,「於是飲酒樂甚」

    2. interrogative pronoun, "what?" "why?" (late usage):「漢開邊，功名萬里，甚當時健者也曾閑」

矧 *shěn*

    adverb, "all the more so":「智能知之，猶卒以危。矧今之人，曾不是思」

胡 *hú*

interrogative, "how," "why":「人盡夫也，父一而已，胡可比也」

曷 *hé* (**g'ât*)

interrogative pronoun, largely indistinguishable from the phonologically different 何 (**g'â*):「況復已朝餐，曷由知我飢」

十畫

奚 *xī*

1. used like 何以, "by means of what?":「死生既齊，榮辱奚別」
2. interrogative pronoun, used like 何:「或謂孔子曰，子奚不爲政」

盍 *hé*

1. fusion of 何不, "why not . . . ?":「王欲行之，則盍反其本矣」
2. interrogative pronoun, used like 何:「盍不出從乎，君將有行」

烏 *wū*

1. clause-initial interrogative:「遲速有命，烏識其時」
2. 烏呼, an exclamation, "alas":「烏呼，天禍衛國也夫」

豈 *qǐ*

clause-initial interrogative for rhetorical questions, usually requiring a negative answer, "How can it be . . . ?":「雖曰天命，豈非人事哉」

匪 *fěi*

a rarely used early equivalent of 非:「朕祇懼潛思，匪遑啟處」

俾 *bǐ*

a causative pivot verb:「敢終布之執事，俾執事實圖利之」

倘，儻 *tǎng*

1. modal marker, "perchance":「而樓屋傾頹，倘能壓人，故令整修」

2. marker of supposition, "if perchance":「倘復請之，吾輩無生理矣」

徒 *tú*

1. adverb, "merely," "just":「吾不見人，徒見金耳」

2. adverb, "in vain," "pointlessly":「大丈夫當爲忠義鬼，無爲徒死也」

特 *tè*

1. adverb, "especially," "in particular":「今天下尚未定，此特求賢之急時也」

2. adverb, "merely," "no more than" (often used in negative constructions with 豈, 非, etc.):「今楚國雖小，絕長續短，猶以數千里，豈特百里哉」

3. adverb, "in spite of all else" (all commentaries and dictionaries gloss this usage as "in the end," which I do not think is right):「以臣所行多矣，周流無所不通，未嘗見人如中山陰姬者也，不知者特以爲神，力言不能及也」

益 *yì*

adverb, "increasingly":「毛血日益衰，志氣日益微」

差 *chā*

adverb, "in comparison more," "in contrast more":「官爵功名，不減於子，而差獨樂，顧不優耶」

殊 *shū*

1. adverb, "especially":「居蠻夷中久，殊失禮義」

2. adverb, "entirely," "to the last":「丞相特前戲許灌夫，殊無意往」，「軍皆殊死戰，不可敗」

3. 殊未 adverb, "still not yet":「園景早已滿，佳人殊未適」

容 *róng*

1. modal auxiliary, "ought to":「臣今在假，不容詣省」

2. clause-initial marker of hypothetical cases, "if perchance":「諸王子在京，容有非常，宜亟發遣，各還本國」

十一畫

率 *shuò*

1. modifier, "all":「進是謀者，率以爲是，固不可解也」

2. modifier, "on the whole":「一歲中往來過他客，率不過再三過」

旋 *xuán*

adverb, "soon":「臣意即以寒水拊其頭，刺足陽明脈，左右各三所，病旋已」

脫 *tuō*

1. modal auxiliary, "perhaps":「事旣未發，脫可免禍」

2. clause-initial marker of a hypothetical:「脫有一人能知翱憂者，又皆疏遠與翱無異」

庸 *yōng*

1. verb, "use":「敷奏以言，明試以功，車服以庸」

2. adjective, "normal," "average":「庸言必信之，庸行必慎之」

3. clause-initial interrogative expecting negative answer, "how [can it be that . . . ?]":「士有偏短，庸可廢乎」,「雖王之國，庸獨利乎」

庶 *shù*

1. modal marker of predicates, "so that perhaps":「君姑修政而新兄弟之國，庶免於難」

2. modal, a stronger version of (1), "wish that . . . ":「死而有靈，庶慰冤魂」

3. modifier, "almost":「回也其庶乎，屢空」

將 *jiāng*

1. modal auxiliary of aspect, "about to":「孟之反不伐，奔而殿，將入門，策其馬，曰非敢後也，馬不進也」

2. modal, "must surely be that . . .": 「神所馮依，將在德矣」,「八神將自古而有之，或曰太公以來作之」

3. modifier, "almost": 「今滕，絕長補短，將五十里也，猶足爲善國」

4. in contrastive rhetoric, "instead"

   a. in statements: 「古之善爲道者，非以明民，將以愚之」

   b. in questions: 「人生受命於天乎，將受命於戶邪」

5. coverb, "to take": 「茲謹將所見聞者條陳於後」

6. very rarely, marker of noun coordination [weakened version of (5)]: 「月既不解飲，影徒隨我身，暫伴月將影，行樂須及春」

唯 *wéi*

1. used like 惟 (1) and (2) below

2. read *wěi*, an exclamation, "yes": 「子曰，參乎吾道一以貫之。曾子曰，唯」

惟 *wéi*

1. modifier, "only": 「顧望無所見，惟睹松柏陰」,「今王亦一怒而安天下之民，民惟恐王之不好勇也」,「豈惟口腹有飢渴之害，人心亦皆有害」

2. "is"

   a. verb of identity: 「彼爾維何，維常之華」,「知我者其惟春秋乎」

   b. modal, "let it be . . .": 「故敢略陳其愚，惟君子察焉」

   c. concessive, "although it be . . .": 「知人則哲，惟帝其難之」

3. verb, "to think about": 「佚而不思其終，安而不惟其始」

許 *xǔ*

1. noun, "this way": 「相送勞勞渚，長江不應滿，是儂淚成許」

2. verb, "be like [this]": 「如今老嬾那能許，臥聽鄰齋夜讀書」

3. modifier, "approximately": 「山有石壁二十許丈」

設 *shè*

marker of supposition, "if": 「莊王死，子般弒，閔公弒，比三君死，曠年無君，設以齊取魯，曾不興師，徒以言而已矣」

假 *jiǎ*

1. modifier, "false," "falsely": 「盛服將朝，尚早，坐而假寐」

2. verb, "to borrow": 「夫死人不能假生人之形以見，猶生人不能借死人之魂以亡矣」

3. verb, "to rely on" (extension of [2]): 「道假辭而明，辭假書而傳」

4. marker of hypothetical (often counterfactual): 「假有人焉，舉我言以復 於我，亦必疑其誑」

既 *jì*

1. verb, "to complete": 「吾與汝既其文，未既其實，而固得道與」

2. auxiliary of perfective aspect, "finished . . . ," often used in time topics: 「既出，得其船，便扶向路，處處誌之」

3. the usual rhetorical role is an extension of (2): "since it is [already] the case that . . . ": 「愛之欲其生，惡之欲其死，既欲其生，又欲其死，是惑也」

4. 既 而: "once/since [that] was done, then . . . " > "soon thereafter": 「既而歸，其婦請去」

從 *cóng, zòng*

1. read *cóng*, verb, "to follow": 「堯舜帥天下以仁而民從之」

2. modal auxiliary, "leave it be . . . ": 「池上有門君莫掩，從教野客看清山」

3. coverb

   a. "from": 「旦日，客從外來，坐談」

   b. "following": 「乃以刀決張，道，從醉卒直隧出」

4. read *zòng*, see [縱] below.

莫 *mò*

1. distributive, "in no case": 「一府中皆慴伏，莫敢起」
2. negative imperative, "don't . . .": 「君有急病見於面，莫多飲酒」

焉 *yān*

1. anaphoric locative pronoun, "at that place": 「積土成山，風雨興焉」
2. interrogative pronoun, see [安]: 「未能事人，焉能事鬼」
3. extension of (1), "at this point," used like 於是: 「吾道路悠遠，必無有二命，焉可以濟事」
4. in descriptive binomes, used like 然: 「忠飲顧昔心，悵焉若有失」

孰 *shú*

1. interrogative distributive, "which," often used where the choices are already defined: 「父與夫孰親」,「與其殺是人也，寧其得此國也，其孰利乎」
2. used for 熟, "thoroughly": 「明日徐公來，孰視之」
3. 孰與: "how can it be better than . . .": 「然不伐賊，王業亦亡，惟坐而待亡，孰與伐之」

第 *dì*

adverb, "just," "merely": 「君第去，臣亦且亡，避吾親，君何患」,「江山之外，第健風帆沙鳥煙雲竹樹而已」

逐 *zhú*

coverb, "do [action of main verb] in succession on": 「山中咸可悅，賞逐四時移」

十二畫

幾 *jī, jǐ, jì, qǐ*

1. read *jī*, adverb, "almost": 「匈奴大圍貳師將軍，幾不脫」

2. read *jǐ*, interrogative modifier, "how many," "how much":「越信隔年稀，孤舟幾夢歸」「總把春山掃眉黛，不知供得幾多愁」

3. read *jì*, used like 冀, "to hope":「爲國求福，幾獲大利」

4. read *qǐ*, used like 豈, "how?":「古之眞人，其覺自忘，其寢不夢，幾虛語哉」

惡 *wū*

a clause-initial interrogative pronoun, "how?" "where?":「雖有江河，惡足以爲固」,「子獨惡乎聞之」,「居惡在。仁是也」

詎,巨,渠 *jù*

1. modifier of aspect, "once," "already":「爾祭詎幾時，朔望忽復盡」

2. interrogative expecting negative answer (like 豈), "how?":「君軍適至，馬未秣，士未飯，詎可戰耶」

3. marker of hypothetical (rare usage), "if":「詎非聖人，不有外患，必有內憂」

然 *rán*

1. verb, "to be like this," often described as a fusion of 如安:「何必高宗，古之人皆然」

2. nominalized form of (1), "this manner":「無若宋人然」

3. bound form in descriptive binomes, "in the manner of . . .":「天油然作雲，沛然下雨，則苗浡然興之矣」

4. resumptive topic (然 [則]) or verb (然 [而], marking antecedent condition), extension of (1), "it being like this, then . . .":「神農非高於黃帝也，然其名高者，以適於時也」

   a. [然而] "Even though this is so, . . .":「性也者，吾所不能爲也，然而可化也」

   b. [然則] "since this is so, . . .":「是進亦憂，退亦憂，然則何時而樂耶」

爲 *wéi, wèi*

1. read *wéi*, verb, "to make," "to become": 「及即位，爲章華之宮」，「高岸爲谷，深谷爲陵」

    a. verb, "to deem to be": 「唯君子爲能貴其所貴」

    b. verb, "to enact the role of" > "to be": 「桀溺曰子爲誰。曰爲仲由」

    c. marker of hypothesis, "were it to be": 「王愛子美矣。雖然，惡子之鼻，子爲見王，則必掩子鼻」

    d. passive marker: 「城小而固，勝之不武，弗勝爲笑」

2. sentence-final marker

    a. question: 「天之亡我，我何渡爲」

    b. exclamation: 「予無所用天下爲」

3. read *wèi*, "to be for the sake of": 「仕非爲貧也，而有時乎爲貧」

    a. coverb, with object: 「庖丁爲文惠君解牛」

    b. coverb, without object: 「白鵠遂不來，天雞爲愁思」

無 *wú*

1. verb, "there does not exist": 「人無遠慮，必有近憂」

2. mild negative imperative, "don't . . .": 「無友不如己者」

3. 無乃 "how can it not be . . ." ("surely it is . . ."): 「居簡而行簡，無乃太簡乎」

4. 無以 equivalent to 無所以, "there is not that by means of which": 「不學禮，無以立」

斯 *sī*

1. pronoun, "this"

    a. as noun: 「逝者如斯夫，不舍晝夜」

    b. as modifier: 「天之未喪斯文也，匡人其如予何」

2. marker of comment, "this [being the case, then]": 「王無罪歲，斯天下之民至焉」

猶 *yóu*

1. verb, "to resemble" (or perhaps a copular function word): 「以若所爲，求若所欲，猶緣木而求魚也」

2. adverb, "still"
   a. time word:「往者不可諫，來者猶可追」
   b. "both . . . still":「天地所罰，小大猶發，鬼神所報，
      遠近猶至」

3. adverbial marker of hypothetical, "if [as before(?)]":「鬼猶求
   食，若敖氏之鬼，不其餒而」

復 *fù*

1. verb, "to repeat"
   a. "to return":「昭王南征之不復，寡人是問」
   b. "to report":「管仲會國用，三分之二在賓客，其一
      在國。管仲懼而復之」
   c. "to give in turn" > "to avenge":「非富天下也，爲匹夫
      匹婦復讎也」

2. adverb, "again":「甚矣吾衰也。久矣吾不復夢見周公」

曾 *zēng, céng*

1. read *zēng*, modifier, "to the very end," often followed by 不:
   「既醉而退，曾不吝情去留」

2. read *céng*, aspect marker, "once":「臣少曾遠遊，周覽九
   土，足歷五都」

厥 *jué*

anaphoric pronoun, used as a modifier like 其:「唐虞建官，厥
可稽已」

十三畫

寖,浸 *jìn*

adverb, "gradually":「久之，寖與中人亂，出入驕恣」

滋 *zī* adverb, "increasingly":「若獲諸侯，其虐滋甚」

微 *wēi*

1. modifier
   a. "slightly":「洞庭始波，木葉微脫」
   b. "imperceptibly," "unseen":「解使人微知賊處」

2. negating function word

  a. modifier, "not":「雖讀禮傳，微愛屬文」

  b. clause-initial negative counterfactual, "if it were not . . . ": 「微管仲，吾其被髮左衽矣」

會 *huì*

1. verb, "to meet together":「永和九年，歲在癸丑，暮春之初，會於會稽山陰之蘭亭」

2. clause-initial function word (partially grammaticalized verb) often used in narratives, "it so happened that . . . ":「親故多勸余爲長吏，脫然有懷，求之靡途。會有四方之事，諸侯以惠愛爲德，家叔以余貧苦，遂見用於小邑」

3. modifier, "it inevitably happens that . . . " (derived from [2]): 「秋高八九月，白露變爲霜，終年會飄墜，安得久馨香」

遂 *suì*

modifier, "subsequently"

  a. "thereafter, to the end . . . ," "thereafter, in the end . . . ": 「及高祖貴，遂不知老父處」,「曹操比於袁紹，則名微而衆寡，然曹遂能克紹，以若爲強者，非唯天時，抑亦人謀也」

  b. "following that, . . . ":「由是感激，遂許先帝以驅馳」

十四畫

與 *yǔ, yú*

1. read *yǔ*, verb, "to give":「欲與大叔，臣請事之」

2. verb, an abstraction of (1), "to be in [some particular] relationship with":「中國與邊地，猶肢體與腹心也」

3. coverb, "to give" > "to [do] with . . . ":「夫地大而不墾者，與無地同」

4. conjunction for nouns, "and" (derived from [3]):「富與貴，是人之所欲也」

5. modifier, "all," related to 舉：「兵不得休八年，萬民與苦甚」

6. read *yú*, clause-final question particle, see [歟] below.

寧 *níng*

verb, "would rather"

    a. 「與其害於民，寧我獨死」

    b. in questions, "how could [I] not rather . . . "：「此壯士也。方辱我時，我寧不能殺之邪。殺之無名，故忍以至此」

    c. in alternating questions：「王寧亡十城耶。將亡十國邪」

    d. "is perhaps to be considered"：「爲壽爲夭，寧顯寧晦，銘誌湮滅，姓字不傳」

嘗 *cháng*

1. verb, "to taste" > "to try"：「君子有酒，酌言嘗之」,「諸侯方睦於晉，臣請嘗之。若可，君而繼之。若不可，收師而退」

2. auxiliary verb, "to try to"：「雖然，請嘗言之」

3. aspect mark, "once did" (derived from [1])：「吾嘗終日不食，終夜不寢，以思，無益，不如學也」

誠 *chéng*

modifier, "sincere," "sincerely"

    a. "in fact," "in truth," "indeed"：「利誠亂之始也」

    b. clause-initial marker of hypothetical, "if in fact . . . "：「楚誠能絕齊，秦願獻商於之地六百里」

蓋 *gài*

1. a modifier to indicate less than complete confidence in the statement to follow, often used to allow an author to politely state a conclusion, "in all probability," "probably"：「屈平之作離騷，蓋自怨生也」,「舜葬於蒼梧之野，蓋三妃未之從也」

2. used for 盍, "why not . . . "：「夫子蓋少貶焉」

輒 *zhé*

modifier indicating regularity of sequence, "thereupon invaria-bly":「張負女五嫁而夫輒死，人莫敢娶」，「賊初逼城急，光弼作大炮，飛巨石，一發輒斃二十餘人」，「目所一見，輒誦於口」

爾 *ěr*

1. pronoun, "this":「彼有取爾也，赤子匍匐將入井，非赤子之罪也」

2. verb, "to be like this":「汝乃我家出，亦敢爾邪」

3. used as bound-form in descriptive binomes:「如有所立，卓爾。雖欲從之，末由也矣」

4. sentence final, like 而已矣:「幸而無恙，是殆有養致然爾」

十五畫

輩 *bèi*

pluralizing suffix:「奴輩利吾家財」

蔑 *miè*

negating modifier, sometimes with a slight imperative:「封疆之削，何國蔑有」，「寧事齊楚，有亡而已，蔑從晉矣」

審 *shěn*

1. modifier, "in fact":「審如說雷之家，則圖雷之家非」

2. modifier, "carefully," "thoughtfully":「兵者，凶器也，不可不審用也」

適 *shì*

1. modifier, "by chance":「先主斜趨漢津，適與羽船相會」

2. modifier, "just at the time":「今賊適疲於西，又務於東，兵法乘勞，此進趨之時也」

3. clause-initial marker of hypothetical, "if it so happens that . . .":「國羊謂鄭君曰，臣適不幸而有過，願君幸而告之」

十六畫

諸 *zhū*

1. pluralizing prefix, "the assembled," "the group of": 「諸大夫皆曰賢，未可也」

2. fusion of 之乎

   a. "it" + locative marker:「孔子時其亡也，而往拜之，遇諸途」

   b. "it" + question/exclamation marker: 「文王之囿方七十里，有諸」

3. used as a replacement for 於:「撥亂世反諸正，莫近諸『春秋』」

獨 *dú*

1. verb, "to be old and without children," "to be alone": 「存幼孤，矜寡獨」

2. modifier

   a. "alone":「與世皆濁，我獨清，舉世皆醉，我獨醒，是以見放」

   b. "privately," "to oneself":「其母將行卜相，言當大貴，心獨喜」

   c. "particularly":「呂氏春秋曰，人固不能自知，人主獨甚」,「夫德不得後身而特盛，功不得背時而獨彰」

十七畫

雖 *suí*

clause-initial concessive marker: "even though" (the clauses seem to act as the object of an abstract verb, much like 既)

   a. "even though it be" (hypothetical):「果行此道矣，雖愚必明，雖柔必強」

   b. "even though it is . . ." (factual):「雖有君名，寡人弗敢與聞」

縱 *zòng*

1. verb, "to unbind," "to let loose":「一日縱敵，數世之患也」,「超乃順風縱火」

2. modifier

    a. "unbridled," "unrestrained":「荒飲縱獵，不復設備」

    b. "unhampered":「欲遊目縱覽，究其有無」

3. clause-initial marker of concessive hypothetical, "even if it is/were the case . . . ":「今縱弗忍殺之，又聽其邪說，不可」

彌 *mí*

1. modifier, "increasingly":「佩繽紛其繁飾兮，芳菲菲其彌章」

2. modifier, "everywhere":「財貨連轂，彌竟川澤」

十八畫以上

歟, 與 *yú*

phrase-final marker, perhaps a fusion of 也乎

    a. question:「其將往而全之歟，抑將安而不救歟」

    b. exclamation:「論者之言，一似管窺豹歟」

藉, 借 *jiè*

clause-initial marker of hypothetical:「藉使子嬰有庸主之材，僅得中佐，山東雖亂，秦之地可全而有，宗廟之祀，未當絕也。」

靡 *mǐ*

1. verb, "there is no . . . ":「室靡棄物，家無閑人」

2. modifier, "in no case":「朕聞蓋天下萬物之萌生，靡不有死」

顧 *gù*

1. modifier, "on the contrary," used like 反:「民者固服於勢，勢誠易以服人，故仲尼反為臣而哀公顧為君」,「若既得位，欲分吳國予我，我顧不敢望也」

2. modifier, "however," "and yet," "but still": 「彼 非 不 愛 其弟，顧有所不能忍者也 」,「此在兵法，顧諸君不察 耳 」

屬 *shǔ, zhǔ*

1. read *shǔ*, pluralizing suffix:「雍齒尚爲侯，我屬無患矣 」

2. read *zhǔ*, modifier

   a. "just when . . . ":「屬到市，觀見所斥賣官奴婢，年皆 七十 」

   b. "just now":「屬 方 有 公 事，君 且 去 」,「丈 人 屬 有 念，事業無窮年 」

   c. "it so happened/happens that just then . . . ," used much like 適 and 會:「若屬有讒人交鬥其間，鬼神而助之，以 興其凶怒，悔之何及 」

Index

Index

C

當 *dāng* (v), to be at, 118 > (adj), contemporary, 56; > (v), to block, 154 ; (v), to be appropriate, 131

導 *dǎo* (v), to lead, 201

悼 *dào* (v), to mourn, 217

盜 *dào* (n), thief, 49

盜跖 Dào Zhí, "Robber Zhí," whose evil deeds are described in the chapter "盜跖," in 莊子, 210

道 *dào* (n), road, 130; > the Way, 96; (v), to say, convey, 223; > to speak of, describe, 164

道故 *dào gù* (v+o), to speak of former [matters], 167

蹈 *dào* (v), to tread, step on, 211

得 *dé* (v), to obtain, 56; equivalent to 德, to acknowledge receipt of virtuous action, 159

德 *dé* (n), virtue, 108

等 *děng* (n), "etc.," 215; [pluralizing fw], 154

敵 *dí* (v), to be a match for (an opponent of equal strength), 146, 186

砥 *dǐ* (n), whetstone > (v), to polish, 212

弟 *dì* (n), younger brother, 82

帝 *dì* (n), emperor, 90

顛 *diān* (n), top [of tree, etc.], 225

典職 *diǎn zhí* (v), to preside at a post, 208

殿 *diàn* (n), the rear guard (that protects a withdrawing army), > (v), to serve in the rear guard, 43

凋 *diāo* (v), to wither, 211

釣 *diào* (v), to fish (with hook), 126

丁 *dīng* (n), (1) "man" [of lower class]; (2) a name, 200

東方朔 Dōngfāng Shuò, a Hàn dynasty man of letters, 194

東海 Dōnghǎi, a place, 111

凍 *dòng* (v), to freeze, 146, 150

凍餓 *dòng è* (v), to freeze and starve, 146

斗 *dǒu* (m), measure of volume, 1.94 liters, 166

豆 *dòu* (n), a footed platter, 158

獨 *dú* (v), to be alone > (adv), privately, 155; (adv), in particular, "precisely," 185

髑髏 *dú lóu* (n), skull, 150

睹 *dǔ* (v), to see, to discern, 167; to look at carefully, 209

篤 *dǔ* (v), to be earnest, 211

端 *duān* (n), tip, beginning, 180

對 *duì* (v), to face > reply, 108

盾 *dùn* (n), shield, 72

多 *duō* (v), many > (adv), mostly, 154

多辨 *duō biàn* (v), disputatious, 164

奪 *duó* (v), to take by force, 146, 178

度 *duò* (v), to calculate, 154; to measure length, 185

墮 *duò* (v), to drop, 167

G

J

孫綽 Sūn Chò (ca. 301–80), a gentleman at leisure, 215

孫叔敖 Sūn Shú'ào, a minister to Chǔ Zhuāng Wáng, 107

損抑 *sǔn yì* (v), to be dispirited, 135

所 *suǒ* (n), place, 154; > (adj), [points to object], 65

索 *suǒ* (n), string, 166

T

撻 *tà* (v), to hit, 146

太公 Tài Gōng, Lǚ Shàng 呂尚, 209

泰山 Tài Shān, a sacred mountain in Shāndōng Province, 185, 196

太守 *tài shòu* (n), [military] prefect, 223

太史公 *Tàishǐ gōng*, "The Grand Scribe," refers to either Sīmǎ Qiān 司馬遷, the author of the 史記, or to his father, Sīmǎ Tán, 司馬談, who started the project, 164, 208

太元 Tàiyuán, an Eastern Jìn reign period (376–97), 222

貪 *tān* (v), to covet, to desire, 150, 211

談 *tán* (v), to chat, 150

嘆惋 *tàn wàn* (v), sigh with surprised sorrow, 223

湯 Tāng, sage emperor, founded 商 dynasty, 196

堂 *táng* (n), hall, 127

堂上 *táng shàng* (n), the upper end of the audience hall, 184

螳螂 *táng láng* (n), praying mantis, 139

儻 *tǎng* (fw), if, 211

逃 *táo* (v), to flee, 112, 208

陶潛 Táo Qián (365–427), a famous poet, 219

騰躍 *téng yuè* (v), to leap, 197

蹄 *tí* (n), foot, hoof, 166

題 *tí* (v), to evaluate, 142

悌 *tì* (v), to behave as a proper younger brother, 145 > (n), brotherly affection, 187

天 *tiān* (n), sky, heaven, 49

天理 *tiān lǐ* (n), Heavenly Principle, an important 道學 concept, 178

天下 *tiān xià*, all under heaven > the realm, 97

田 *tián* (n), cultivated field, 56

田完 Tián Wán, i.e., Chén Wán, son of 陳厲公 Duke Lì of Chén, who fled to Qí and whose descendent was appointed marquis of Qí, 165

蜩 *tiáo* (n), cicada, 195

髫 *tiáo* (n), bangs (worn by children), 222

條理 *tiáo lǐ* (n), articulated order, 180

庭 *tíng* (n), courtyard, 165

亭長 *tíng zhǎng* (n), head of a 亭, a Qín administrative unit of 10 villages, 154

蚤 *zǎo* (v), to be early = 早, 210

造 *zào* (v), [unusual usage] to begin, 219

躁 *zào* (v), to be agitated, easily excited, 217

則 *zé* (fw) [explicit topical], 112

擇 *zé* (v), to select, 184

澤 *zé* (n), a marsh, 154

賊 *zéi* (v), to steal, 180

曾 *zēng* (fw), to the very end, 219

曾參 Zēng Shēn, disciple of Confucius, 111

乍 *zhà* (adv), suddenly, 179

宅 *zhái* (n), home, household, 219

沾 *zhān* (v), to moisten, 139

斬 *zhǎn* (v), to cut in half at the waist, 154

戰國策 *Zhàn guó cè, Strategies of the Warring States*, 90

暫 *zhàn* (adv), for a brief time, 179

章 *zhāng* (n), section [of text], 178

彰明 *zhāng míng* (v), to be brilliantly clear, 211

長 *zhǎng* (v), to grow, 97 > (v), be an elder (leader), to, 90

長上 *zhǎng shàng* (n), elders, superiors, 145

長者 *zhǎng zhě* (n), old person, 185

長子 *zhǎng zǐ* (n), oldest son, 145

掌 *zhǎng* (n), palm of the hand, 179

招 *zhāo* (v), to summon, invite, 219

召 *zhào* (v), to summon, 166

趙 Zhào, a state in north China during the 戰國 period, 165

趙簡子 Zhào Jiǎn Zǐ, i.e., Zhào Yǎng 鞅, minister to the duke of Jìn 晉 during late Chūnqiū, 114

趙岐 Zhào Qí (d. A.D. 201), late Hàn dynasty editor of the only extant version of *Mèng Zǐ*, 177

折 *zhé* (v), to break, 56, 195

折枝 *zhé zhī* (v+o), lit, "to break a limb," perhaps means "massage," 185

輒 *zhé* [fw: invariably then . . .], 219

者 *zhě* (n), a bound-form abstract noun that requires a modifier, 43, 56

貞 *zhēn* (v), to be pure, honest, 142

枕 *zhěn* (n), pillow, 150

振驚 *zhèn jīng* (v), to alarm and frighten, 165

徵 *zhēng* (v), to be verifiably true, 197

征 *zhēng* (v), to attack in a punitive campaign, 146

征利 *zhēng lì* (v-o), to compete for profit = 爭利, 177

正 *zhèng* (v), to stand straight > to set straight, 97; > (v), to be impartial, 130

政 *zhèng* (n), governance, 56

Harvard East Asian Monographs

(*out-of-print)

21. Kwang-Ching Liu, ed., *American Missionaries in China: Papers from Harvard Seminars*

22. George Moseley, *A Sino-Soviet Cultural Frontier: The Ili Kazakh Autonomous Chou*

23. Carl F. Nathan, *Plague Prevention and Politics in Manchuria, 1910–1931*

*24. Adrian Arthur Bennett, *John Fryer: The Introduction of Western Science and Technology into Nineteenth-Century China*

25. Donald J. Friedman, *The Road from Isolation: The Campaign of the American Committee for Non-Participation in Japanese Aggression, 1938–1941*

26. Edward LeFevour, *Western Enterprise in Late Ching China: A Selective Survey of Jardine, Matheson and Company's Operations, 1842–1895*

27. Charles Neuhauser, *Third World Politics: China and the Afro-Asian People's Solidarity Organization, 1957–1967*

28. Kungtu C. Sun, assisted by Ralph W. Huenemann, *The Economic Development of Manchuria in the First Half of the Twentieth Century*

*29. Shahid Javed Burki, *A Study of Chinese Communes, 1965*

30. John Carter Vincent, *The Extraterritorial System in China: Final Phase*

31. Madeleine Chi, *China Diplomacy, 1914–1918*

*32. Clifton Jackson Phillips, *Protestant America and the Pagan World: The First Half Century of the American Board of Commissioners for Foreign Missions, 1810–1860*

33. James Pusey, *Wu Han: Attacking the Present through the Past*

34. Ying-wan Cheng, *Postal Communication in China and Its Modernization, 1860–1896*

35. Tuvia Blumenthal, *Saving in Postwar Japan*

36. Peter Frost, *The Bakumatsu Currency Crisis*

37. Stephen C. Lockwood, *Augustine Heard and Company, 1858–1862*

38. Robert R. Campbell, *James Duncan Campbell: A Memoir by His Son*

39. Jerome Alan Cohen, ed., *The Dynamics of China's Foreign Relations*

40. V. V. Vishnyakova-Akimova, *Two Years in Revolutionary China, 1925–1927*, tr. Steven L. Levine

*41. Meron Medzini, *French Policy in Japan during the Closing Years of the Tokugawa Regime*

42. Ezra Vogel, Margie Sargent, Vivienne B. Shue, Thomas Jay Mathews, and Deborah S. Davis, *The Cultural Revolution in the Provinces*

*43. Sidney A. Forsythe, *An American Missionary Community in China, 1895–1905*

*44. Benjamin I. Schwartz, ed., *Reflections on the May Fourth Movement.: A Symposium*

*45. Ching Young Choe, *The Rule of the Taewŏngun, 1864–1873: Restoration in Yi Korea*

46. W. P. J. Hall, *A Bibliographical Guide to Japanese Research on the Chinese Economy, 1958–1970*

47. Jack J. Gerson, *Horatio Nelson Lay and Sino-British Relations, 1854–1864*

48. Paul Richard Bohr, *Famine and the Missionary: Timothy Richard as Relief Administrator and Advocate of National Reform*

49. Endymion Wilkinson, *The History of Imperial China: A Research Guide*

50. Britten Dean, *China and Great Britain: The Diplomacy of Commercial Relations, 1860–1864*

51. Ellsworth C. Carlson, *The Foochow Missionaries, 1847–1880*

*82. George A. Hayden, *Crime and Punishment in Medieval Chinese Drama: Three Judge Pao Plays*

*83. Sang-Chul Suh, *Growth and Structural Changes in the Korean Economy, 1910–1940*

84. J. W. Dower, *Empire and Aftermath: Yoshida Shigeru and the Japanese Experience, 1878–1954*

85. Martin Collcutt, *Five Mountains: The Rinzai Zen Monastic Institution in Medieval Japan*

86. Kwang Suk Kim and Michael Roemer, *Growth and Structural Transformation*

87. Anne O. Krueger, *The Developmental Role of the Foreign Sector and Aid*

*88. Edwin S. Mills and Byung-Nak Song, *Urbanization and Urban Problems*

89. Sung Hwan Ban, Pal Yong Moon, and Dwight H. Perkins, *Rural Development*

*90. Noel F. McGinn, Donald R. Snodgrass, Yung Bong Kim, Shin-Bok Kim, and Quee-Young Kim, *Education and Development in Korea*

91. Leroy P. Jones and Il SaKong, *Government, Business, and Entrepreneurship in Economic Development: The Korean Case*

92. Edward S. Mason, Dwight H. Perkins, Kwang Suk Kim, David C. Cole, Mahn Je Kim et al., *The Economic and Social Modernization of the Republic of Korea*

93. Robert Repetto, Tai Hwan Kwon, Son-Ung Kim, Dae Young Kim, John E. Sloboda, and Peter J. Donaldson, *Economic Development, Population Policy, and Demographic Transition in the Republic of Korea*

94. Parks M. Coble, Jr., *The Shanghai Capitalists and the Nationalist Government, 1927–1937*

95. Noriko Kamachi, *Reform in China: Huang Tsun-hsien and the Japanese Model*

96. Richard Wich, *Sino-Soviet Crisis Politics: A Study of Political Change and Communication*

97. Lillian M. Li, *China's Silk Trade: Traditional Industry in the Modern World, 1842–1937*

98. R. David Arkush, *Fei Xiaotong and Sociology in Revolutionary China*

*99. Kenneth Alan Grossberg, *Japan's Renaissance: The Politics of the Muromachi Bakufu*

100. James Reeve Pusey, *China and Charles Darwin*

101. Hoyt Cleveland Tillman, *Utilitarian Confucianism: Chen Liang's Challenge to Chu Hsi*

102. Thomas A. Stanley, *Ōsugi Sakae, Anarchist in Taishō Japan: The Creativity of the Ego*

103. Jonathan K. Ocko, *Bureaucratic Reform in Provincial China: Ting Jih-ch'ang in Restoration Kiangsu, 1867–1870*

104. James Reed, *The Missionary Mind and American East Asia Policy, 1911–1915*

105. Neil L. Waters, *Japan's Local Pragmatists: The Transition from Bakumatsu to Meiji in the Kawasaki Region*

106. David C. Cole and Yung Chul Park, *Financial Development in Korea, 1945–1978*

107. Roy Bahl, Chuk Kyo Kim, and Chong Kee Park, *Public Finances during the Korean Modernization Process*

108. William D. Wray, *Mitsubishi and the N.Y.K, 1870–1914: Business Strategy in the Japanese Shipping Industry*

CPSIA information can be obtained at www.ICGtesting.com
Printed in the USA
BVOW08s2130280914

368572BV00005B/5/P